HISTORY OF CRIME AND CRIMINAL JUSTICE
David R. Johnson and Jeffrey S. Adler, Series Editors

Certain Other Countries

*Homicide, Gender, and National Identity
in Late Nineteenth-Century England,
Ireland, Scotland, and Wales*

Carolyn A. Conley

The Ohio State University Press
Columbus

Library of Congress Cataloging-in-Publication Data
Conley, Carolyn A., 1953–
  Certain other countries : homicide, gender, and national identity in late nine-
teenth-century England, Ireland, Scotland, and Wales / Carolyn A. Conley.
      p. cm. — (History of crime and criminal justice)
  Includes bibliographical references and index.
  ISBN-13: 978-0-8142-1051-2 (cloth : alk. paper)
  ISBN-10: 0-8142-1051-1 (cloth : alk. paper)
  ISBN-13: 978-0-8142-9131-3 (cd-rom)
  ISBN-10: 0-8142-9131-7 (cd-rom)
  1. Homicide—Great Britain—History—19th century—Case studies. 2.
Criminal behavior—Great Britain—History—19th century. 3. Murderers—
Great Britain—Psychology. 4. Prejudices—Great Britain—History—19th
century. 5.   Social status—Great Britain—History—19th century. 6.
Marginality, Social—Great Britain—History—19th century. I. Title.
  HV6535.G4C66 2007
  364.152'3094109034—dc22
                                              2006031692

Cover design by Larry Nozik
Type set in Adobe Garamond
Printed by Thomson-Shore, Inc.

9 8 7 6 5 4 3 2 1

TO JOHN DOUGLAS CONLEY
WITH MUCH THANKS

Contents

Acknowledgments

One of the ironies of studying violent crime for twenty-five years is that I have met very nice people. I am enormously grateful to Jeff Adler, for encouraging this project as well as for his friendship and his sage advice about history, teaching, and dogs.

The Criminal Justice Network of the Social Science History Association and its international counterpart, the International Association for the History of Crime and Criminal Justice (IAHCCJ), are made up of the pleasantest group of working scholars I have ever encountered. I wish to thank members who have read and commented on various parts of this work, especially Martin Wiener, who must have felt at times that he could not go to a conference without having to read yet another draft of my work. I am also very grateful for the suggestions and encouragement of John Archer, Andrew Davies, Clive Emsley, Kim Stevenson, Judith Rowbotham, and Shani D'Cruze.

Thanks to my colleagues at UAB, especially Michael McConnell, who never fails to provide keen insight even when presented with the most garbled prose. A number of graduate assistants have also helped along the way: Howard Fox, Kurt Kinbacher, Averil Ramsey, John Springer, Pam Jones, Brian Barsanti, Nilanjana Majumdar, Tim Pittenger, Autumn Wilson, Joshua Bearden, Christopher Null, and John Kevin Pocus. I am also very grateful for the patience, skill, and good cheer of Tamekka Hayden.

The staffs at the National Library of Scotland and at the British Newspaper at Colindale were particularly helpful. Some of my research was funded by The American Philosophical Society and the NSF ADVANCE program.

My friends and family continue to tolerate a process which does not get any easier. Their amazing patience keeps the issue of domestic discord a purely academic one.

Finally, thank you so much to Wendy Gunther-Canada, who has saved me both literally and figuratively more times than I can count. She is a wonderful scholar and the best friend imaginable.

Introduction

No money is wasted which is employed in maintaining the administration of justice in the highest degree of efficiency. That administration is probably the one effectual check upon the ungoverned and ungovernable passions of rough and rude life. It is the great educator of the ignorant and the violent. (The *Times*)[1]

Welshmen believed that if God ever did delegate his privilege of depriving a human being of his life to a man or a society, that this prerogative was withdrawn by his only son . . . it is no wonder that Welshmen are horrified at the idea of giving evidence against a guilty fiend in human form, being that the evidence will be the means of consigning him reeking with the innocent blood of his victim into the presence of his offended Maker, therefore to be hurled headlong into that abyss of torment. But the abolition of capital punishment would solve the problem, sponge out once and for ever that damned and infernal law by which poor, frail, impotent mortals usurp the power of the Omnipotent—a law conceived in revenge and executed in iniquitous cold-bloodedness. Let this be done and no murderer shall be screened or harbored in Wales. (*Carmarthen Weekly Reporter*)[2]

By common consent of all thinkers on the subject of criminal jurisprudence, it is not the severity of punishments which deters from crime; it is the increasing certainty of detection and conviction which is really efficacious. To attain this certainty in ever increasing degree it is essential to convince the minds of witnesses, injured parties, and jurymen not merely that the general spirit of the law is mild, but that punishment is likely to be awarded not more than fairly proportionate to the crime. Capricious leniency occurring along with occasional unexplained severity is as injurious to the due operation of Criminal Courts as the bad system of excessive punishment. . . . Nor is there any great difficulty in seeing the general principles upon which punishments might be reduced to system, these being mainly two-fold—to weigh the mischief done by the criminal act and also the malice or anti-social nature displayed by the offender. (The *Scotsman*)[3]

1

The moral of this occurrence is very trite. The case is not one for which a remedy can be suggested, as if it sprung out of any form of oppression, with which the legislature might deal. . . . The affair is rather an example of that passionate disposition which, we fear, marks the Irish character in some excess. Such passion will certainly be restrained to some extent by the certainty that punishment will follow its indulgence. Until, however, society is wonderfully improved, it would be too sanguine to entertain any confidence that we shall be quite free from the occasional blot upon our records of such melancholy transactions. (*Cork Examiner*)[4]

Homicide has always held a special fascination for the public. Understanding what drives one human to take another's life has been the stuff of countless works ranging from pulp fiction to scientific treatise. Ultimately determining why one individual killed another is always an act of speculation. The excuse offered by the killer, the motive suspected by the arresting officer, and the explanations offered by the prosecuting and defending attorneys rarely correspond exactly. If a caregiver kills an elderly, wealthy, and cantankerous relative, whether the perceived motive was greed, mercy, fatigue, or resentment will depend as much on the observer's assumptions about human nature as the killer's actual incentive at the time. Which assumptions dominate determines the fate of the accused killer and reveals a great deal about the values and beliefs of the large society. By examining homicide trials, their outcomes, and the rhethoric surrounding them, it is possible to glean a good deal of information about both common wisdom and practical realities.[5] In the nineteenth-century United Kingdom, homicide trials provided a forum for discussing such issues as class, respectability, gender roles, family life, the role of the state, individual responsibility, the definition of insanity, the costs of industrialization, and the effects and regulation of firearms and alcohol. This book will compare the response to and perceptions of criminal homicides in England, Ireland, Scotland, and Wales between 1867 and 1892.[6]

After the Act of Union abolished the Irish parliament in 1801, the four nations of the United Kingdom shared a common parliament for the first time. The last third of the nineteenth century was a time of considerable change in the United Kingdom. The Second Reform Bill of 1867 created the largest increase in the electorate in British history. Though the political changes arguably had little effect on the homicide rate, the post-Reform Act

Parliament did pass a great deal of legislation aimed at addressing social problems. Laissez-faire Liberalism was being challenged by a philosophy which accepted the ameliorative role of the state. Trade unions enjoyed greater legal protections and the working classes were becoming better organized and more vocal. Economically, though British preeminence was being challenged by Germany and the United States, the British people were still among the most prosperous in the world. Given the relative political, social, and economic stability of the period, homicide was almost completely limited to the personal. Even in Ireland where the Land agitation of the years 1879 to 1882 and the Home Rule crisis of the late 1880s inspired headlines in the British press referring to civil war in Ireland, fewer than 15 percent of homicides were in any way linked to the politics, land, or sectarian battles.

Throughout the United Kingdom, the temperance movement; reforms in education, housing, and public health; societies dedicated to the more humane treatment of women and children; as well as other cultural influences were leading to a decline in the overall number of homicides. The long-term trend throughout Europe toward a more civil and humane society in which interpersonal violence was increasingly condemned is part of what Norbert Elias has called "the civilizing process." Though a number of factors may have contributed to the change, it is well established that the number of homicides being committed was declining. A number of historians have examined this process and the reasons for it.[7]

This work, however, has a different focus. Rather than trying to determine the actual number of homicides and why that number was declining, I am interested in the responses to homicides and what those responses reveal about the comparative cultures of the four nations of the United Kingdom. The quantitative evidence used in this study deals almost exclusively with homicide trials.[8] While the incidence of homicide is obviously an important consideration, it is also very difficult to determine. The correlation between official statistics and the actual number of cases in which one human being willfully or recklessly killed another is problematic. Recent work has highlighted the problems historians face with English homicide statistics, and the Irish, Scottish, and Welsh figures are also uncertain.[9]

Instead of trying to explain homicide rates, this work will examine the way various factors influenced the reactions to homicides in the four nations of the United Kingdom. Despite the union of the parliaments, the late nineteenth-century images and experiences of the nations of the United Kingdom were strikingly different. While Ireland presented a constant problem for English politicians, Scotland was a bastion of good order and Wales was largely overlooked. The Irish were regularly portrayed in the British press as violent barbarians, incapable of showing gratitude for the blessings of British rule.[10] The Scots, on the other hand, were presented as progressive, well mannered, and seemingly happily assimilated. The occasional political or sectarian confrontations in Scotland were but pale imitations of the problems of Ireland. As for the Welsh, they seemed to suffer from the national version of coverture—like married couples in Blackstone, England and Wales had become one entity—England, except for those occasions when Welsh quaintness was a source of amusement.

There are of course complex historical explanations for the differences as well as many exceptions to the generalizations.[11] England had conquered Wales in the late thirteenth century, which meant Wales had no modern political history as a separate nation. Nevertheless the Welsh language and cultural identity had survived.[12] Wales had been particularly hard hit by the industrial revolution. Arguably the economic relationship between Wales and England was a colonial one with Welsh coal and Welsh miners providing the raw material to enrich English mine-owners and industrialists. Welsh industrial cities were also subject to some of the worst hardships of industrialization. In an 1876 article on crime statistics in the various regions of the United Kingdom, the *Times* noted that the crime rate in Glamorgan was the highest in Britain but chose to drop it from discussion as an exception. According to the leading historian of crime in nineteenth-century Wales, "In industrial Wales serious injury, and manslaughter were half-expected on pay nights, weekends and holidays, during industrial strife."[13]

Part of the United Kingdom since 1707, Scotland had enjoyed economic prosperity, had seen its citizens play a disproportionate role in the growth of the British Empire, and, despite occasional tensions, had enjoyed a greater sense of partnership with its southern neighbor than had Ireland. Scotland's union with England had been peaceful if not completely voluntary. Scottish politicians took an active part in British politics and while there were certainly divisions in Scottish society, the differences had not been complicated by a conflation of religious or economic identity and Englishness. The breaking of the Highland clans, for all its pains, had largely been a conflict among the Scots themselves. Scotland had participated fully in the industrial revolution and while by no means an unmixed blessing, by the late nineteenth century Scotland had attained economic parity with England.[14]

In stark contrast, when Ireland was brought into the United Kingdom in 1801 after a violent rebellion, the Catholicism of the majority of the Irish had still barred them from political office and the Protestant minority owned a vastly disproportionate share of the land. Discriminatory legislation had also stifled Ireland's economic development. In the late nineteenth century,

Ireland was still 78 percent rural.[15] Further, the Great Famine of the late 1840s had enhanced the long-held resentment.

Despite the common parliament, the four nations often reacted to very similar casese in very different ways which reflect fundamental distinctions in cultural values and assumptions. The first chapter examines procedural differences and general trends in trial outcomes. Chapter 2 looks specifically at issues of national identity. The third chapter focuses on class and gender and how these categories intersected in reactions to homicides in brawls. Chapter 4 further explores class and gender issues as they impacted trials of homicides within the family and involving courtship. In the late nineteenth century definitions of both masculinity and femininity were being challenged and the courts were heavily involved in both determining the definitions and in dealing with situations that contradicted the commonly accepted definitions. Chapter 5 carries the gender discussion into the relationship that was most likely to lead to homicide—marriage. Finally, chapter 6 looks at the ways that courts dealt with the many homicides involving children.

Sources

In order to be as comprehensive as possible within the realistic confines of time and space I have tried to find accounts of as many homicide trials as possible. In order to do so I relied heavily on the *Times* for English and Welsh trials. After going through the *Times* index for the period and reading every account of a murder or manslaughter trial, a coroner's inquest, or a magistrate's hearing on an alleged homicide, I then did further investigation in Welsh provincial newspapers when possible. For Scotland I initially read through the index of all criminal trials heard at the High Court of Judiciary and then looked for trial accounts in the *Scotsman*, the *Glasgow Herald*, and provincial newspapers. For Ireland I relied on the Outrage papers for a list of homicides and then traced those cases as possible in the Irish press. My final database consists of over seven thousand homicide reports and nearly six thousand homicide trials.

This work is heavily based on these primary sources. While I am enormously indebted to the contribution of other scholars, my bibliography is by no means exhaustive and I have consciously chosen not to engage in lengthy historiographical discussions in the text. There are three reasons for this choice. The first is that the field of criminal history has reached the stage where a full synthesis of current scholarship would require a longer work than this. I have tried to consult and cite those most relevant to this particular work but omission is by no means intended as disrespect. Second, I hope, perhaps naively, that this work will appeal to readers beyond the growing but still small circle of scholars in the field. Academic conferences allow us to debate to our heart's content. Finally, while the secondary works are readily available, much of the primary material is not. I wanted to focus on the trials themselves and contemporary reactions to them.

CHAPTER 1

Homicides—Procedures, Perceptions, and Statistics

FORTUNATE AND UNFORTUNATE MURDERS. It is difficult to account for the differences in the amount of interest displayed with regard to murders. The body of a murdered person is found one day stabbed to the heart, and all England is convulsed by the intelligence: latest particulars are given by the papers and eagerly devoured by the public, a large reward is offered by Government for the discovery of the murderer and all Scotland-Yard is on the alert. The body of another murdered person is found the next day with the skull fractured and little or no notice is taken of the circumstances the jury returning an open verdict, no reward is offered by Government the body is perhaps never identified but is buried in a nameless grave and there is an end of the matter. (*Pall Mall Gazette,* 1871)[1]

The question of which homicides are significant and which are not is one that has plagued both contemporaries and historians of Victorian Britain. All too often the social history of homicides has focused on cases that inspired a fascination inversely proportional to their representativeness. But relying on quantitative evidence is equally problematic. Despite how difficult it might seem to ignore a dead body, a homicide victim does not exist in the official records simply because one person has killed another. A number of assumptions, decisions, and actions have to be taken by policemen, government officials, and even family members before a death is recorded as a homicide. Consequently homicide statistics are always suspect. The Victorians were aware of the discrepancy. In 1876 in an article examining the official judicial statistics, the *Times* insisted: "The absolute number of [recorded] murders tells us nothing. It only says how many murderers have been brought to justice."[2]

In a suspicious death in England, Ireland, or Wales, the initial decision about whether the death was to be treated as a homicide lay with the coroner's inquest—an ancient proceeding which was subject to considerable human error. Nineteenth-century coroners were not required to possess any medical or legal expertise.[3] In addition to simple ignorance, they might also be influenced by external pressures. Homicide investigations were expensive and officials might be reluctant to spend public funds to investigate the deaths of unimportant persons. For example, authorities in Kent were pleased when a stranger found with two stab wounds to the back was conveniently ruled a suicide.[4] In 1882 the *Times* complained that during a five-year period coroner's juries had returned a simple verdict of "found drowned" in nearly six hundred cases in which corpses had been found in the Thames. "Unhappily our careless English way of dealing with the bodies and effects of persons found drowned renders it improbable that the mystery which surrounds these deaths will ever be cleared up. . . . It is not a pleasant thing to reflect that there may be many ruffians prowling about London who have already committed riverside outrages with impunity."[5] But while the *Times* found the coroner's juries lax, some judges found them overly zealous. English coroner's juries regularly reported twice as many murders as did the police. One judge complained that "the members of the coroner's jury were very often led away by sympathy or some surrounding incident to return a verdict or to express censure without real justification."[6]

In addition to the coroner's jury, magistrates heard homicide charges. Even if the coroner's jury failed to indict, the magistrates could send the accused before a grand jury for indictment. The redundancy could be an additional source of confusion and annoyance. In 1875 the *Carmarthen Weekly Reporter* noted that "the inhabitants of Carmarthen have happily but little knowledge of the official method of procedure in cases of manslaughter or murder." But, the editorial continued, "to their unsophisticated minds" it seemed strange that after a coroner's jury ruled a death accidental "the magistrates should then take up the same case and send the men for trial." When the men were acquitted the newspaper complained that "[t]he law—that curious admixture of contradictions and absurdities, that emanation of the accumulated judicial wisdom of the past has insisted on a trial for no other reason that we can see except to increase the amount of the county rates."[7] But others complained that magistrates were too intimidated by ratepayers' concern. The *Spectator* complained that magistrates in Northern England had been demoralized "by a false theory of social necessities that the few among them who think that murder by torture should at least be sent before tribunals empowered to give heavy sentences are censured by other magistrates for want of judgment, forgetfulness of local circumstances and indifference to the permanent interests of the taxpayer."[8] After 1879 the newly instituted office of the public prosecutor could also begin homicide proceedings. Again the proponents of efficiency and economy were not necessarily pleased. When informed that "[t]he Public Prosecutor said he felt it to be his duty to take up any case in which a life had been lost," one judge warned that "[i]f the Public Prosecutor does what you state, all I can say is that it will very soon become a public nuisance."[9]

But however expensive and redundant the proceedings of magistrates and coroner's juries in England, Ireland, and Wales might be, they were public. In Scotland suspected homicides were investigated privately by the procurator fiscal of each county who decided whether or not to bring charges. As a Scottish judge pointed out to the House of Lords, "If the investigation did not result in a trial, then the whole evidence was kept secret. The number of such cases in which no trial took place was naturally very large, and of the merits of such cases or why they were not pushed to trial, the public always remains ignorant."[10] The system preserved privacy, but the *Scotsman* suggested, "Many retain that conviction that [the Scottish criminal justice system's] benefits would be enhanced by increased publicity in the proceedings connected with its operation."[11]

In addition to coroner's juries and magistrates, homicides in Ireland were also reported in the Outrage papers prepared for the chief secretary by the police of each Irish county.[12] These reports were predicated on the assumption that Irish homicides represented a level of sedition that was unknown in England and Wales. The Irish press often complained that the Outrage figures were exaggerated in order to justify coercive policies by the government. But by the late nineteenth century the figures were also indicative of a lack of clear instructions. The Outrage Papers included the name of the victim and the killer (if known) and a brief summary of the circumstances for every homicide the police deemed an outrage. However, there was no clear definition of "outrage."[13] In some counties the police reported every nonnatural death as an outrage, including cart accidents. Others reported only what they considered truly "outrageous conduct" and even failed to include domestic homicides. Unlike the Scottish records, which only reported cases if someone was formally charged with homicide, and the English and Welsh ones that depended on the decisions of coroners and magistrates, the Irish records included all violent deaths the local police deemed outrageous.

Given the vagaries involved in the official homicide records, it seems safer to base statistical comparison among the nations on the outcome of homicide trials rather than the number of reported homicides. Obviously the number of homicide trials will vary according to the efficiency of the police, the willingness of authorities to spend money on investigations, and the willingness of coroner's juries and magistrates or procurator fiscals to indict. But the statistics relating to trial outcomes are more likely to be an accurate reflection of what they purport to record than are estimates of the actual number of homicides. The rate of homicide trials per 100,000 population varied significantly among the nations and was changing over time.[14] In the late 1860s, England and Wales had the highest rate of homicide trials per population, but that rate had fallen by 36 percent by 1892. The Irish had the lowest rate in the UK for the late 1860s, but their rate rose by 20 percent during the period so that by 1892, Ireland had the highest rate in the UK. Scotland was in the middle in 1867, but saw the steepest decline over the period. The Scottish rate dropped over 40 percent so that by 1892, its rate was the lowest in the UK, a full 20 percent lower than that of England and Wales.

In addition to the fact that the numbers are more reliable, jury trials provide at least some indication of public opinion. Though juries were limited to male property owners, the very premise of the jury trial assumes that they will represent community standards. Sentencing patterns reveal the views and concerns of authorities. Often capital sentences were carried out not so much because of the heinousness of a particular crime as because there was a sense that a particular type of offense was happening more frequently and the Home Office believed an example needed to be set.[15] Public reactions to sentences as reflected in the press and sometimes in the streets are also particularly illuminating.

When a verdict failed to meet public expectations, the reaction was usually vocal. Applause or hisses within the courtroom often infuriated judges. When an acquittal was met with applause in an Edinburgh courtroom, the judge angrily announced, "We don't sit here for marks of approbation or disapprobation."[16] But the vehemence inspired by unpopular verdicts indicates that on the whole the courts were expected to reflect the views of the larger community. After a case in Liverpool the *Times* reported, "[A]lthough his Lordship concurred with this verdict, there is no question that it is not in accord with general opinion. It was received with hissing, an unmistakable signal of disapprobation when it was delivered in court . . . the verdict was generally condemned."[17]

Comparing trial outcomes among the four nations presents a number of challenges. In England, Ireland, and Wales juries consisted of twelve men who were impaneled to reach a unanimous verdict. One dissenting voice meant no conviction. But, under the terms of the 1707 Act of Union, Scotland had maintained its own distinct legal system. Criminal trials in

Scotland were heard by a fifteen-member jury with the verdict determined by a simple majority. A vote of eight to seven could and did decide the fate of persons accused of capital murder. Scottish juries were not required to reveal their vote but in the majority of homicide cases between 1867 and 1892 the vote was recorded. In 41 percent of the cases in which a Scottish jury convicted the accused of some form of homicide, the verdict was not unanimous. Scottish juries also had three possible verdicts—guilty, not proven, and not guilty. While both of the latter two led to the liberation of the accused, juries clearly felt the distinction was significant. In crimes in which more than one defendant was involved, the same jury might find one of the parties not guilty while the verdict for another was not proven. The not-proven verdict provided a means of avoiding an unacceptable conviction without fully exonerating the accused.

Courts in Ireland and Wales operated under the rules of the English Common Law, but not always happily. For centuries English law had been used to coerce the Irish people, to confiscate their land, and to maintain religious discrimination. Even though de jure discrimination in Ireland had ended by the late nineteenth century, a legacy of bitterness and mistrust remained.[18] The judges and jurors were Irish but the law was still English. In 1872 an Irish judge assured the Tyrone Grand jury: "I shall continue as I have done heretofore faithfully and fearlessly to administer and expand the laws of *England* [italics mine] and no other."[19] Irish defense attorneys regularly played on jurors' fears that the system discriminated against the Irish. The need for jury unanimity meant that only one juror had to be persuaded that the accused was a victim of English law. In about 7 percent of homicide trials in Ireland, authorities eventually chose to release the accused rather than go to the expense and trouble of retrying a case in which a jury had failed to agree. Crown authorities chose not to prosecute at all in another 12 percent of cases in which an indictment had been brought when they felt it was unlikely that any Irish jury would convict. The central government also routinely moved trials from one district of Ireland to another in the hopes "persons who commit outrages can no longer rely upon the certainty of absolute impunity when they are tried in a place where neither intimidation nor favor can have any effect on the minds of the jury."[20]

Technically, there was no difference between English and Welsh procedures. In fact, Welsh and English cases were often heard at the same assize, and even when separate assizes were heard for Welsh districts, the judges were English. However, the Welsh faith in English justice was in some instances as limited as that of the Irish. The leading scholars on Welsh justice have concluded that in nineteenth-century Wales "two concepts of order, the official and the popular" were in effect. Though homicides are less amenable to popular justice than lesser offenses, there is ample evidence that Welsh communities often believed in extralegal solutions.[21] In addition to the question of homicides that were deliberately kept from official scrutiny, trials in Wales also faced serious language problems. Perhaps one of the most chilling lines from reports of Welsh trials is: "The sentence of death was then translated into Welsh for the information of the prisoner."[22] The issue of bilingualism in Welsh courts came to the forefront in 1874, when a county magistrate in Carmarthenshire reduced the local jury list from 164 to 45 names by striking all those who did not speak English. He explained that not speaking English was analogous to being deaf and dumb and it was "impossible to approve of men being left on the lists to try prisoners for their lives and liberties who would not understand what the English speaking witnesses, the council and the judges said to them. Keeping Welsh speakers is no doubt why Welsh juries have been and are spoken of with such contempt as to have become a proverb." The editor of the *Carmarthen Journal* was quick to respond that "the true and indeed only function of the jury is 'to give a true verdict according to the evidence' and the mass of evidence heard in our courts was given in Welsh."[23]

Given the language problems, it is not surprising that Welsh juries were notorious for giving eccentric verdicts. A Welsh attorney wrote to the *Times* explaining that "of any twelve common jurors in mid-Wales, from one-half to three-fourth are absolutely ignorant for speaking purposes of more English than the monosyllables Yes and No. . . . The foreman, probably has as much knowledge as will enable him if you speak very slowly with a strong Welsh accent, and use none but the commonest words to follow a very brief and very clear statement of facts." The attorney stressed that the English spoken in Welsh courtrooms was largely lost on the juries. "It is through the evidence of the Welsh-speaking witnesses only that the least glimmering of the matter in hand reaches the mind of the jury. . . . [T]he evidence of English witnesses is not translated at all." The words of the legal experts were also largely wasted. "The eloquent speeches of counsel delivered in the most refined English accent and filled with technicalities and rhetorical flights are as absolutely unintelligible to the majority, if not to the whole of the jury as similar speeches in Welsh would be to the counsel of the Judge." After the judge instructed the jury in unintelligible English, "the poor puzzled peasants put their heads together and come to a thoroughly independent decision."[24] It is hardly surprising that as the *Carmarthen Weekly Reporter* noted, "Stupid findings are invariably attributed to the Welsh jurymen."[25]

The language difficulties created problems for judges and jurors alike.[26] In

Table 1.1. Homicide Trial Outcomes

England	Total	67–75	76–84	85–92
%ng	27	31	27	26
%murder	21	16	20	27
%insane	8	7	7	10
Ireland	Total	67–75	76–84	85–92
%ng	29	35	27	25
%murder	5	3	7	6
%insane	7	6	9	8
Scotland	Total	67–75	76–84	85–92
%ng (including not proven)	28	35	28	21
%murder	5	5	4	7
%insane	5	6	4	5
Wales	Total	67–75	76–84	85–92
%ng	32	29	32	21
%murder	11	6	16	17
%insane	5	1	4	11

1871 the lord chancellor rejected a petition requesting that county court judges in Wales be required to be fluent in Welsh on the grounds that "a Judge selected for his Welsh requirements would become subject to mistrust on the part of an English litigant." A Welsh MP responded that in mid-Wales four-fifths of the Welsh who appeared in court spoke Welsh as their primary language and probably half of them spoke no English. "I cannot but think that a Welsh litigant would have at least an equal ground for distrusting the decision of a Judge who cannot understand a word of his own language."[27] Even the *Times* recognized the problem. The absence of Welsh speakers on the bench "absolutely saps the public confidence in it. . . . The Judge has practically to grope his way as best he can almost in the dark as it were."[28] Like most disagreements between the Welsh and the English, the dispute was carried on politely but the miscommunication was serious.

As can be seen in table 1.1, the percentage of trials ending in acquittals did not vary much among the four nations. Between 1867 and 1892 English juries acquitted in 27 percent of homicide trials, Welsh jurors in 32 percent, and the Irish in 29 percent. Scottish juries found 16 percent of defendants not guilty and the charges not proven in 13 percent of cases. Everywhere but Wales the trend was toward fewer acquittals. In England the percentage acquitted fell from 31 percent in the late 1860s and early 1870s to 26 percent by the early 1890s. Irish juries were also becoming less likely to acquit, with the figures dropping from 35 percent in the late 1860s to 25 percent by the early 1890s. The biggest change was in Scotland where the percentage of homicide defendants receiving verdicts of not guilty or not proven fell from 35 percent to 21 percent. However, which sorts of cases resulted in acquittal varied considerably from nation to nation.

Which types of trials were most likely to lead to acquittals did vary however. Other than in accidents, English juries were most likely to return a not-guilty verdict if the death had occurred while the killer was delivering what the jury perceived as a justified chastisement to a prisoner, an asylum inmate, or an unruly servant, apprentice, or student. Irish and Scottish juries were most likely to acquit when the motive for the homicide had been issues of land or politics. Welsh juries were most likely to excuse homicides that occurred during pranks.

These differences are particularly interesting when compared with which defendants were least likely to be acquitted. In England juries were least likely to acquit if the motive for the killing had been thwarted romance. This is in part because the killer in these cases was likely to use a lethal weapon, but it also points to some interesting assumptions about gender. A man might chastise his wife, his child, or his subordinate but *not* a woman he was courting. The Irish were hardest on defendants who had killed while seeking revenge. A planned assault based on a grudge did not square with the Irish assumption that homicides were the inadvertent result of uncontrolled passions. The Scots were hardest on poachers whose guilt was compounded by the combination of theft and homicide.

Trial outcomes throughout Britain were also very much affected by the common law tradition which allowed considerable leeway to judge and jurors in determining what the law actually was. Despite efforts at codification of the law and the regularization of procedures, the outcome of any late nineteenth-century homicide trial depended very much on the individual judge and jury. Lord Chief Justice Coleridge explained that he did not like to direct juries to particular verdicts. "It was impossible to devise an intellectual formula which would cover all the varying circumstances of different cases."[29] In 1884 the *Times* observed that Baron John Huddleston in advising a jury "had to do what English judges have frequently to do—under the guise of interpreting the law he had to make it."[30] Baron William Channell even acknowledged that the jurors were also lawmakers when he told a jury, "[T]he law was an abstraction; in reality it meant the verdict of a jury, upon which depended its practical enforcement."[31]

DEFINING MURDER

Among the most contentious issues was the distinction between the capital offense of murder and the lesser crimes of manslaughter in Ireland, England, and Wales and culpable homicide in Scotland. The written law left considerable leeway for both judge and jurors in deciding between murder and manslaughter or culpable homicide. Manslaughter was formally defined as "unlawful and felonious killing of another without any malice express or implied."[32] Culpable homicide was defined as "a killing caused by fault falling short of the evil intention required to constitute murder."[33] But *malice* and *evil* were fairly flexible terms in practice, and the judges often disagreed.

English Justice George Bramwell seemed to imply that no prior intent was required: "If a man without lawful cause and without circumstances to reduce it to manslaughter inflicted a deadly wound he was guilty of murder although the thought of doing it never entered his mind until the moment he gave it the fatal blow."[34] Justice James Stephen argued that the method was crucial. "The rule he should lay down for their guidance was that if a man kills another by means which in all probability must cause his death, that crime amounted to murder unless there were circumstances which reduced it to manslaughter or justified the act."[35] But his colleague Justice William Brett suggested jurors must consider the killer's state of mind: "[I]f at the time he had command of his passions so as to have command also of his will and intention he would be guilty of murder; but if he had not much command of his passions, it would be open to the jury to convict him only of manslaughter."[36] However, Justice Huddleston assured a jury that "the fact that the prisoner's mind was distorted by evil and wicked passions was no defense."[37]

Provocation and self-defense were the most obvious mitigating factors. The degree of provocation required was also subject to debate. Justice Lush insisted that "mere quarrel of words did not constitute a provocation nor a single blow but a series of savage blows."[38] Justice Cleasby concurred that "neither opprobrious language nor even a slap in the face would reduce the offence from murder to manslaughter but when a man was kicked and knocked down and blood made to flow it might be otherwise."[39] But Justice

Mellor seems to have believed that the issue was the immediacy of the provocation: "Whether their verdict should be one of manslaughter or murder depended on whether the prisoner's acts causing death were done in the heat of passion, arising under reasonable provocation, or not until after an interval of time sufficient either in fact or in legal presumption to allow the passion to subside and the control of reason to be resumed."[40]

Self-defense and the defense of others were also considered mitigation. But even so, prior intent was significant. Chief Justice Coleridge told a jury "if they believed the prisoner went out with the deliberate intention of taking someone's life it would be murder, no matter whether he himself was attacked or not; but if they believed he had a bona fide belief that his life was in peril, but that such belief was unreasonable it was manslaughter and finally if he had grounds to believe his life was in danger then acquit."[41] In a case in which a man had killed in defense of his sibling, Justice Field told the jury, "If they believed the deceased did no more than was necessary to prevent the prisoner beating his brother it was not manslaughter; but if he did more than was necessary, looking at the excited state of the prisoner's mind at the time, than it would be manslaughter."[42]

Ultimately the issue was malicious intent, which was difficult both to define and to detect. In practice the jury's assumptions about the killer's state of mind were frequently based on the relationship between and status of the killer and the victim. When both were working class and the setting was a pub on Saturday night, authorities may have been less willing to assume malice. As the *Times* reported in one case, "Yesterday Samuel Chipperfield, a laborer, is alleged to have killed another laborer, named Samuel Betts, in a pub in Beerstreet, Norwich on Saturday night but the police have not found that Chipperfield had any ill-will against Betts and under these circumstances it seems probable that the case will resolve itself into one of manslaughter."[43]

English juries returned for manslaughter rather than murder in nearly half the convictions resulting from murder indictments, in some cases over the strong objections of the judge. In one case Justice Martin told a jury: "I am bound to tell you that your verdict is directly contrary to the evidence."[44] With only slightly less censure, Justice Denman told a Warwick jury that had returned a manslaughter verdict that ninety-nine out of one hundred juries would have said the crime was murder.[45] Justice Martin insisted in a charge to a Chelmsford jury: "[I]t is your duty to act upon the law. You do not sit there with discretion to find this man guilty of murder and that man guilty of manslaughter as you may think proper according to your own view of the law. It is your duty to act upon the law as laid down by a judge."[46] But what law was laid down depended very much on which judge was presiding. In

England 32 percent of homicide convictions were for murder, but among judges who heard over fifty trials the percentage of convictions that were for the full offense ranged from just 10 percent for Justice Gillery Piggott to over 58 percent for Justice Montagu Smith.

In addition to the fact that different judges might offer different opinions, juries always had the option to disregard their instructions. After an English jury acquitted a man who had stabbed a neighbor who interfered when he was beating his wife, Justice Henry Keating told the prisoner: "The jury have found you not guilty on what grounds I am utterly at a loss to conceive but it is their province and not mine to decide. I merely make these observations in order that this verdict may not be an encouragement to you to commit acts of violence."[47] An Irish judge told a Limerick jury: "It was nothing to him if the jury discharged the prisoner, but it was everything to the county."[48] Another Irish judge was unable to show such sangfroid. When a Tipperary jury failed to convict, he shouted: "Take back that verdict. I will not take it. Do you think fracturing a man's skull is nothing? If you do I'd like to see it tried on yourself."[49] Similarly after the judge explained that there was no way to reach a verdict of culpable homicide, a Glasgow jury promptly returned a verdict of culpable homicide.[50]

Despite the variations among judges and juries, English trials were still four times more likely to result in murder convictions than were homicide trials in Ireland and Scotland. Irish juries were so reluctant to return murder convictions that prosecutors often chose to indict only for "very serious manslaughter."[51] With the death sentence out of the equation, presumably it was easier to persuade an Irish jury to convict. Irish courts were also more willing to accept that homicides were the result of either accident or uncontrollable passion.[52] An Irish judge explained that "[m]anslaughter was killing another without any malice."[53] According to Irish law books, "[I]n every case of proved homicide the law presumes malice but such presumptions may be rebutted."[54] But Irish courtrooms routinely ignored the presumption.[55] Only 5 percent of Irish homicide trials led to murder convictions. Unless the motive was political, the Irish tendency to see homicides as unfortunate accidents meant that punishment should be light. In fact, 65 percent of persons convicted of homicide in Ireland between 1866 and 1892 served less than two years.

Scottish juries rarely returned murder convictions, though the figures are somewhat skewed by the fact that Scottish murder defendants were much more likely to plead guilty than were those of the other nations. Nearly a quarter of those indicted for murder in Scottish courtrooms pled guilty to culpable homicide as compared with fewer than 5 percent of English and

Irish defendants. This may be because the defendants felt that, given the
thoroughness of the investigation before the trial, it was foolish to fight the
charges. At any rate, when the decision was left to the jury in Scottish murder trials, the jurors returned a conviction for the full offense in 15 percent
of cases.

As in England, the judges in Scotland sometimes disagreed on the distinction between murder and culpable homicide. Trials heard by Justice
Moncreiff were over twice as likely to end in murder convictions as were
those heard by Justices Deas or Young. Scottish jurors also chose to ignore
instructions on occasion. For example, after the judge assured a Glasgow jury
that he "did not see a single thing in the case that could lead to any other verdict than murder," the jury returned a unanimous verdict of culpable homicide.[56] In another case a man pled guilty to culpable homicide after he
stabbed a man on a footpath. The defendant was drunk and belligerent and
simply attacked the first person he saw. The prosecution accepted the plea on
the grounds that there could have been no prior malice since "they were complete strangers." The presiding judge, Lord Young, announced that the attack
was "what we are in the habit of calling murder," but he sentenced the man
to only fourteen years.[57] In another case in which a strolling piper had
stabbed a man he encountered on the road, the defense attempted to claim
that the stabbing was the result of a quarrel, but Lord Ardmillan insisted
"there were no degrees of malice in the Scottish law" and insisted on a murder verdict.[58]

Though the numbers were small, the Welsh were more likely to return
murder convictions than were the Irish or Scots but less likely than the
English. The *Carmarthen Weekly Reporter* insisted that Welsh juries were
reluctant to return murder convictions because of their religious conviction
that the death penalty represented a usurpation of God's sole authority over
life and death.[59]

Everywhere a murder conviction carried an automatic death sentence,
though the Crown through the Home Office could commute the sentence.
Juries gave their recommendations regarding mercy with their verdict and the
presiding judge passed them on with his recommendations. In prominent
cases, communities often presented petitions as well.

Even though the Home Office in London made the ultimate decision in
all capital cases, there was considerable variation among the nations.[60]
Between 1867 and 1892 the Home Office allowed 58 percent of English
death sentences to be carried out. Though the percentage of English death
sentences being carried out remained relatively constant, the percentage of
homicide trials in England which led to execution went from 16 percent for

the period 1867–1874 to 27 percent for the period 1885–1892. Death sentences were most likely to be carried out when the murder had been committed in the course of another felony such as robbery or rape or when the killer had been taking revenge on a woman (other than his wife) who had spurned his romantic advances. About half of Welsh murder convictions resulted in executions, but the numbers are so small it is hard to reach many conclusions.

Irish juries were the least likely to return a murder conviction, but the Home Office was also least likely to commute an Irish death sentence. Irish defense attorneys routinely warned against "the foulest of all crimes, namely the bringing about of judicial murder."[61] In one particularly grisly case in which the accused had broken into a home and hacked a woman to death, two jurors admitted they believed the defendant was guilty but as members of the Anti-capital Punishment Society they would never vote to convict.[62] Only 4 percent of Irish homicide trials ended with murder convictions. But 67 percent of those sentenced to death for murder in Ireland were executed. There is a chicken-and-egg aspect to these figures. Because Irish death penalties were the most likely to be carried out, it would seem wise for Irish juries to be particularly cautious in risking them. On the other hand, given the difficulty in obtaining a murder verdict in Ireland, it might be that those who were convicted were particularly deserving of harsh punishment. In fact, those most likely to be executed in Ireland were convicted of murders in connection with land or politics.

Scottish death sentences were the least likely to be carried out. Only 34 percent of the condemned in Scotland were executed. Given the fact that a murder conviction in Scotland could be based on a majority of one, the need for mercy may have been greater. But over half of the death sentences that were commuted had been based on unanimous verdicts. Further, the jury had been split in over a third of the cases in which the death sentence was carried out. Nor was it simply a matter of the Home Office correcting for overzealous verdicts. Only 2 percent of all persons tried for homicide in Scotland between 1867 and 1892 were executed. Those most at risk of actual execution in Scotland were those convicted of murder while poaching.

The sentences in manslaughter and culpable homicide convictions could range from immediate release to life in prison. As the Scottish Justice Lord Deas explained, culpable homicide "sometimes may be quite properly visited with a few weeks improvement and at other times it is a crime which meets the highest punishment of the law short of death."[63] Though sentencing in manslaughter cases was at the discretion of the judge, the general sentencing patterns give some indication of the relative weight given to various types of homicide according to circumstances. The national averages varied. Sentences were lightest in Ireland, where the average sentence was three years (this includes all cases where the initial charge was homicide, though the conviction might have been for assault or a lesser charge). The Scottish average was nearly two years longer than the Irish, and the English and Welsh another year longer than that of the Scots. Of course, within nations judges varied as well.

INSANITY

The other possible outcome was a finding of insanity. The percentage of cases ending in insanity verdicts was remarkably similar among the four nations, all falling between 5 and 8 percent of cases. Everywhere domestic cases were the most likely to result in insanity verdicts, followed by cases involving blighted romances. But all of the complexity, indeterminacy, and ambiguity of the British legal system is clearly evident in the issue of insanity.[64] There was no statutory definition of insanity. The definition given in the M'Naghten Rules[65] that "the accused at the time of committing the act was labouring under such a defect of reason, from disease of the mind, as not to know the nature and quality of the act he was doing: or, if he did know it, that he did not know he was doing what was wrong" was often cited in English cases.[66] But in fact the definition of insanity in any given case was very much at the discretion of the judge and jury. The definition most often applied in Scottish courts derived from Hume, who stated that "[t]o serve the purpose of a defense in law, the disorder must amount to an absolute alienation of reason, such a disease as deprives the patient of the knowledge of the true aspect and position of things about him, hinders him from distinguishing friend or foe—and gives him up to the impulse of his own distempered fancy."[67] But, as in England, the definition was ultimately in the hands of the jury.

The instructions given by English judges indicate a considerable degree of disagreement. As an attorney explained to a Central Criminal Court jury in 1869, "[T]he question of insanity as applied to the criminal law was exceedingly difficult and one with respect to which many learned judges had differed in opinion."[68] Justice Brett insisted that the mere fact that the accused was insane or delusional did not suffice. While hearing a case in which a man had suddenly killed a coworker with an adze with no apparent motive, Brett told the jury: "No doubt the man was in a sense insane, that is he was probably under the influence of delusion and no doubt the act was sudden and there was no apparent motive for it; . . . but the question was not whether he was of unsound mind, but whether he was so insane as not to know the nature of the act." The Maidstone jury returned a verdict of "guilty but not accountable for his acts." Since this was not a legal verdict, the clerk of the Assize asked, "[T]hat is you acquit him on the grounds of insanity?" When the jury agreed, Justice Brett then asked, "[I]nsanity in the sense I have explained to you?" Once again the jury agreed.[69]

The confusion over the meaning of the jury's initial verdict was addressed in the Trial of Lunatics Act of 1883, which changed the procedures so that persons found insane were no longer declared "not guilty on grounds of insanity," but rather "not responsible." The change was largely semantic and at least one judge claimed that its impact was minimal. Justice Williams described the act as a "curious illustration of the way things were done in this county. For although it was his duty to go to the court to preside over the trial, it was only by the merest accident that the fact that such an Act had been passed was made known to him and he became aware of that fact by reading it in the newspaper. A copy of the Act was not delivered to him." Williams went on to add that "he was not aware of the reasons for passing the Act."[70] His comment is particularly significant. All too often the statute books and legal commentary seem to be only minimally connected to the realities of courtrooms.

The *Times* suspected that English judges and medical experts were too lenient. In 1883 a leading article described the case of a man who had murdered his child as "only too fairly representative of a class of cases frequent in English courts." After outlining the man's history of violence, the newspaper noted that "those not uncommon symptoms of lawlessness and ruffianism satisfied one doctor that the defendant was 'a typical lunatic with dangerous delusions.'" But to the newspaper's satisfaction, "the jury were not convinced by the familiar argument that a man who does anything particularly wicked must be insane. . . . For years the plain men who sit in jury boxes have been assailed by medical theorists who seek to discredit all the old homespun ideas as to responsibility."[71] Three weeks later, when the sentence was commuted on grounds of insanity, the *Times* suggested that the Home Office would do well to ignore "theorists who gauge the extent of a criminal's insanity by the magnitude of his crime."[72] Cases in which the jury rejected an insanity plea but the Home Office intervened after the fact and had the killer transferred to an insane asylum were particularly galling as they seemed to undermine the jury system altogether.[73] But in England the trend favored the medical men. Though the actual number of homicide trials ending in insanity verdicts was constant, the percentage of homicide trials resulting in insanity verdicts rose from 7 to 10 percent in the late 1880s.[74]

One of the main problems many people had with insanity pleas was that they suggested a lack of will and control, two key virtues for the Victorians. When a grocer who had killed his wife and brother-in-law out of unfounded jealousy claimed, "[I]t wasn't me, it was my brain,"[75] his plea exemplified the detachment between self and actions that many found objectionable. Justice Honyman complained that "uncontrollable impulse was 'the cant of the day.'"[76] Justice Huddleston cautioned a jury against "taking a cowardly refuge" in insanity verdicts. "It was not any idle frantic humour, not any eccentricity or something unanswerable or unexplained which would justify a verdict of insanity."[77] Justice Bramwell appeared to share this view. When a witness spoke of "homicidal mania," Justice Bramwell interjected: "[Y]ou mean a morbid appetite to do wrong. If an insane man knew he was committing murder that man was responsible. It was not enough to have a homicidal mania. The object of the law was to guard against mischievous propensities and homicidal impulses. He did not believe in uncontrollable impulse at all." But, as was often the case, the judge's rhetoric during the trial did not square with the outcome. The accused was found insane and Justice Bramwell voiced his support of the verdict. "It would have been impossible, gentlemen, for such a man to be executed—too shocking and cruel. It is a very sad case and the man is deeply to be pitied."[78]

Some scholars have argued that this link between strength of will and insanity had rendered the insanity question a highly gendered one.[79] Gender will be discussed in depth in chapter 3, but regarding insanity the homicide records indicate that the link between insanity and feminine nature may have been overstated. While women homicide defendants were more likely to be found insane than men (16 percent of female killers compared to 6 percent of men), 60 percent of accused killers who were found insane were men. Much has been made of the link between infanticide and insanity verdicts, but in fact the likelihood of an insanity verdict for a defendant accused of killing his or her own child was not highly influenced by gender. Twenty-three percent of English mothers accused of killing children were found insane, but so were 18 percent of English fathers.

The Irish were even less inclined to link insanity with femaleness.[80] Nearly 90 percent of the Irish killers who were found insane were male. The killer most likely to be found insane in Ireland was a man who had killed his lover or an adult relative. Given the presumption that homicide was often the result of uncontrolled passion, it might be expected that the Irish were particularly likely to find insanity verdicts. But that was not the case; instead, Irish courts often saw uncontrollable impulses as a universal problem. Also, since sentences for manslaughter in Ireland were lighter than in other countries, an insanity plea might have been counterproductive. One judge even recommended that defendants not plead insanity "since it could mean being kept in an asylum for an extended period."[81]

Scottish homicide trials were the least likely to end in insanity verdicts. This may have been in part because Scottish courts were willing to find diminished capacity as a mitigating factor in homicide cases. In the *Dingwall* case in 1867, Lord Deas told a jury that while the defendant could not be found insane, they might return a finding of culpable homicide since his chronic drunkenness indicated diminished responsibility. This precedent was not always followed, however, even by Lord Deas.[82] In fact, in 1875 the superintendent of the Glasgow Royal Asylum complained in the *Times* that "it is a grave defect in our criminal law that it does not recognize degrees of insanity and corresponding degrees of culpability. A jury should have the power not merely to commend a culprit to mercy and so mitigate his punishment, but to declare him entitled to a mitigation of punishment when they are satisfied that there exists mental weakness, although not to the extent of irresponsible insanity."[83] The likelihood of an insanity verdict in a Scottish homicide trial was the same for men and women.

DRINK AND RESPONSIBILITY

In addition to the possible precedent of diminished responsibility, the *Dingwall* case was also cited as a precedent for accepting drunkenness as a form of mitigation. Everywhere alcohol was a frequent factor in homicides. In England and Wales alcohol was specifically mentioned in about a quarter of homicide cases. But Justice Huddleston told a jury that "[f]ive/sixths of cases in the calendar throughout the country might be traced to intoxication, for which there was no excuse whatsoever."[84] It might well be that Huddleston's estimate was closer as alcohol may have been so common in homicides that it was not thought worthy of mention. Alcohol was reported as a contributing factor in 28 percent of Irish homicide cases, though, again, in many situations the presence of alcohol was probably deemed too obvious to mention. Parliamentary reports on crime in Ireland concluded that "[t]he great problem indicated by the statistics of Irish crime is how to deal with drunkenness and the crimes connected therewith."[85] The Scots were the most likely to record the presence of drink in homicides. Either the killer, the victim, or both were reported to have been intoxicated in 40 percent of Scottish cases, but even this may be an understatement.

Despite the temperance movements found throughout the British Isles during the late nineteenth century, drunkenness was still often taken for granted.[86] After hearing a case in which two young men had killed a third during a fight in a pub, English Justice Grove "commented on the frequency of crimes of violence which arose from drunkenness, but he added that this vice was regarded unfortunately in so venial a light by a large class of the more uneducated people, that such an expression of opinion seemed to be wasted on them." The punishment in the case was also venial—three months each.[87] These circumstances were by no means unique to England. In Crieff, in central Scotland, a stabbing victim bled to death on his own front porch as neighbors and even a policeman passed by, assuming he was drunk. In a case from Glasgow in which a man had killed his wife using a hammer, a poker, an iron bar, and clogs, witnesses explained that both the accused and the victim were addicted to drink, "though otherwise they had borne a respectable character."[88] The same sorts of comments were heard in Irish courts. In Kilkenny, a man who had murdered his own child was described as "a very good man—with one exception— that he drank."[89]

Given these views, how much and whether drunkenness mitigated a homicide was always a moot point and judges themselves seemed ambivalent. When a man in Manchester was convicted of killing a friend by kicking him in the stomach, Justice Lopes told the jury the man had acted "while under the influence of drink and not from any feeling of animosity. Still life must be respected." To show this respect, he sentenced him to three months.[90] But other English judges felt differently. Justice Lush told a jury "if a man were lying in the road dead drunk waving a sword about and he thereby caused death he would not be guilty of murder, but nothing short of that would reduce the crime to manslaughter."[91] An English defense attorney argued that "while drunkenness is no legal excuse for crime, no man should in my judgment be put to death for murder committed while drunk."[92] But Justice Bovill staunchly announced the rationale for not accepting that argument: "Drunkenness voluntarily caused by a person was no answer whatever to a charge of murder and it did not reduce what would otherwise be murder to the crime of manslaughter. That was the law of the land and if it were not so, there would be no protection to society."[93]

But other judges did feel that drunkenness worked against a murder conviction. Justice Day told a jury, "I have ruled that if a man were in such a state of intoxication that he did not know the nature of his act or that his act was wrongful, his act would be excusable." The prosecuting attorney cited a ruling by Justice Manisty that "disease brought about by a prisoner's own act, e.g. delirium tremens caused by excessive drinking—was no excuse for committing a crime unless the disease so produced was permanent." Manisty had told a Manchester jury that "if the prisoner's insanity was only temporary and produced by his own excesses the law did not excuse him."[94] But Justice Day explicitly rejected the precedent insisting that "the issue was insanity not its cause or whether it was temporary or permanent."[95] Lord Chief Justice Coleridge apparently agreed with Justice Day. In 1886 he told a jury that a "principle of the law was that a man must be taken to intend what was the natural consequences of his act . . . drunkenness was no excuse for acts done. . . . They must administer the law as they find it and it could not be perverted to meet any feelings of mercy."[96]

English juries were less likely to acquit drunken killers than sober ones. However, they did seem to find some mitigation in drunkenness as sober killers were more likely to be convicted of the full crime of murder than were drunken ones. However, the Home Office was more likely to let an execution go forward if the killer had been drunk. Welsh juries were slightly more likely to acquit drunken killers than sober ones. They were also nearly twice as likely to convict sober killers of *murder* as drunken ones. When a Welsh jury acquitted two men who had beaten and kicked a friend to death during a drunken fight, the judge said the verdict was proper but "gave them a severe caution for this mingling themselves up in a drunken row in which a fellow creature was sent unprepared to his great reckoning."[97] Though English and Welsh juries were less likely to return *murder* convictions if the killers had been drunk, judges were harsher in sentencing. In manslaughter convictions, the average sentence given to a drunken killer in England and Wales was eighteen months longer than for a sober one. English authorities may have been more concerned about drunken violence than were middle-class jurymen who were rarely threatened by it.

The situation was reversed in Ireland where defendants who had been drunk at the time of the homicide served shorter sentences and were much less likely to be executed. Only one of the fifty-four persons hanged for murder in Ireland during the period was reported to have been drunk at the time of the crime. Irish judges and jurors seemed to accept that drink was a good man's failing. As one Irish judge said, "[I]t was very hard to know what punishment to mete out to a man who was ordinarily quiet and well behaved as long as he was sober but violent and uncontrolled when drunk."[98] This also follows general trends in which Irish courts were likely to see killers as victims of circumstances who were not fully accountable for their actions.

Despite the *Dingwall* precedent, the Scots were less tolerant of drink as an excuse for homicide. Killers reported as having been drunk at the time were convicted 82 percent of the time versus only 50 percent of those who had not been reported as drunk. Drunken killers in Scotland were seven times more likely to hang than sober ones. When convicted of culpable homicide, 24 percent of those who had been drunk were sentenced to more than ten years in prison versus only 4 percent of the sober. Generally then, English, Irish, and Welsh jurors were more likely to see drink as mitigation whereas Scottish juries saw it as worsening the offense. This corresponds with a general trend for Scottish juries to be more likely to stress individual responsibility and the need for atonement.

ACCIDENTAL DEATHS

The focus of this book is on the relationships between killers and victims, but there were two categories of homicide in which there was no relationship. In 1873 an article in the *Daily News* titled "The Annual Massacre in England" noted, "In England and Wales, a population as large as that of the city of Winchester, is every year swept away by violent deaths, accompanied in many cases by mutilation." The article went on to make some rather striking comparisons. First, it compared the slaughter to that of revolutionary France: "If every inhabitant of the two towns of Margate and of Melton Mowbray had been guillotined or drowned on the first of January 1871 there would have been hardly a larger number of violent deaths than actually occurred in this country during the year in question, while the total sum of suffering and torture endured by the victims would undoubtedly have been considerably smaller." The next comparison was to the primitive outposts of the empire: "In 1871 an Englishman runs from seven to eight times as great risk of a violent death than an East Indian does from wild animals." The article then returned to the French as the standard for horror. "The English are being slaughtered, steadily, certainly and remorselessly slain at a rate which every two years sacrifices as many victims as the Massacre of St. Bartholomew." Clearly few things could be more outrageous than that Englishmen were as much in danger as Frenchmen or Indians.

The statistics were shocking: "Every day of the year forty-seven English people are killed with suffering and mutilation of the most excruciating kind." What is most remarkable for our purposes is how little of this slaughter fell under the heading of homicide. Criminal homicides accounted for only 2.5 percent of the violent deaths in England and Wales. The inspiration for this hysterical rhetoric was the number of deaths in mining and railway accidents and the fact that the authorities seemed to be doing very little to prevent them. "Are the fitful and momentary outbursts of impatience such as are exerted on the occasion of some unusually fatal colliery or railway disaster the only signs of concern we shall ever see in the face of the tragedies occurring every day and everywhere around us?"[99]

For the United Kingdom as a whole, more than 7 percent of deaths reported as criminal homicide trials dealt with accidents, though the distribution varied considerably. While accidents constituted 5, 6, and 8 percent of homicide trials in Ireland, England, and Wales respectively, they made up 14 percent of the criminal homicides tried in Scotland. The Scots were much more likely to use the criminal court to investigate deaths from industrial or railway accidents—tragedies that authorities in the other countries were more likely to see as misadventures rather than crimes. Because there were no coroners' juries to investigate such deaths, Scottish judges often praised the use of the criminal courts as a scene for public investigation. Juries sometimes acquitted the defendants but passed resolutions condemning the industry for lax practices.[100] But Scottish courts were also slightly more likely to convict in such cases than were other British courts. Even when there was no malice, the Scots were more likely to hold someone accountable. Scottish courts believed in atonement even when the sin had been unintentional. Lord Young summarized the situation at a Glasgow court: "They were cases of neglect on the part of persons of respectable character, but neglect which had been attended by serious and unexpected consequences."[101]

Predictably the number and types of accidental deaths which were treated as criminal varied among the nations. An investigation by the Statistical Society of Great Britain published in 1886 found that the accidental death rate in Scotland, England, and Wales was more than twice that of Ireland.[102] Since most of the accidents were related to either mining, railway, or construction, the low Irish rates reflect that Ireland was so much less industrialized. Seventy-one percent of the homicide trials resulting from accidents in Ireland involved carts colliding or running over pedestrians. In most cases the driver had been intoxicated. But the Irish courts were very tolerant. Fewer than 20 percent of persons charged with criminal homicides in a traffic accident served any jail time as a result. However, as is often the case, the Irish figures are highly suspect as some county police departments chose to report vehicular homicides in the outrage figures and some did not. Nearly half of the reported cases were in Ulster where vehicular homicides were the subject of more than 6 percent of homicide trials.

Thirty-nine percent of English trials for accidental homicide resulted from road traffic accidents. Justice Bramwell complained to an Old Bailey jury that there was a "mistaken notion which drivers of vehicles too often entertained that the road belonged to them and that they had a sort of right to run over anybody that happened to come in their way."[103] When a cabdriver ran over

and killed a woman in 1874, the *Times* reported that "[t]he only fact weighing against the prisoner was that he was intoxicated at the time, but he was
driving at a steady, if not slow, pace and the scene was intensely dark." The
jury acquitted him.[104] But this jury was more lenient than most. In England
70 percent of cart drivers tried for killing a pedestrian while driving drunk
were convicted as opposed to only 25 percent of sober drivers. However, the
sentences were always light.

Nor was negligence always considered criminal. English judges were divided over the criminality of negligent homicide. Justice Lindley told a jury
hearing a manslaughter case in which an elderly man had died of complications after being run over that it "did not necessarily follow that they ought
to convict because the prisoner had been guilty of some degree of negligence."[105] On the other hand, when two brewers were accused of running
over an elderly deaf woman, Justice Stephen insisted that it was the "duty of
those who drove to take care of the public and not the duty of the public to
look out for persons who were driving at an excessive or dangerous pace."
The jury acquitted them, leading Justice Stephen to say that had they been
convicted, he would have given them a severe sentence.[106] Stephen never got
a chance to act on this threat. The accused were acquitted in every accidental homicide case he heard during the period.

Judges were sometimes more condemnatory in their rhetoric than in their
sentencing. John Baker, a fish hawker at Grays, drove his cart through a
crowd of people, killing a pedestrian. When told he had killed a man, he said,
"And a good job too! What business had he to be there?" Justice Hawkins
said, "People had a right to walk in the road and were not to be driven over
recklessly even if men were lying in the road drunk, anyone deliberately driving over them was guilty of murder." However, after the jury convicted Baker,
Hawkins sentenced him to only three months although he had several prior
arrests.[107] Two months later, a drunk who had driven over and killed a man
while speeding was sentenced to five months. The judge said, "The public
highways were open to all her Majesty's subjects[,] the public had a right to
pass along them and if the prisoner drove fast he did it at his own peril."[108]
The pronouncement is interesting since it would seem the greater peril was
for his victim. In England the average sentence for a homicide involving a
horse-drawn vehicle was less than four months, and nearly 20 percent of convictions resulted in no jail time at all.

Only twelve Scots were tried for cart homicides, but half of them were
convicted and all of the convicted served jail time. In 1869 at Peebles, Hames
McGrath was sentenced to twelve months for running over a deaf and dumb
woman in his gig. Two of his passengers were given nine months each as

accessories.[109] But in another case, a drunken car driver who had killed a three-year-old child who was standing on a sidewalk won a not-proven verdict by a vote of eight to seven.[110]

Cart accidents were more likely to lead to criminal charges, even though trains were far more lethal. The average annual death toll in rail accidents was more than a thousand.[111] In 1869 a *Times* editorial urged, "A more punctilious reverence for human life must be encouraged. Homicidal negligence must be frowned down by society as well as homicidal anger. Railway companies are guilty as Companies, when they pound to pieces their passengers in one train by the engine of another."[112] But many English judges felt that carelessness on the railways was not criminal. Justice Cleasby told a jury if an engineer "was attending to his business and carrying out the regulations of the company in the ordinary way, he could not be held criminally liable because he had made a slight error in speed." The man who had been driving a train at thirty miles per hour when he should have been going fifteen was acquitted.[113] In another case, Justice Bramwell explained: "A man was not liable necessarily because he was unskilled or careless. He was criminally liable if the act was so negligent or careless that his fault could only be properly punished by a criminal conviction."[114] Of the fifty-three men tried for criminal negligence resulting in deaths on English and Welsh railways, only six served any jail time. The longest sentence—twelve months—went to a stationmaster who had left a teenager in charge. The collision had killed thirteen people, and Justice Hawkins said it had been "inexcusable to leave a fifteen year old boy who was working twelve hour days at 7 shillings, 6 pence a week in charge of the station."[115]

After a trial for a rail accident resulted in acquittals all around in 1869, the *Times* complained that the result demonstrated a flaw in the English character: "Foreigners who edify their countrymen with Letters on England may find a rich subject for their comments in a story which came to an end last week. With all our Anglo-Saxon recklessness we are not indifferent to human life, and the sacrifice in this case was so appalling that the whole machinery of our institutions was instantly set in motion for the purpose of detection and retribution." But the efforts of the system had come to naught. "Nobody is punished for it is nobody's fault. . . . What a picture of inconsequence, heedlessness and failure. Was there ever a people like these English?"[116] Six months later the circumstances were repeated. After a railway collision at Nottingham was ruled accidental, the *Times* concluded: "Thus there has been a loss of seven human lives, an enormous amount of terror and suffering and no one is to blame."[117]

The worst rail accident in England during the period was at Thorpe in

September 1874 when a train collision killed twenty-five. The night manager of the station was convicted and sentenced to eight months.[118] The *Times* was not content. "We do not know whether anybody is satisfied with this result. It has always seemed to us scarcely worth the trouble to hunt down such small game as station masters, engine drivers and telegraph clerks while the system which renders their blundering fatal escapes any effectual criticism."[119]

The *Scotsman* shared the concern of the *Times,* complaining that the railways were conducted with the "most common and culpable carelessness." Officials, the editorial complained, played with lives "as a juggler plays with balls." The *Scotsman* even suggested that the miracle was that more people were not killed. "Every day's experience show men how much they are dependant for their safety upon the simple exercise of care on the part of other men and the wonder really is that so many people in places of responsibility do exercise the care necessary to avoid danger."[120] A third of the criminal charges brought for accidental deaths in Scotland stemmed from rail accidents, and Scottish juries often concluded that the problems were systematic. For example, in a case from Edinburgh, the jury acquitted the engineer and added their "disapprobation of the laxness which appears to have existed in the supervision of the working of this particular train."[121] Another jury passed a resolution "condemning the lax practice that has been proved particularly disregarding the rules of the railway company."[122] In 1878 an Edinburgh jury found the driver and signalman in a collision guilty, "but recommended them to the leniency of the court in respect the company were to blame in not having enforced the rule as to lighting the lamp at the distant signal post."[123]

But Scottish judges were also wary of letting individuals off. Justice Deas probably had this case in mind when a week later he heard charges against a stationmaster and a railway point man for a railway collision in Inverness. Justice Deas charged against the accused. "Even supposing the company were to blame for not strictly adhering to their published rules, that would never do away with the blame of the servants in plainly neglecting their duty. He held it would be dangerous to the public to go on encouraging acquittals in cases of this sort where such neglect was clearly proved."[124] The issue of personal responsibility was also stressed in a case heard by Lord Ardmillan in 1873. After hearing a stoker who had been involved in a collision testify that the engineer had "said someone should go back for the purpose of signaling the passenger trains to stop I considered that it was the brakeman's duty and not mine to do this," Lord Ardmillan promptly spoke up: "Allow me to tell you that where there is the slightest chance of danger every man should do what he can to prevent any accident taking place, and if you saw that the right man was away you would never have been the wrong man to have done it, and you ought to have done it." The brakeman also told the court, "I have been in the employment of the Railway Company for four years and have never got a rule-book." Again Justice Ardmillan interrupted: "Allow me to recommend to you first to get a rule-book and then to make yourself master of what it is your duty to do, and just act like a man of sense and do your duty for it is not like a man of sense not to have a rule-book, and still less of those who employed you not to have supplied you with one." Lord Ardmillan had no opportunity to issue a sentence in the case as the jury acquitted the accused brakeman and the stationmaster.[125] However, Lord Ardmillan's direction to "act like a man of sense and do your duty" was a frequent theme in Scottish courts.

Though rail accidents were more frequent in Britain, the deadliest railway accident of the period occurred in Armagh, Ireland, in 1889. Extra cars had been added to a Sunday school excursion train to carry six hundred extra passengers, but the locomotive was not powerful enough to carry them all up a hill. To correct the problem the engineer had the last ten cars detached so that he could get the front part over the hill. During acceleration, the front part of the train reversed slightly, tapping the back part which then rolled backward down a hill, crashing into an oncoming train. The passengers had no means of escape because the doors of the train cars had been sealed to prevent people entering without paying. Eighty-eight people were killed, many of them children. Four railway officials were tried for manslaughter and the prosecuting attorney urged the jurors to return a guilty verdict as "he was sure that it would be a lesson to other officials in the future. If [they] were found guilty, it would be for the Judge to pronounce punishment, which would be as lenient as possible." But the Dublin jury acquitted them all.[126] As in the cases from England and Scotland, the point of the trial seemed to be primarily to allow a public investigation of the circumstances rather than to punish those responsible.

MURDEROUS STRANGERS

At the other extreme was murder by strangers, including robbers, rapists, serial killers, and lunatics. Such crimes accounted for only 6 percent of homicide trials on the island of Britain and only 4 percent in Ireland. However, since such crimes are often the hardest to solve, the gap between the number of crimes and the numbers of trials is probably higher in this category than others. Certainly the popular image of "murder" conjured up a monstrous stranger. In describing a tramp who had been arrested and charged with the murder of a family at Denham, the *Times* claimed, "[T]he man, seen any-where and under any circumstances would be judged to be of a particularly brutal type. His head indicating a thoroughly animal organization."[127]

But the assumption that killers looked different from other people was also challenged by the *Times*. In an article titled "Mild-Looking Murderers," the newspaper described how surprising it was for observers at a murder trial to see "a mild-looking lad in the place of the ruffian they expected to behold. The disposition to suppose that men guilty of base crimes must necessarily look as brutal as their deeds is so common that novelists, who follow in this respect the temper of mankind, do not venture to portray murderers pos-sessed of a comely countenance." The *Times* warned that "the human visage is not altogether a trustworthy indication of character; heavy brows do not always stand for foul motives and frank and pleasant countenances are some-times the masks of viler sorts of men."[128]

In addition to giving a false impression of how murderers looked, writers were also suspected of inciting further violence through sensationalism.[129] Murder in late Victorian England usually brings to mind Jack the Ripper, perhaps the most famous multiple murderer in history. But the Ripper's fame has as much to do with the media as with the crimes themselves.[130] As the *Scotsman* pointed out in February 1891 when a woman was murdered at Whitechapel eighteen months after the Ripper cases, "there is, unfortunately nothing abnormal in the occurrence of a murder in a locality like Whitechapel. Or in the fact that the victim was a friendless and almost name-less street waif. Had the report come from any other quarter where crime and vice abounds, it would have attracted only passing notice."[131] At least sixty-eight women other than the known Ripper victims were found murdered and mutilated in England between 1867 and 1892. In 1873 the *Times* reported the accumulation of female body parts along the Embankment. After the corpse was more or less reassembled, the woman was buried without ever being identified.[132]

Though the crime was not unprecedented, the publicity given the Ripper case did inspire imitators. In fact, over a third of the stranger murders com-mitted in England between 1867 and 1892 happened in the three and a half years after the Ripper cases. Though some of these murders were clearly inspired by the Ripper case, it may also be that reporting became more vigi-lant. As the literacy rate rose and along with it the availability of the penny press, there were concerns that sensational coverage served to increase crime. When six months after the Ripper murders a young man was convicted of murder after nearly decapitating a ten-year-old girl, Justice Wills said the case was "mysterious, very unusual and exceptional, an aimless motiveless crime, probably the morbid result of reading the accounts of the horrors which of late have appeared in the newspaper."[133] In 1892 the *Times* complained that "for many minds revolting crimes possess an unwholesome fascination, which appear to be irresistible. Their owners positively gloat over stories of cruelty and bloodshed. They crave for the minutest details of such histories and are eager for the amplest information as to the lives, characters and antecedents of the actors and the victims in all sensational crimes." Nor was such voyeurism limited to the masses: "The prurient curiosity which leads large numbers of respectable people to saturate their minds with every incident they can collect relating to whoever happens to be the most notorious scoundrel of the hour and to hanker for still further knowledge as one of the most striking characteristics of this age."[134] Of course, the Victorian press was lively before the Ripper case and murder had always made good copy. In 1878 a sailor who had murdered a shipmate explained: "For the last twenty years I have read all kinds of books about all kinds of murders and I always thought I would be hung."[135] A seventeen-year-old who murdered his landlady in 1870 said he was led to it "by reading of recent murders and that he had long taken a marked interest in perusing narratives of murders."[136]

The public was also drawn to visit the sites of horrific crimes. After a double murder in London, the *Times* reported, "The two squares where the murders were perpetrated have been visited by immense crowds, but of course there is nothing to be seen there, the houses being closed up and under the charge of the police."[137] When a man cut his sweetheart's throat and then his own in Wolverhampton, "hundreds of people were allowed to view the body, which was laid out in a concert-room adjoining a publichouse."[138] Fifty thousand people attended the funeral of a murdered boy in Liverpool.[139] After a murder in Kent, "upwards of 20,000 persons visited the scene of the murder on Sunday, the majority coming from London."[140] In another case "the marked desire to possess some memento of the horrible crime has shown itself very prominently among the visitors to the cottage . . . a fir tree has nearly been stripped and many loose articles abstracted. Buses and pleasure vans provided for the trip."[141]

But when it came to morbid curiosity, the *Times* believed the English were superior to other nations. The newspaper offered the public reaction to the execution of a murderer in America as an "illustration of the morbid interest in criminals which has of late years been displayed in this country and in France but which may perhaps claim America as the country of its origin." Sensationalism could all too easily lead to glorification. "A murderer, after all, is a person of whom a civilized country may reasonably be ashamed but according to another method of procedure, the commission of a murder is a direct road to an amount of notoriety which many feeble-minded persons would rush into crime in order to obtain."[142]

Among the horrifying aspects of stranger murders was that the victims were often completely defenseless. Though the Ripper murdered prostitutes, children were the victims of many of his imitators. Over a third of the victims of mutilation murders in England were children between the ages of two and fifteen. An old man who murdered a twelve-year-old boy in Liverpool confessed to his crime, insisting, "I was impelled to the crime while under the influence of drink by a fit of murderous mania and a morbid curiosity to observe the process of dying."[143] Less than two weeks after the Liverpool cases, "a murder similar in some respects to those of Whitechapel" was reported from Leeds where the mutilated body of a five-year-old girl was discovered. A local man was arrested after his mother discovered the child's body in their cellar. The autopsy revealed forty to fifty wounds on the child's body.[144] Six months later another five-year-old girl was found raped and strangled in Brighton.[145] A man who had been seen speaking with the child was arrested. Though his attorney argued that the "[c]rime was so revolting to humanity, that of itself it indicated insanity," the jury convicted him after a six-minute deliberation.[146] Not only were children victims of crimes inspired by the coverage of the Ripper murders, sometimes children committed the crimes. At Winchester an eleven-year-old boy was accused of murdering an eight-year-old boy in a deliberate copycat of the Ripper crimes.[147] The reported rate of child murders by strangers was more than twice as high in England as it was in Ireland or Scotland. But the judicial responses were predictable. Everywhere, when an arrest was made, the accused was either convicted of murder or found insane. In England, when the victim of a stranger murder was a child, two-thirds of convictions led to execution. Another 20 percent of the English cases led to insanity verdicts. Three trials for child murder by strangers were held in Scotland. Two led to murder convictions and the third to an insanity verdict. There were two Irish cases: a man who had raped and murdered a six-year-old was executed and a young lady who had murdered a little girl was found insane.

Motiveless murders were (and are) particularly frightening. However wrong it may be to blame the victim, it is only human to derive comfort from the notion that the victim demonstrated some behavior or characteristic which can somehow be avoided by the rest of us. When a gang in Liverpool beat a respectable working man to death when he refused to give them money, suggesting that they "might work for their money, the same as he had to," the *Spectator* warned that such crimes were a sign of the end of civilization. "The murderer had no grudge against the victim, did not so far as appears attempt to rob him, was not drunk to the point where he could understand nothing, but acted from sheer love of brutality, the pleasure of feeling his own power to kill." Murder without a rational motive was "the most dangerous, perhaps, if not the wickedest of all crimes. The brave who kills for revenge, or the burglar who kills for booty [,] even the man who kills out of mere temper is easy to deal with, compared with the man who will commit murder almost in sport, out of a wanton desire to realize his own power."[148] In England, in cases where no clear motive was discovered in a murder between adult strangers, nearly two-thirds of those convicted were executed. Slightly less than a quarter of those tried were found insane. In Ireland 43 percent of the convicted were executed and 45 percent found insane.

Despite the implication in the English press that murders inspired by greed were preferable to motiveless ones, homicides during robberies also inspired shock and horror.[149] When a middle-aged woman in Oxford was murdered in a public street by a beggar, Justice Brett commented that "it was strange that in this country a respectable woman, void of offense, apparently protected by an advanced civilization and organized police on a high road near her own home should meet her death by murder."[150] After hearing four cases of violent robberies, Justice Bramwell complained about the needless violence: "Why were they not content with robbery? Why did they hurt them? It was such an unreasonable piece of cruelty; it was such a savage, barbaric thing, it was unendurable." Ironically, the judge suggested that violence was the best response. "People would be better off if they lived in a place where there was no law at all, and each man defended himself when he was attacked by shooting the person who did it."[151] In England 49 percent of those convicted of killing during a robbery were executed. For those convicted of manslaughter during a robbery, the average sentence was nearly twice as long as the average for all manslaughters. The Irish courts were also particularly hard on robbery homicides. A third of those convicted were executed, and sentences for robbery manslaughters were nearly two years longer than the average.

But the Scots seemed to have taken a different approach. The *Scotsman* suggested that expecting killers to have rational motives was unrealistic. "It is curious and a singular instance of the faith in humanity that human nature is unwilling to believe [murder] was committed except at the pressure of some powerful motive. We all find it hard to believe that human blood could ever be shed for the sake of shedding it . . . whether for example there may not be monsters who, when they have tasted blood, are impelled by a purposeless passion to go on sipping it." Failure to accept that some killers might "take a delight in their deeds such as a wild beast experiences in slaughter" was naïve. "Why so gratuitously and commonly assume that all murders are traceable to vengeance and a desire of plunder?"[152] Only twelve of the Scottish homicide trials involved cases in which an adult had killed an adult stranger without any explanation. None of the accused were executed and nearly half were found insane. Apparently the beastlike delight rendered them less culpable.

The Scottish courts were also more sympathetic to those who killed for plunder. Only one Scot was executed for killing someone during a robbery compared to seven Irishmen and thirty-four Englishmen. The average sentence given a Scot who killed someone during a robbery was less than half the average for England and only a third of the average for Ireland. For example, in Glasgow a young man had knocked an old woman down to steal her purse. She had died from injuries. He told police, "I am guilty of trying to snatch the old woman's bag, but not of trying to hurt her in the least." Though he had clearly acted with violence, the defense argued that she had died "of nervous shock acting on a weak, diseased heart." The presiding judge said, "[I]t was a dreadful thing that old or infirm persons were not safe walking the streets of Glasgow in broad daylight." But the young man was sentenced to only eighteen months.[153]

The other major felony that often occurred in connection with a homicide was rape.[154] In England 46 percent of those convicted of killing a woman during a rape were executed. If a weapon was involved, the number rose to 88 percent. On the other hand, when no weapon was involved and the victim died of exposure or from the effects of trauma, a third of those convicted served less than two years. For example, in 1881, when five young laborers raped a drunken widow and then pushed her down the stairs, the murder charges against them were dropped after it was revealed that she had died of peritonitis. One man whom the victim had named before her death served sixteen months, two others were sentenced to six months each for indecent assault, and two were acquitted. However, Justice Hawkins did comment "on the atrocious aspect in which the case presented itself and also upon the unmanly and unfeeling way in which they had behaved."[155] In another case, a young woman had jumped into the canal to escape a young man who had attempted to rape her. He had made no attempt to rescue her and had watched as she drowned. The grand jury threw out the homicide charges against him but "desired to express the abhorrence which everyone must feel at such infamous conduct."[156]

The Scottish courts were even less likely to take a hard line in rape homicides. Only one rape homicide in Scotland led to a murder conviction, and half of the accused were acquitted outright. A master-builder in Edinburgh who raped a deaf-mute woman who was dying of heart and liver disease was initially accused of murder as her death "it is believed was hastened by the injuries she received." But he was convicted only of assault and sentenced to fifteen months.[157] Another man who confessed to smothering a widow with a pillow after raping her with a brush was allowed to plead guilty to culpable homicide and sentenced to five years. It was explained in mitigation that the man had been "drunk and dissipated since his return from India."[158] Another man who was charged with raping and killing a young woman in her father's house was acquitted after it was revealed that her death was "from syncope caused by nervous trepidation."[159] Five miners were seen going into the home of a single woman in Glasgow; "the woman was not again seen till the following day when a neighbor found that she had received very severe usage from the men, her face and head being badly cut and swollen. She died Monday night." They were all acquitted of all charges as were two miners charged with murdering a woman by "inserting a tin whistle into her private parts."[160]

The Irish courts took a much different stance. When a homicide victim had been raped, the accused was more than four times more likely to be convicted of murder and executed in Ireland than in Scotland. The average sentence given to an Irishman convicted of manslaughter during sexual assaults was six times longer than the average sentence in Irish manslaughter cases. Even when no weapon was used, as was true in 90 percent of Irish cases, a quarter of those convicted were executed and the average sentence for manslaughter convictions connected with sexual assaults was over fifteen years.

The number of homicide trials dealing with rapes and robberies is small, which makes drawing larger conclusions from the trial results particularly perilous. However, it does appear that the English and Irish courts were much more likely to accept the premise that such crimes were more heinous than other homicides, whereas the Scots were apt to see deaths that occurred during robberies or rapes as unfortunate accidents unless the presence of a weapon provided proof of intent. The results may represent the fact that the accused in the Scottish cases, though not necessarily acquainted with the victims, were usually local men. Even when a murderer was shown to be a native, he was often presented as a member of a brutal alien subspecies.

Of course, most homicides were not committed by homicidal strangers or robbers or rapists. In fact, most killers had no prior record of criminality. The defendant in most homicide trials was a friend or relative of the victim, and this is what makes the criminal courts such an important source in examining basic cultural values. How do judges and jurors respond when the killer is not inherently Other but is a local man or woman responding to difficult circumstances? The choices made reveal a great deal about underlying assumptions regarding gender, power, class, and the boundaries between public and personal responsibility.

Verdicts, Sentences, and National Culture

The verdicts and sentences in homicide trials were made by a great many different people who were rarely of one mind, but the overall patterns do reveal certain assumptions. The English courts were increasingly willing to use the full extent of the law's power. The percentage of homicide trials which led to executions rose from 9 percent to 15 percent between 1867 and 1892. By contrast, Irish homicides tended to be seen in two ways—one was as the unfortunate result of a drunken brawl. The sentences in such cases (which made up nearly half of all Irish homicide trials) were very light. More worrying to officials were political assassinations—such crimes were often impossible to prosecute, but when a conviction was obtained, the killer almost invariably hanged. In Scotland the number and types of homicides being tried changed very little during the period. The number of homicide trials remained very low and most involved deaths that were unintentional if not purely accidental. Scottish courts insisted on atonement for the loss of human life, but the sentences on the whole were moderate. The rate of executions per 100,000 population was about two and a half times higher in England, Ireland, and Wales than it was in Scotland where the lower rate of reported homicides may have assured people that harsher measures were not needed.

Within these general trends, the most socially and culturally revealing elements are the respective social status, ethnicity, gender, age, familial ties, provocative behavior, and prior reputation of the killers and victims. The interaction between killer and victim was crucial in determining not only which deaths were considered criminal homicides, but also how judges, jurors, the press, and the public viewed them. However, the same factors that might make execution more likely in one nation might be considered mitigation in another. Despite the Union of Parliaments, the United Kingdom was still a collection of diverse cultures.

National Identity:

Foreigners and Strangers

In offering these opinions I do not desire to suggest what
indeed my experience negatives, that a foreigner as such has
any monopoly of brutality over an Englishman. There are
forms of brutality which are committed by Englishmen
which a Frenchman or an Italian, for instance would never
dream of. But there are also idiosyncrasies of crime which
are, as it were, peculiar to particular countries, both in their
conception and mode of execution. (The *Times,* 4 October
1888, 10d)

In the nineteenth century for the first and only time, the four nations of the
British Isles were united under one parliament in Westminster. The nationalities of the English, Irish, Welsh, and Scots were, at least in theory, subju-
gated to a greater identity as Britons. Though the extent to which the new
nationality was ever a reality in Ireland is certainly a moot point, the dominant interpretation has been that at least in Wales and Scotland the dual
identity was accepted for the most part.[1] But the political union did not mean
that the differences among the nations were erased. In fact the union sometimes heightened tensions as the various nations defined themselves in opposition to their neighbors.

The largest nation, England, faced the most difficult task of self-identification.[2] At a Metropolitan Choral Schools concert at the Crystal Palace, three
thousand children sang "The Campbells Are Coming" in honor of Scotland
and "Men of Harlech" in honor of Wales. "The children also sang 'Home
Sweet Home' which is almost the only English melody which may truly be
termed national."[3] Even the *Times* admitted that "there is no Englishman in
history or now living who has not the blood of many races in his veins."[4] The

explanation was simple. "An Englishman has but one patriotism because England and the United Kingdom are to him practically the same thing."[5]

In keeping with the idea that the United Kingdom had superseded other identities, the *Times* frequently suggested that nationalism in the Celtic nations was either nonexistent or ludicrous. When the Irish nationalist Charles Stewart Parnell accused Scotland of having lost her nationality, the *Times* replied, "Scotland has lost her nationality in Mr. Parnell's sense by accepting her place as a constituent member of the greater nationality of the United Kingdom; Ireland has not lost her nationality for she never had a nationality to lose." The *Times* went on to suggest that the Irish were not capable of true nationalism. "Ireland apart from her connection with Great Britain has either no history or no creditable history. She has done nothing, she represents nothing and she gives promise of nothing."[6] Though the tone was slightly less acidic, the *Times* was also sure that Welsh nationalism did not exist. An article headlined "What Is Wales, and Who Are the Welsh?" concluded, "The differences which exist between some Welshmen and some Englishmen are those gradually shaded off distinctions which exist between a partly and imperfectly assimilated fraction of a nation and the main body of the same people. They are not the deep and well marked lines which sever nations."[7] The *Times* did acknowledge that the good sense of the Scots might render them capable of maintaining dual loyalties. "A Scotchman has two patriotisms, but he is sensible of no opposition between them. He is none the less loyal to the United Kingdom because he is also loyal to Scotland."[8]

ENGLISH AND *NOT* ENGLISH

Though the English often saw Britain and England as synonymous, there was little question that they also saw themselves as the superior breed. In a House debate on capital punishment, MPs concluded that the English were inherently better behaved than other people, though they were not infallible. "It was no doubt in large measure owing to the calm temperament of the British people that murder and assassination were so much less frequent in this country than in many others. But it was also owing to the certain knowledge that if life was maliciously taken the penalty would be death."[9] During the Jack the Ripper terror a *Times* correspondent argued that the killer must be of foreign origin because

> in the whole record of criminal trials there is no instance of a series of crimes of murder and mutilation of the particular character here involved

committed by a person of English origin; whereas there are instances in some foreign countries of crimes of this peculiarly horrible character. The celerity with which the crimes were committed is inconsistent with the ordinary English phlegmatic nature.[10]

The assessment was factually inaccurate. The *Times* reported at least nineteen cases in which the body parts of mutilation victims were found in England between 1867 and the beginning of the Ripper murders in the fall of 1888 (not including cases in which husbands had used mutilation to dispose of their wives). But even at the height of the Ripper hysteria, the *Times* still described Ireland as the land of murder: "Another shocking murder is reported from Kerry, though so far it appears to have been more the outcome of a family quarrel than of an agrarian dispute."[11] The total numbers of homicide victims in Kerry in 1888 was only one more than the number of victims of the Ripper.

But the belief persisted that violent crime was un-English as was tolerating it.[12] After convicting a man who had kicked a drinking companion to death, an Exeter jury added a criticism of the bystanders that "we cannot separate without expressing our indignation that any English men should have run away when this brutal conduct was committed."[13] English criminals were often accused of behaving like uncivilized foreigners. The *Times* reported an assault in Birmingham under the headline "English Savages."[14] When a young man was murdered by a gang in Regent's Park, the *Times* recorded a sense of shock. "It was not generally realized that London is the theater of systematic local feuds almost as real as the tribal feuds of the Arabs and the Red Indians."[15] After the discovery of the corpses of eleven infants in London, the *Times* admitted, "Had such a discovery been made in any other country than our own, most of us would have drawn harsh inferences as to the condition of feeling which made such indecorum and indignities to the dead possible."[16]

The *Times* sometimes implied that civility declined with distance from London. In 1872 the *Times* took the Winter Assize for the North of England as its subject. "A succession of murder and minor outrages has presented a picture of drunken brutality such as might be more fitly expected in some savage island in the far Pacifics where the natives had just tasted for the first time the terrible poison of drink." In describing the crimes of Durham, the *Times* suggested the people were barely human: "They are not Murders of the deliberate and malignant class but simply outbreaks of brute ferocity which indicate an existence little better than that of savage animals." Such behavior brought into question whether the North belonged to England. "Are these not a sufficiently sad collection of scenes from common life in a country which boasts to be civilized, Christian and the enlightener of the world? In the sort of existence thus revealed there is not even a trace of the commonest feelings of humanity."[17] Over a quarter of all executions for murder in England were in the northern district.

The *Spectator* described the workingmen of Liverpool as a separate species:

> Naturally a rough race, habituated to violence, always armed—for the steel-tipped shoe on a strong man's foot is a deadly weapon—feel themselves almost above the law and begin gradually to delight in the exercise of their powers. In Liverpool murder is committed without motive of any sort, except a kind of enthusiasm of ruffianism, a delight in a monstrous exercise of physical power.[18]

In 1890 the *Times* reported a murder which "illustrated the manners and customs of Birmingham Corner-men."[19] But such cases were not taken as evidence of flaws in English character or society but rather as evidence that alien savages were peopling the North. The *Pall Mall Gazette* suggested that the North of England should be treated as a foreign country.

> A body of police should patrol the district to make the inhabitants aware that there is not an angry word or a loud cry or a rough jostle which will not bring the eye of a constable upon them. These are the methods by which disorder has been put down in Ireland and India, and there is no reason why the disease should be harder to control in Liverpool.[20]

As the analogy between Liverpool and Ireland suggests, in the English press the Irish were more likely to be viewed as aliens than as fellow citizens of the United Kingdom. At best the Irish were unfathomable. An editorial asked in 1877, "How often will it have to be confessed that Ireland is England's enigma? Before we have half understood the meaning of one Irish mood, Irishmen are out of it and well-nigh through another. Their haste bewilders us." The editorial suggested that the Irish might have attributes the English lacked. "While we are slow, Irishmen are quick, while we are anxious and careworn they are careless and negligent of the future; and so it follows that our forecasts of Irish conduct are empty delusions." Ultimately, however, the Irish failed to live up to English standards. "Our unwritten law is that everything is to be done in the best way possible, and that everybody is to act up to the most exalted canons of duty."[21]

The English press rarely missed an opportunity to expose the "revolting cruelty which is the distinguishing note of Irish crime." Though English crimes were attributed to deviant individuals who were alien to the true English nature, Irish crimes were inevitably interpreted as a reflection of national character. In 1882, when an entire family was murdered at Maamtrasna in rural Galway, the *Times* suggested that the murder "differs in degree rather than in kind from the crimes which are, unhappily, only too common over a great part of Ireland. . . . When all due allowance has been made for agrarian motives, there remains an element of savage ferocity." After pointing out that poverty and squalor were found all over the European continent, the *Times* complained, "Yet in none of these countries do we find anything to compare with the violence and cruelty which are the standing disgrace of Ireland . . . when there are no longer landlords to plunder it will not be found easier than now to restrain the indiscriminate brutality which ignores the claims alike of race and humanity."[22] The Maamtrasna murders were horrifying.[23] They were also unique. The only other case in which an entire Irish family was murdered involved a police officer who killed his sergeant and the sergeant's family before killing himself. The Irish homicide rate of reported homicides was lower than England's for most of the period and the Irish were the least likely of all the nations to kill children. In the initial report, even the *Times* had acknowledged that the Maamtrasna murder was not typical. "It is very much within the truth to say that it has no parallel for absolute barbarity."[24] Further, the locals helped with the investigation. "Never was there an occasion in which the public of all classes were so penetrated by an earnest desire that the perpetrators of a crime should be made to feel the avenging arm of justice."[25] Yet in editorials the *Times* insisted that the crime represented the unique savagery that was innate to the Irish character.

But if the Irish were perceived as savages, the Scots were exceptionally well behaved. "The quietness, not to say the neglect with which Scotland had become used after the experience of years, is the penalty for which an orderly, reasonable and on the whole well-behaved country must lay its account."[26] In fact, Scottish prudishness was sometimes the subject of jokes. In an article titled "Scotland's Weak Points," the *Times* reported that "Scotland is proverbially a staid, sober and thrifty nation and for general respectability of demeanor and observance of the Sabbath, among the whole family of nations there is not one which bears so high a reputation. At the same time it must be confessed even Scotland has her weak points." The article went on to mockingly quote a Free Church report on "religion and morals," which warned that "[s]ome London journals of a sensational character are occasionally sold and read. Dancing during the winter is reported to be a 'great hindrance to the young.' A growing class in the towns are addicted to

Sabbath walking, dog coursing and excursions to the seaside for bathing purposes." After citing other complaints about such things as "balls about the
time of New Years," and the fact that in Glasgow "the general community are
remarkable for profane swearing, intemperance and uncleanness," the article
wryly concluded, "With the exception of these little shortcomings the general condition of Scotland appears to be satisfactory."[27]

Most often when the Welsh were mentioned, it was to report an example
of their bumptiousness.[28] Under the headline "Welsh Humanity," the *Times*
reported that a man who had fallen off a cliff and dragged himself to the door
of an inn "was refused admission because the Lord Lieutenant was staying
there."[29] An article headlined "A Welsh Wedding" reported that a pair of
"well-to-do" farmers coming home from a wedding had gotten into a drunk-
en scuffle and that one of the men had died from his injuries.[30] Deaths from
drunken scuffles after celebrations were hardly unique to Wales, but the tone
of the item indicates that there was something particularly comical about
"tipsy" Welsh farmers. A year later the *Times* also reported that "[a] Welsh district newspaper devotes a considerable space to reporting the proceedings of
an Eisteddfodd held last week at Ynyaybwl, which, to insure identification is
described as being 'near Llanwonno.'" Having established the remoteness of
the area, the article then described the sorts of honors that might appeal to
such folk. "Adjudications were made upon a wide range of subjects, prizes
being awarded, inter alia, for the best pair of white stockings; the best pair of
black stockings; and for the best essay upon 'the duties of ratepayers with
regard to the Reform Bill.'"[31]

Except for such odd human-interest stories, the Welsh merited little attention in the English press. "The principality indeed seems the chosen home of
the commonplace. For some reason which we cannot here attempt to pene-
trate, Wales does not turn out her due proportion of great men."[32] However,
another editorial suggested that there was some comfort in Welsh backwardness.

> They do not excite the jealousy of the English by dashing to the front as
> the Irishmen do, or by slowly and safely working their way to that posi-
> tion, with the certainty of success as Scotchmen do. It is pleasant to
> glance over the shoulder and see at least one of our neighbors always
> steadily in the rear, and more than satisfied with that position.

The implication was that they might make good mascots. "They are a pic-
turesque ingredient in our too tame and matter of fact community. Truth to
say their most charming quality in English eyes is their pretty little vanity;

their sweet self-complacency, their lovely self-conceit [,] their absolute satisfaction with what they suppose to be their poetry and history." Welsh backwardness was attributed to their failure to assimilate. "Scotchmen and Irishmen are great as far as they are also Englishmen. They are not great without us and apart from us, but as members of our own family and sharers of our unsurpassed stock of common words, ideas and associations. . . . The Welsh language, like the Englishman's home, is his castle and his prison."[33]

A *Times* correspondent despaired of the difficulties "in dealing with a language which treated by the process of literal translation yields such phrases as 'Boys, I must break my hair, she is too fat.'"[34] However strange their language, he was certain that the Welsh were "prudent patriots." Welsh loyalty to the crown was never in question. "They quite understand the value of belonging to this United Kingdom, to say nothing of such minor matters as prestige. They value the English market for their cattle, their ponies, their coal, their slate. They do not despise the English tourists who every year fill their watering places."[35]

THE WELSH

The fact that they were generally either ignored or patronized by their neighbors was not lost on the Welsh. The Welsh press warned that "journalists must not believe all they hear about Welsh doings. Much that they publish is spiced for the English market."[36] The *North Wales Chronicle* thought that "the manufacture of Welsh news paragraphs for the London papers is singularly curious and at times amusing."[37] An editorial in the *Carmarthen Weekly Reporter* stressed that the Welsh valued their distinctiveness. "The Irishman has no patriotic objection to conversing in English. The Highlander is as ready to give up his Gaelic as to give up the kilts which have for years been abandoned to gamekeepers, children and English tourists. But the Welsh behind the shelter of the mountains, into which they retired before the Saxon invader, have tenaciously preserved their national language." But while they had maintained their distinctive language, they were also the best of neighbors. "The Welsh are a satisfied, industrious, law-abiding people who have long ago accepted their connection with England as the best thing that could have happened to them."[38]

The Welsh were also certain that they were the most law-abiding characters in the British Isles. "Murders are rare in Wales—would they were rarer—and no witness has need to fear assassination for giving evidence against the destroyer of human life. Welshmen may poach, may steal, may commit minor offenses yet it appears that they do less of these things then our English, Irish and Scottish neighbours do."[39] The point was well made. Judges frequently remarked on light calendars at Welsh Assizes. While on circuit in Wales, Justice Cleasby said that "in most of the [English] counties I have visited I should have thought the calendar before me was a light one, but it seems that here it is regarded as a heavy one."[40] Justice Cockburn told the grand jury at the South Wales Assize that "its population is one which is entitled to the highest possible praise for order, good conduct and obedience to the law."[41] Even the *Times* occasionally admitted the Welsh were a peaceful lot: "It was certainly remarkable and gratifying circumstances that in the four counties [on the South Wales circuit] there should not have been one case in which any violence had been offered to any man or woman."[42]

Welsh newspapers were full of sensational reports of crimes among their neighbors. The headline for a report of two murders, one of them on the Isle of Man, was "Two Typical English Tragedies."[43] The Welsh also shared the English assumptions about Irish behavior. The *North Wales Chronicle* announced that "we daily hear of Irish murders. Cut-throats are increasing in number and loyal and obedient subjects go about in fear of their lives."[44] Welsh newspaper editors also seemed to take particular delight in stories which reflected badly on the Scots. In an editorial headlined "Our Country's Crime" (throughout Britain, references to "our country's crime" almost invariably referred to one of the other nations), a Welsh newspaper warned that "Scotland makes us fear that there is no crime too revolting for wicked men to commit for the sake of gain."[45]

In addition to featuring the crimes of their neighbors, the Welsh press sometimes took on the tone of a slighted sibling. "There are a few old fogies so blinded with prejudice that everything Welsh is bad. On the other hand, England is all good and especially Scotland, the latter being held up to our gaze as all but the pink of perfection while Ireland and Wales are fit only to point a moral or adorn a tale." The editor of the *Carmarthen Weekly Reporter* was determined to show that the Scots were overrated. "Scotland, the most cultivated and civilized portion of her Majesty's dominion and with the most conservative and religious people in the world—so it is assumed—can still set some of the worst examples possible to the present age. One of these is drunkenness." However, in the desire to show the Scots in the worst light, the editor did seem rather desperate for ammunition: "[T]here was cock-fighting in Glasgow. If this be civilization and proper work for any day we have no wish to partake. Better run naked and sink into barbarism than be guilty of such deeds."[46]

THE SCOTS AND THEIR NEIGHBORS

Though the Scots may have ignored such criticism from the Welsh, there was a concern that their southern neighbors remained willfully ignorant of Scottish concerns. Edinburgh's leading newspaper, the *Scotsman,* complained, "We want some credit for our country and we want it on the true facts of the case and not upon these strange and persistent mistakes as to persons and places which our London counterparts in particular seem somehow to prefer making up for themselves."[47] The complaint may have been well founded. In 1872 the *Times* reported that a school board committee member in Birmingham insisted that educated Scots did not speak English.[48] According to the *Scotsman,* part of the problem was a lack of comprehension. "The truth is that of all classes of men in the British dominions your genuine Londoner has the least perception of either wit or humour."[49]

Regarding the Scottish character, the Scottish press was critical but only mildly so. The *Glasgow Herald* acknowledged that "[w]e are apt to have too much work and too little play in Scotland."[50] An editorial in the *Scotsman* began: "Perhaps it is well not to deny that we Scotch have as much conceit on certain subjects as we are entitled to or is as good for us and that we are occasionally under obligation to our English friends for taking some of it out of us." But national pride was clearly justified. "The national institutions of Scotland were preserved from demolition by no generous sufferance on the part of the English nation, but for the fact that Scotland, although a little nation, merely by the moral power that animated it, contrived to inspire fear and respect in one much its superior in numbers and every other element of strength."[51] In an editorial arguing for the placement of a memorial at Bannockburn,[52] the *Scotsman* argued: "We cannot really afford to forget that at terrible odds we fought against our great neighbor throughout twelve generations for our existence as a nation, and that at last we won it on that spot whereon we hope the ruddy lion rampant in gold will float as long as men shall class patriotism as a virtue and freedom as a blessing."[53]

But the union on the whole was a good thing. "We have not felt that we did ourselves dishonour or disservice by becoming part, not of England but of the United Kingdom." Certainly the Scots felt morally superior to Irish nationalists. The *Scotsman* proudly pointed out that no Scots "political philosopher ever presumed so far upon our want of rationality or our superabundance of nationality as to suggest that it would have been justifiable, if not preferable to have betaken ourselves to murder and arson, as a means to the restoration of disunion and conflict."[54] Instead, Scotsmen preferred "the nationalism of a poet and a patriot—a fine and in some respect noble sentiment with which all true

Scotsmen of whatever politics have sympathy."[55] Despite the Scots' retention of a separate legal system, they were also willing to see the commonality of Britons: "The minds of prisoners are much the same on both sides of the Tweed, and so are the minds of juries."[56]

Regarding the Irish, the editorial position of the *Scotsman* changed dramatically over time. In 1869 the newspaper recognized Irish grievances and looked to Irish progress. "The task we have before us is to create in the Irish character a respect for law, and this can only be done by separating the law from all alliances with injustice."[57] But the *Scotsman* also portrayed the Irish as whiners who needed to buck up. "Irishmen show a wonderful incapacity for helping themselves, and a wonderful capacity for getting others people's help. . . . An infusion of Scotch habits and characteristics would we rather think be a great blessing to Ireland, not even excepting Kerry."[58]

In 1879, as the Land League movement began in Ireland, the *Scotsman* took a measured approach. "The circumstances of Ireland are to a great extent different from those of Great Britain and different because of past misgovernment of Great Britain." It had been hoped that better treatment would make Ireland "as orderly and easily governed a country as Scotland." Unfortunately the Irish had still not given up "foolish agitations for impossible objects. The reasons, it may be assumed, are first, the character of Irishmen, and secondly their feelings as to the land." But even so, the *Scotsman* admitted that Irish character "is very much though not wholly what it has been made and it may be expected to change, in process of time with good and just government."[59]

During the height of the Irish land agitation in 1881, the *Scotsman* echoed the Irish press in warning that reports of crimes in Ireland might be exaggerated. "There was a greater necessity at this time to receive the news which comes from Ireland with much allowance. Outrage and disorder are common enough in that country, and they do not need exaggeration to make them matters for serious consideration." The *Scotsman* also offered a sophisticated analysis of the problem. "The Reason is three-fold. It begins in the imaginative tendency of the Irish mind; and inaccuracy is encouraged by the Parnellites on the one side and by the Conservatives who are crying for more coercion, on the other."[60] A year later, while a little more skeptical about Irish character, the *Scotsman* was still willing to blame the British for much of the problem. "The lawlessness of the criminal class in Ireland may be due in some measure to the hot recklessness of the Celtic blood. It is certainly largely due to the bad laws under which Irishmen have been forced to live. Ireland is now receiving better and fairer laws but the character of a race cannot be changed in a day or in a year."[61]

By the mid-1880s, however, the patience with the historic suffering of the Irish had been exhausted. "How long is this whine about the penal laws to continue: . . . Irishmen instead of putting their shoulder to the wheel, fall into the cant about the penal laws and tell us that in Ireland they have nothing to be loyal to but coercion."[62] Not only was history no longer an excuse, even the history was being rewritten. "It should be understood once and for all that the people of Ireland have and have had their times and chances just as good and as bad as the people of the rest of the three United Kingdoms. They have been raised from tribal barbarism into comparative civilization and decency, much more by their connection with Great Britain than by their own unaided efforts." Complaints about prior injustice would no longer be tolerated.

> It will not do to have this everlasting harping upon past mistakes or references to a golden past in Ireland which never existed. The most skilled and civilized observer of Ireland before the English law was introduced are at one in the opinion that there was nothing to be found but oppression by native chiefs and utter barbarism among native occupants.

The nationality card was also rejected. "The nationality which every reasonable person desires to cultivate is the great nationality common to the Englishmen, Scotsmen and Irishmen alike." Regarding the purely Celtic Irish, "It would be a dereliction of clear duty as well as a want of political sense not only to leave these ignorant people to themselves, but to give them power to reduce their better countrymen to their own level."[63] The Celtic Irish were inferior and dangerous. "Irishmen are not fit to possess in existing circumstances the ordinary freedom of British citizens." Without reference to past problems, the editorials now claimed that the Irish character was fatally flawed. "It is the misfortune of most Irishmen that they cannot conceive the possibility of arguing a case without resort to violence. Their first action against the man they believe to be wrong is, not to try to convince him of his error by arguments, but to attack and beat him down by noise or outrage."[64] After sectarian riots in Belfast in June 1886, the *Scotsman* concluded that "nothing short of a political miracle could suddenly transform the Irish people into a sober, self-restrained, self-governing nation." But the condemnation was evenhanded. "The Orangeman would probably be as little to be trusted with supremacy as the nationalist."[65]

By the late 1880s, headlines in Scotland reported "Civil War in Ireland."[66] The newspapers regularly reported murders in Ireland in sensational terms. A case in which a mentally unbalanced young woman in rural Ireland had killed her mother was reported in the *Scotsman* with the largest possible head-line: "Irish Matricide."[67] But two cases of matricide by women in Scotland that same year, one of which included the use of a hatchet, were not report-ed in the *Scotsman* until they came up for trial and then in minimal detail. Further, many of the homicides reported as dreadful agrarian murders in the Scottish press in the late 1880s do not appear in any official records and appear to have been exaggerated versions of minor assaults. The *Times* cor-rected some of the erroneous reports of nonexistent Irish homicides, but no such retractions appeared in the *Scotsman*.

The *Scotsman* rejected the idea that all Celts were doomed to be savages, insisting that only the Irish had perversely clung to bad habits. If the Irish chose to behave as irredeemable savages, the Welsh were civilized. "The Welsh farmer though Celtic to the core, is unlike his Irish kinsman in that he prefers honest work to agitation; he is industrious and frugal almost to a fault, and would willingly if he were left alone, return to the peaceful culti-vation of his farm."[68]

THE IRISH

For their part, the Irish accepted that they might be particularly prone to pas-sionate outbursts. The editor of the *Cavan Weekly News* admitted that "in Ireland the religious tendencies and moral habits are stronger and more ele-vated . . . but the passions are more easily excited."[69] The passions meant that the Irish may have been more inclined to violence. As Justice Battersby explained to the Kilkenny Assize in 1875, "Although the people, as far as regards larceny, are the most moral and less guilty of offences of the kind, still in some parts of this country, the people seemed not to consider murder under certain circumstances a crime at all and cannot be got to assist the ends of justice."[70] Another judge warned that "there was a class of persons in this country who considered picking a man's pocket a grievous offence, but the breaking of a neighbor's head was of no consequence."[71]

But there were also suspicions that British authorities deliberately inflated the Irish crime figures to justify coercive policies against the Irish population. The *Roscommon Journal* reported that the police had been ordered to manu-facture agrarian outrages.[72] The *Limerick Reporter* complained in 1881, "No well informed person now believes a word about the alleged perilous condi-tion of Ireland. What possibly can be the cause of all his misrepresentation as to our condition and of the actual facts before our eyes?"[73] Indeed the Irish criminal records reflect a very different situation from that reported in the

British press. In 1892 Justice O' Brien reported from the Tipperary Assizes, "I think its present condition would compare favorably with any shire in England or any country in Scotland."[74]

Irish newspapers not only complained about the unfair treatment of the Irish in the British press, they also took every opportunity to report on crimes in England. In 1889 the *Kilkenny Journal* pointed out that "never was the business for the Winter Assize so light. . . . How different it is in England."[75] The *Munster News* argued that the English made excuses for English criminals but were determined to see every Irish crime as proof of sedition and barbarism.

> The English and Orange organs do not triumph when they receive accounts of the British shootings and stabbings, throat cuttings, poisoning and infanticides . . . no, they would treat you to homilies containing palliatives and sets off in this or that class or condition. But there is no allowance for crime in this kingdom. They raise a cry for the enactment of indiscriminate despotism.[76]

The Irish press also argued that the English were particularly cruel. An editorial in the *Kilkenny Journal* offered "as plain proof of beastly brutality, the love of the lash as a government institution in England."[77]

IRISH IMMIGRANTS

In each of the British nations there was a suspicion that crime within their country was largely the fault of Irish immigrants. Confronted by statistics showing that crime rates were markedly higher in England than in Ireland, the *Times* suggested that "the Irish make up for their innocence at home by an excessive criminality abroad."[78] But after a lengthy analysis of the claim that the Irish were responsible for crime in Britain, the *Times* reluctantly concluded that "the theory of a supposed excessive criminality of persons of Irish birth in England and Wales as accounting for the greater number of crimes is erroneous." The article also acknowledged that "among persons over the age of twenty in London, Liverpool and Manchester the Irish born were less criminal than the natives."[79]

But despite the statistics, to many in Britain, the simple fact was that the Irish were savages.[80] During a trial at the Old Bailey in which an Irish laborer was accused of killing his roommate, the *Times* reported that "the victim was one of ninety-seven people, all of them Irish who lived in the same lodging house and the landlady said it was a point with her not to keep a poker in the house."[81] In newspaper accounts "Irish" was often shorthand for "violent" or "disreputable" even when no Irish were involved. A London magistrate told a nineteen-year-old pauper charged with using threatening language toward a relieving officer, "He must be taught that such violence would not be tolerated in England, whatever might be the case in Ireland."[82] When an Irish woman was charged with assaulting an English neighbor "for no cause other than some little water spilt in the hall and because she was an Englishwoman," the magistrate said he "was satisfied that an unprovoked and violent assault had been committed. It was but too characteristic of the class of Irish to which the defendant belonged to commit savage assaults and then try to screen themselves by falsehood. He would never allow such things to be done with impunity."[83]

The initial reports of crimes involving the Irish always assumed the worse. In September of 1868, under the headline "Brutal Murder Near Altrincham," the *Times* reported that a gang of Irish laborers "without any provocation set upon the foreman at the tile works and batted in his head with bricks and palings. The murder is one of unprecedented atrocity."[84] But the trial testimony revealed that Irish and English laborers had been throwing brickbats at each other and the victim had been caught in the crossfire. Justice Lush instructed the jury to acquit the accused as they were "defending themselves from the violence of English people who were following with clubs and sticks to capture them."[85] Though fewer than 7 percent of those tried for killing someone in a brawl in England were described as Irish in the *Times,* 11 percent of those who were sentenced to penal servitude or death for killing someone in a brawl were from that group.

The Scots also distrusted the Irish among them.[86] Irish immigrants were suspected of being responsible for much of the violence in Britain. The suspicions in Scotland were perhaps more well founded. Thirty percent of the persons tried for homicides in brawls in the western circuits of Scotland were Irish. The *Scotsman* complained that the Irish immigrants were not only belligerent, they also used foul tactics. "A peculiarity of an Irish disturbance is that no fair play is given or expected."[87] Irishmen accused of homicide in brawls in Scotland were more than three times more likely to be convicted of murder than were Scottish defendants.

The *Scotsman* also complained that the Irish were never content to fight one on one: "[T]he man who is down is certain to be kicked and maltreated not only by his immediate opponents but by the latter's friends."[88] "Agrarian crime in Ireland, with its cowardly shooting without warning or opportunity for defence is repeated in the assaults, robberies and house-breaking which disgrace the Irish population in such centers as Glasgow."[89] Southwestern

Scotland had received an enormous influx of Irish immigrants during the nineteenth century. Driven by rural poverty in Ireland and attracted by better wages in the heavy industry of Scotland, the Irish were an important source of cheap labor but they also inspired considerable resentment. "It is painful; the Scotch Census Commissioners say 'to contemplate what may be the ultimate effect of this Irish immigration on the morals and habits of the people and on the future prospects of the country.'"[90] Twenty-three percent of homicide defendants in Glasgow between 1867 and 1892 were Irish. The *Glasgow Herald* concluded a report on capital crimes in Glasgow, "[I]t is perhaps not unworthy of note that of eight culprits, six were Roman Catholic." Roman Catholic was certainly code for Irish.[91]

During the 1870s, Irish Protestants poured into the area, creating a situation in which the sectarian tensions of Northern Ireland were played out in the streets of Glasgow.[92] Two homicide trials in Scotland between 1867 and 1892 could be traced to sectarian violence and both involved Irish immigrants. One victim was Catholic, the other Protestant. The outcomes were very different. In 1870, in Linlithgow, a gang of drunk Protestants shouting "Down with Papists! Down with Fenians!" attacked the house of James Docherty, a Roman Catholic. Docherty was dragged from his home and beaten to death. Their defense attorney claimed that one of the Protestants had been struck by a man who had run into Docherty's house. The jury returned a unanimous verdict of not proven, the verdict often used to give the benefit of the doubt to sympathetic defendants.[93]

Two years later the roles were reversed. On 12 July 1872, the Orangemen held a procession in Wisham in North Lanarkshire. Later that night two Catholics were pretending to duel with railroad ties when John Skillen joined them. The next morning Skillen was discovered dead of head wounds. According to the *Glasgow Herald*, Skillen was not an Orangeman but "may have used provocative language." The two men with the railway ties were accused of murder. Both said they remembered being drunk and in a fight, but that was all. Their defense attorney stressed "the unlikelihood of their assaulting in the manner described a man they did not know, without the slightest provocation and against whom they could have no malice." But the judge was indignant: "These party processions were a disgrace to a civilized country. Drink had put Wisham into a state of tumult and disorder. Parties of men ready for a quarrel and perhaps not caring very much what the conclusion might be were strolling the street." Despite the fact that the party procession had been by Orangemen and the defendants were Catholic, the judge charged for conviction. He also discounted the defense's suggestion that the case could not be one of murder.

If the accused struck these blows with the weapon intending to do serious bodily injury, it was of no merit, in regard to the legal character that
he did not intend to kill or that he had no malice. . . . He could only say
that except in a case where a clear personal motive had been adduced, he
had seldom seen proved in a court of justice a more cold-blooded, brutal
and savage homicide.

By a vote of fourteen to one the jury returned a murder conviction.[94]

The Scottish courts were determined to restrain the Irish. When accused
of homicide, the Irish were more likely to be convicted and the sentences
were heavier than those given to native Scots. The differences were clear in
two cases involving the death of police constables. In 1869 James Gallin, an
Irish shipbuilder, got drunk and created a disturbance in a candy store. When
asked to leave, he punched the owner in the mouth and ran. A police inspector in plain clothes encountered Gallin in the street and urged him to go
home. They struggled and Gallin stabbed him under the left ear. The man
bled to death within ten minutes. At his murder trial, Gallin tried to plead
guilty to culpable homicide but the advocate general refused to accept the
plea, insisting that "neither absence of malice, nor intoxication, nor previous
good character would suffice to reduce the charge." The defense pointed out
that the struggle had lasted for ten minutes and Gallin had not known that
the victim was a policeman. Eight of the jury members voted to convict
Gallin of culpable homicide; seven voted to convict him of murder. He was
sentenced to twenty years.[95] The attitude of the advocate general and the
heavy sentence given to Gallin were in marked contrast to the response when
a respectable farmer in Inverness fatally stabbed a uniformed policeman who
had tried to stop him from smashing hotel windows during a drunken spree.
He was sentenced to just five years and the judge announced that the purpose of the sentence was that "he should learn to live without liquor."[96]

In 1886 the *Scotsman* insisted that it was the racially suspect Irish aborig-
ine who was responsible for most of the crime and violence in Great Britain.
"The lower Irish race whether they are Celts or aboriginal pre-Celtic Irish are
well known in the great cities and mining districts of England and Scotland
where they are to be found the cause of a large proportion (one-half or one-
third) of the worst crime." The Irish Celts represented a particularly reprehensible sort of violence.

It is they who have demoralised the mob by their frightful examples of
brutal assaults on men when down to the utter forgetfulness of English
and Scottish notions of fair play. It is not enough for an Irish combatant

as he is known in this country, to knock his man down, he must proceed
to kick and stamp upon his opponent when helpless in a way which
betrays the savage.

Irish criminals were also a drain on revenues. "Every Criminal Court in
England or Scotland knows of such brutalities and but for this Irish immi-
grant population, low in civilization, there would be no need for many courts
and for many policemen."[97] The conviction rate of Irishmen accused of
homicide in Scotland rose from 66 percent between 1867 and 1879 to 84
percent between 1880 and 1892. The likelihood of an Irishmen arrested for
homicide in Scotland being executed nearly tripled during the 1880s.

Welsh newspaper editors shared the suspicions that crimes were the work
of their neighbors though they were suspicious of Scots and English immigrants as well as the Irish. The *Carmarthen Weekly Reporter* announced that
"it is a notorious fact that the bulk of convictions at Welsh Assizes are of
English tramps."[98] When a young woman was found murdered in a Welsh
port, the local press insisted that "there is not a scrap of evidence to show that
she was murdered by a Welshman or that a solitary Welshman knows who
the murderer was. The probability therefore is that she was slain by one or
more of those tramps from England, Scotland or Ireland who continually
infest Welsh society and who cost the Principality so much for prosecution
and imprisonment."[99]

But, like their neighbors, the Welsh were especially quick to describe the
Irish as savages. The *Llannelly Guardian* reported, under the headline "An
Irish Row," that "in a quarter of town where a race of people live some of
whom are celebrated for breaking each other's heads" a brawl had taken place
inside a house where "about a dozen true sons and daughters of the Emerald
Isle were all jabbering together." Instead of shillelaghs they "took a more
modern course, viz, seize hold of the first earthen utensil that comes to hand
and let fly."[100] When a local gentleman was murdered by his gamekeeper, the
Carmarthen Weekly Reporter suggested that "the fatal shot once fired there
seems to have awakened in [the killer] that wild beast thirst for blood which
(perhaps inherited from some ferocious and barbarian Irish chieftain) had so
long slumbered unsuspected or unnoted in his nature."[101]

The sterling character of the native Welsh was implied in a report of a
stone-throwing riot between the Welsh and Irish. According to the
Carmarthen Weekly Reporter, the incident began when some Irishmen pelted
some Welshmen with stones. "The Welsh remonstrated with them for their
conduct and a fierce quarrel ensued." When the police separated the groups
and attempted to arrest one of the Irishmen, the stone throwing resumed.

"Some of the Welshmen present cried out, 'Don't abuse the police, they are only doing their duty.'" At this point, "a general row took place between the Welsh and the Irish." When the police again separated the crowds, more stones were thrown and the Welsh began to throw stones at Irish houses. The report concluded, "It is not true that the police called on the locals to assist. It is not true that the Welshmen sought revenge on the Irish. They threw the stones at the doors and the windows in self-defence."[102]

ETHNIC BATTLES

Conflicts between locals and outsiders were common throughout Britain though migration within the United Kingdom could create uncertainty as to what constituted an outsider. Under the headline "The Welsh and the Irish," a Welsh newspaper reported that an eleven-year-old Welsh boy was being tried in Liverpool for killing an Irish boy "in a dispute about nationalities." The victim had taunted the boy about being Welsh. "He strongly repelled this insinuation although he admitted that his father was guilty of belonging to that branch of the Celtic race." The victim "remarked that it was just like the Welsh who were a deceitful lot and could not stay in their own country. The prisoner made the obvious retort that the Irish were afflicted with the same roving tendency." The Welsh boy "then kicked out at the deceased who was kicked in a dangerous part of the body and was killed."[103] The report is interesting in the use of passive voice; the Welsh boy "kicked out" and the victim "was killed" but the report does not say that the Welsh boy kicked the victim. The report also demonstrates that ethnic identities were a source of tensions but were also in flux for second-generation immigrants. It is also worth noting that the death of an Irish boy was perceived as humorous.

Riots between workers from the various nations of Britain were frequent. Forty-two homicide trials in England and Wales were the results of ethnic battles. When an Englishman was beaten to death with a brick in a fight between English and Welsh railway workers in 1875, the *Carmarthen Journal* explained that "what took place seems to have arisen from the jealousy of races, and partly from that which so often accompanies crimes of that description the excitement of drink." At the trial a witness testified to hearing one of the accused say "that the next English —— that was out of the hut I'll knock the brains out of his head." Three men were arrested, but the evidence as to who struck the fatal blow was conflicting and the accused all swore that the true culprit had not been apprehended. After a half-hour deliberation the jury acquitted them.[104] The *North Wales Guardian* complained that such behavior was un-Welsh: "The Welsh as a nation have ever had the credit of being hospitable to strangers. It should be remembered that there are many Welshmen working in English districts." The paper also suggested that "it is also silly to find prejudices of race in a land where all are Britons and should live together in good fellowship."[105]

Railway gangs were particularly likely to fight. Work on the Midland railway near Carlisle led to at least two fatal riots.

> The men consist of Englishmen, Irishmen and Scotchmen, divided into distinct gangs who work together, drink together and fight together too. The English appear to have fancied that the Irishmen were working for less money than themselves and this suspicion engendered much ill-feeling, which vented itself in a very forcible manner when the men had drunk deep.

Three young Englishmen had gone to an Irish pub. When they arrived, the publican had taken his wife and children and hidden in the cellar. A battle erupted and an Irishman was killed when he was "held up and kicked in a very savage manner while another man battered his head with a spade." Three Englishmen were acquitted of his homicide.[106] A year later three Irish navvies were convicted of the attempted murder of a Scot. "It appears a feud had sprung up between the Irish and the English navvies with the latter of whom the Scotch navies were classed." An Irish worker was convicted of attempted murder and sentenced to five years.[107]

A report of a Durham murder trial began: "[F]rom the opening statement of learned counsel it appeared that the deceased man was an Irishman and the prisoner was an Englishman and at the time of the deceased meeting with his death there was ill-feeling existing between the English and the Irish in Willington." Both the accused, Joseph Turnbull, and the victim, Martin Hogan, were pitmen attending the races. At the race Turnbull told an Irishman to "go back and tell the Irishmen to prepare for tonight; but let them come in in ones and not in gangs." That night sixty to seventy people gathered for the fight. When Hogan asked for a match, he was knocked to the ground. Turnbull "danced upon Hogan's chest saying 'I'll tramp his Irish guts out!'" Hogan died before they could get him to the hospital. Turnbull was convicted and sentenced to death though the sentence was commuted.[108]

Chief Justice Coleridge was concerned about the pattern after hearing a case from Liverpool in which a gang of Irishmen had killed an Englishman in the streets. The victim had allegedly challenged the Irish, saying, "Come on I'll have satisfaction now, there is plenty of us." Justice Coleridge said: "Prisoners would seem to have engaged in the disturbance from a spirit of

national animosity, which induced them to have recourse to disgraceful violence. Such outrages must be put down by the strong hand of the law, and if
persons engaged in such fighting and sad results followed, they must be
taught that such conduct could not be allowed."[109] The two Irishmen
described as the ringleaders of the group were sentenced to penal servitude.
But there was also a sense that the victims of such violence might not merit
much sympathy. After hearing trials involving riotous brawls between Welsh
and Irish laborers, Justice Bowen said: "[F]or two days they had been engaged
in what was really a war of savages."[110] Forty-five percent of the homicide trials in England involving ethnic brawls ended in acquittals. When the defendant was English, the acquittal rate was 70 percent.[111]

FOREIGNERS

Though the peoples of the United Kingdom fought among themselves, they
agreed that those from outside the British Isles were far more violent. The
Times often devoted more column inches to murders in France or Italy than
to homicide trials heard in London. The commentary usually focused on the
savage nature of the population and the stupidity of their courts.[112] Though
foreigners were assumed to be innately inferior, foreign examples might be
used to encourage the British to mend their ways.

The fate of foreigners in English courts varied considerably by nationality. Foreign nationals tried in England, Ireland, and Wales were entitled to
have their consul present, they were provided with an interpreter, and they
had the option of a jury made up of six British subjects and six foreigners.
When a Belgian servant was tried in London for the murder of her French
mistress, the presiding judge warned the jury that "more patience, attention
and vigilance should be exercised through the trial of a foreigner than in a
similar proceeding against a British subject."[113] Sometimes judges even made
allowances for national failings. When a Greek sailor was accused of stabbing
an Italian sailor, Justice Willes charged against a murder verdict because "foreigners when from home acted differently from what they did when they
were surrounded by their friends and neighbors."[114] Some attorneys argued
that violence came naturally to certain people. When one woman killed
another in a boardinghouse "in a locality almost exclusively inhabited by
Italians," the defense "besought the jury picturing to themselves the scene of
a party of angry Italian of both sexes fighting promiscuously in a dark under-
ground kitchen where it would be impossible to determine what really
occurred." The jury acquitted.[115] When an Italian ice-cream dealer was con-

victed of murder in Glasgow, a memorial was presented to the Home Office for commutation of the death sentence. The *Scotsman* ran an editorial urging the public to sign the petition because, among other reasons, "the prisoner and the deceased are both natives of Italy which has no capital punishment and prisoner belongs to a hotblooded race."[116]

The UK courts were hardest on Americans (a quarter of those tried were executed). There was a consensus that Americans were more savage and placed less value on human life than any of their British or Irish cousins. The *Times* lamented, "[O]ne is sometimes tempted to think that the life of a man is thought little more of in America than the life of a rat."[117] An Irish judge explained one homicide by noting that "the prisoner was sometime in America, and he was afraid the prisoner had learned there to regard other men's lives more cheaply than they were regarded in this country under our law."[118] Continental European defendants were also more likely to hang than British defendants, though they were still thought to be better off than they might be in other courtrooms. When a Swedish sailor was tried for murdering a shipmate he thought was bringing bad luck to their ship, the defense attorney referred to his client as a "wretched creature whose swaying from side to side was sufficient to show he was demented. . . . Happily, he was being tried by a jury composed wholly of Englishmen and they with that innate sense of justice by which Englishmen were always governed would doubtless acquit him." The attorney was disappointed in his hopes as the man was found guilty of murder and sentenced to death though the sentence was commuted.[119] The Scots were also less sympathetic toward foreign defendants. Foreigners were nearly three times more likely to hang than were native Scots.

But though Americans and Europeans were punished severely, only one of the twenty-eight Africans and Asians tried for homicide in England and Wales was executed. English judges also gave lighter sentences to defendants from "uncivilized" countries. Justice Cotton explained that he was reducing a sentence from fifteen to ten years as "the prisoner was a man of colour and therefore the use of the knife under provocation he had received was somewhat more excusable than it would have been had he been a white man."[120] The Scots also sympathized with those from less civilized nations. When a mulatto from Canada was convicted of culpable homicide for killing a local man in a drunken brawl in Dundee, the local newspaper editorialized that "the Jury only embodied the public opinion when they restricted their verdict to one of Culpable Homicide. The Judge's merciful treatment of the negro has been generally approved of by public opinion."[121]

Weapons and National Character

The presumption that the British were less savage than the people of other nations included a belief that the British were less likely to use lethal weapons. The English had long taken pride in the notion that Englishmen fought with their fists.[122] In fact, even judges might share the pride in the notion that the Englishmen used nature's weapons. After hearing a case in which four solders had killed a man in a pub brawl, Justice Brett assured them they would "return to their regiments without a stigma on their character, as it had been a fair stand-up fight and the knife had not been used."[123] Justice Wightman was even blunter, insisting that "during a quarrel" people should use "the weapon with which nature had provided mankind—the fists." [124]

Since the defining feature of murder is intent, whether or not the killer used a weapon was an important factor in trial outcomes. In each nation about a fifth of homicides that came to trial involved no weapon. Everywhere beating deaths were less likely to lead to murder convictions than other types of homicides and sentences were lighter than average (a year and a half lighter in England and Ireland). But if the killer used his or her feet as well as hands the outcomes differed. In England kicking was associated with foreigners and roughs. Officials in England were particularly eager to stop kicking, both as a form of fighting and as a tactic of wife abuse.[125] English juries convicted in 80 percent of homicide trials in which the victim had been kicked to death. Sixteen percent of kicking trials led to *murder* convictions even though no lethal weapon had been used. When the victim had been kicked as well as beaten, the average sentence in English manslaughter cases increased by nearly three years. In Scotland, kicking was taken more seriously by judges than by jurors. Though Scottish juries were no more likely to convict in kicking homicides than in beating ones, the average sentences given by Scottish judges were nearly two years longer when the killer had used his feet. In Ireland there was no significant difference in either conviction rates or sentences when the homicide had been caused by kicking rather than beating. This may give credence to the claims in English and Scottish courtrooms that kicking was characteristic of the Irish.

Beatings either with fists or with handy objects such as rocks or sticks accounted for over half of all Irish homicide trials as opposed to only about a third of homicide trials in Britain. Though such beatings were the cause of death in over a thousand Irish homicide trials, only fifteen of these trials led to murder convictions and only ten of the death sentences were carried out. In Ireland 82 percent of homicide convictions that involved no weapon led to a sentence of less than two years as did 75 percent of cases in which the victim had been beaten to death with an object.

But if fisticuffs were a natural form of combat, the use of a knife was considered alien. In 1880 Justice Grove complained after a case in which a man had been stabbed to death during a brawl, "There was a time when such a use was called un-English, but the term did not apply now having so many cases of this sort where people used weapons, instead of having recourse to the habit when the English fought with their fists."[126] He also implied that some Englishmen were even worse than foreigners. "People were accustomed to speak of Spaniards and Italians being addicted to the habit of using weapons, but he doubted whether there was anything like the homicide and wounding with intent to do grievous bodily harm by the knife in any country greater than in England."[127] Twenty percent of English homicide trials involved stabbing. Seventy-four percent of these trials led to convictions and over a quarter of those tried were executed. Scottish courts were even harder on stabbing deaths. Stabbing was the cause of death in 17 percent of Scottish homicide trials, but it was the cause of death in 54 percent of murder convictions.

The Irish also viewed the use of the knife as alien. As one judge told a Limerick jury, "Now this habit of using the knife is most cowardly it is certainly un-Irish and should be checked."[128] Another judge explained that the increase in stabbing could be "attributed to the great intercourse with America, where people were in the habit of carrying knives in the street and using them with the greatest freedom and there was hardly a quarrel anywhere there in which parties did not take out knives and use them with deadly effect."[129] But even though stabbings were more likely to lead to conviction in Ireland than other homicides, over half of those convicted of stabbing someone to death were sentenced to less than two years. In Ireland the knife was used in brawls— only guns were associated with premeditation.

Though only 11 percent of Irish homicide trials involved guns, they were the weapon in 40 percent of homicide trials involving political, sectarian, or agrarian issues. Because gun deaths in Ireland were so often related to political unrest, the courts took them very seriously. But, for the same reason, finding witnesses was often very difficult. Convictions were 20 percent less likely in gun homicides than in other homicide trials, but a person convicted of killing with a gun was over four times more likely to hang than other convicted killers in Ireland. Not all political shootings were intended to be fatal. Firing into houses (or moonlighting as it was more popularly known) was listed as a separate category in the Irish crime statistics. In fact, the use of guns to make a point rather than to kill was sometimes accepted even in circumstances that might seem highly suspect. Charges against a tailor in Cavan who had fired a double-barreled shotgun at a drinking companion were dismissed because there had been "no bad feeling."[130] The Irish outrage papers regularly noted that some "cases entered in the numerical return as 'firing at the person' are unimportant, intimidation and not injury being the apparent object." The *Cork Examiner* suggested that a local physician who was charged with firing a shot from a revolver was being treated unfairly: "[T]hat a shot was fired there seems to be no doubt whatever but it appears equally certain that it was not fired at anything in particular and it may very well be that some fellow going that way fired off a shot 'in the gaiety of his heart.'"[131]

Gun deaths were rare in England. Only 7 percent of English homicides that came to trial had involved guns. The English press presented gun violence as an American vice. In fact, merely being American sometimes sufficed as a defense in English shooting cases. When Luke Emerson shot William Robinson outside a bar, the defense explained that he "drew a revolver which he was in the habit of carrying in America and fired it for the purpose of frightening him." Emerson was acquitted after the U.S. consul gave him a good character.[132] But in another case Justice Hawkins spoke of what many probably viewed as the crucial distinction between Britain and the United States when he complained of the "impropriety of men in this country where the law is sufficiently strong for their protections, going about armed with revolvers which in the momentary provocation they may be tempted to make use of."[133] Justice Stephen concurred. "A more barbarous practice than that of carrying about loaded arms such as the revolver he could not imagine. . . . There might be places where it was right to carry a loaded revolver but that any man should think it necessary to have a loaded revolver on his mantel-piece in London was almost inconceivable"[134]

Confident that their people were civilized and their law enforcement efficient, English courts saw gun use as an affront to national dignity. The issues were brought to the forefront in the case of Walter Hargan, a veteran of the British army who had spent several years in the United States. Hargan had interfered when two drunks began harassing the landlady of a pub. Once outside, when Hargan saw the two men behind him on the street, he turned around and shot them both in the head though he insisted to police he had merely fired shots in the air to frighten them. When the shooting first occurred, the *Times* reported it under the headline "Double Murder at Kingsland." Hargan was described as a stranger and the *Times* reported that local residents had run to capture him: "[A]n excited mob of men and women was now congregating and whilst one man fetched a rope and want-ed to hang the fellow at once, others kicked and cuffed him. . . . Had it not been for the timely arrival of police constables, the murderer must have been killed." The initial report described the victims as common laborers in their sixties and the incident as an example of American contamination. "The accused is said to have remarked that the deceased affronted him and he served them as they would have been served in America."[135] Hargan was convicted of manslaughter and Justice Charles sentenced him to twenty years penal servitude.[136]

The case did not end there, however. After the Home Office reduced the sentence to twelve months, an MP took up the cause and called for a full pardon on the grounds that Hargan was of good character and the victims were not, insisting that "Hargan in what he did obeyed an older law than any on the Statute book—namely, the law of self preservation." The home secretary replied, "The question of whether the men were of good or bad character had nothing whatever to do with the case. The best man in the world had no right to take the life of the worst man in the world, unless he were in danger of his life." He also cautioned that such notions were not English. "The right hon. gentleman had implied that it was necessary for persons to go armed, and that to use a weapon upon such provocation as Hargan received was justifiable homicide. These appeared to him to be assertions more fitted to the atmosphere of a South American bar than to any district of London." The *Times* warned that were Hargan to escape unpunished it would be "an evil example. . . . If the notion were to be encouraged that 'shooting at sight' was secure of impunity when a man was threatened by 'roughs,' we might soon lapse into the state of private warfare that is said to prevail in the Far West."[137]

The home secretary and *the Times* agreed that the crucial issue in gun deaths was the threat to the state's monopoly on the preservation of law and order. In late Victorian England public safety was preserved by duly appointed authorities. Guns threatened both public safety and the state's position as its guarantor. References to the United States and Latin America demonstrated that citizens needed to carry weapons only in other less civilized countries. When an English farmer was shot to death while riding to market, the coroner's jury "expressed an opinion that the murder could not have been committed by an Englishman."[138] But because the number of gun deaths supported the belief that guns were not the weapon of choice for English homicides, there was no great sense of urgency regarding their availability and use.[139]

But even though gun homicide trials in England were rare, they were increasing. The average number of gun deaths tried as homicides per year in England went from eleven for the period 1867–1874 to eighteen for the period 1884–1892. As a percentage of homicide trials, gun deaths doubled between 1867 and 1892. In 17 percent of gun homicide trials in England the defense argued that the death had been accidental. In the early part of the period such incidents rarely led to convictions. In 1867, when a sixteen-year-old boy was tried for fatally shooting his fourteen-year-old sister, both the judge and the *Times* reporter showed considerable sympathy for the accused. "These children and some others had been playing and laughing together. The prisoner was going to church with his mother, when she sent him back for an umbrella. The prisoner went back, found his sister in the parlor and they laughed together." He then picked up a gun, pointed it at his sister, and pulled the trigger. "The contents entered the poor child's head and she fell dead. The gun had been loaded unknown to the prisoner." The account, with the reference to play and laughter and describing a sixteen-year-old as a child, was exceptionally sentimental. But the view was shared by Justice Willes, who said that "no one would think of punishing the prisoner." After the young man pled guilty, the judge described the case as "a melancholy instance of the danger of playing with firearms. He had no doubt the prisoner had suffered more punishment in his feeling than the Court could inflict. The prisoner, who appeared to suffer very much, was then discharged."[140] The sympathy shown in this case was in marked contrast to the next one in which Justice Willes sent an eleven-year-old boy to a reformatory for five years for stealing a letter.

But as the death toll mounted, such shootings were increasingly viewed as culpable negligence. Though no accidental shootings led to convictions between 1867 and 1875, 40 percent of them led to convictions between 1885 and 1892. The sentences were light but the point was made. In 1881 Justice Hawkins complained, "People seemed to think the reckless use of revolvers was really no crime at all . . . very few days passed without one seeing, reading or hearing of some mischief done by the use of revolvers."[141] The *Times* agreed: "There has been far too much use of the revolver in England of recent years. They are at least as dangerous as poisons and it would be well if their sale could be restricted in a somewhat similar manner."[142] There were also suggestions that the blame be distributed. In 1890 two teenage boys were charged with killing a teenage girl with what they thought was a "toy pistol." Justice Day said the guilt lay "with the man who sold the pistol to a lad of the prisoner's age" and suggested the laws should be changed.[143]

As in Ireland, judges accepted that the use of a gun might not necessarily imply intent to kill. Justice Piggott said about a man charged with killing a friend when he fired into a crowd of people standing outside a pub: "If they thought he only went into the yard in a state of excitement intending only to raise consternation and alarm and not to kill or do harm they might find him guilty of manslaughter."[144] In 1876 George Underhill, "a man of considerable means," shot a passerby because in a drunken haze he thought someone was attacking him. Though there was no evidence that the victim was in any way a threat to Underhill, the judge told the jury: "If a man in a public thoroughfare without calling for the assistance of bystanders uses a dangerous weapon the crime is manslaughter not murder. Merely firing in a place when someone would likely be struck would not be sufficient to constitute the more serious offense." He sentenced Underhill to twelve months.[145] In 1887 Justice Stephen heard a case in which one American had shot another in Woburn Place. He told the jury, "If the jury thought he fired the pistol at the deceased's body intending to hit him, taking the chance where he hit him that would be murder. If on the other hand they thought that he had fired it vaguely, without any special intent at all—that would be manslaughter."[146]

Even when there was evidence of malicious intent toward someone else, English judges were surprisingly tolerant of guns. Alfred Hawse, a lodging house keeper, had been locked in his room with a loaded revolver, prompting a worried servant to fetch a policeman. When the constable knocked on the door, Hawse opened the door and fired the revolver. The shot killed a passerby. Hawse claimed that "he had no animosity to anyone and had been amusing himself with the revolver which he bought to shoot his wife with." Justice Hawkins said that "it was one of those cases in which they all regretted the facility with which people obtained and used revolvers" and sentenced Hawse to eighteen months.[147] English courts were willing to accept that guns were as much symbols as weapons. Guns might be fired "vaguely" or to create consternation. Perhaps because bullets were harder to target than knives, in England the average sentence for manslaughter with a gun was two years less than for manslaughter with a knife.

Gun deaths in Scotland were actually less likely to lead to murder convictions than other types of homicides, and Scots who were convicted of killing with a gun were actually more likely to receive a sentence of under two years than were those convicted of homicides involving beating or kicking. In keeping with Scottish principles, wrongs had to be atoned for, but because the number of trials for shooting homicides was not increasing in Scotland, as it was in England, there was no great concern about using prison sentences as a deterrent. Only 3 percent of Scottish homicide trials involved shootings, and though over three-quarters of the trials ended in convictions, nearly half of the convictions led to sentences of less than two years. Scottish gun deaths most often involved misfires. In other words, the shootings were deliberate—the outcomes unplanned. For example, in 1877 a watchman had fired a shotgun at three boys who were pelting him with stones. He pled guilty to culpable homicide though the defense pointed out that "[h]e had been much provoked. However when firing the gun he had

no intention of hitting any of the boys." The judge "remarked that it could
not be too widely known or clearly understood that the reckless use of
firearms was a very culpable act, but as on the whole he was satisfied that the
prisoner had no intention of harming the lads, he thought this punishment
[three months] was sufficient to meet the ends of justice."[148] In another case
a gentleman staying at a sanitarium in Inverness had shot at a cat and
missed. The bullet struck the managing director of the establishment, who
was killed instantly. The presiding judge explained that "where human life
had been sacrificed, a fine could not be imposed" and sentenced the man to
one month. Again the sentence was a very light one but the principles of
accountability were upheld.[149]

Even in cases in which the recklessness was more culpable, the Scottish
courts took the same moderate approach. In 1878, after a drunken quarrel
with his wife, James Martin found a crowd outside his window hooting him
for being a wife beater. Martin responded by firing his rifle out the window,
killing a seventeen-year-old girl who was walking by. He pled guilty to culpable homicide. The prosecution accepted that he "may have been alarmed
by the crowd and unintentionally loaded bullets instead of blanks; however,
to fire a rifle even loaded with blank cartridges among a body of women is
a most grave offense." He was sentenced to twelve months.[150] Heavy sentences in shooting homicide trials in Scotland were reserved for poachers.
The only nonpoacher convicted of murder with a gun in Scotland during
the period was a fisherman who had deliberately shot his sleeping wife in the
head.

Very few gun accidents appear in the Welsh courts, which may indicate that
such cases were not considered homicides and gun deaths were not considered
a serious problem. In North Wales in 1891 a fifteen-year-old boy was able to
purchase a revolver for five shillings. He had kept the gun hidden from his
mother, but his twelve-year-old brother found the gun and shot his nine-year-
old sister. The coroner's jury ruled the death accidental, but the coroner added
that he "wished to know how the pistol came into the possession of the child
and would not remain satisfied until the affair had been thoroughly investigated."[151] Language problems could also be involved in gun accidents. In 1892
William Morgan was shot to death in Swansea by a seaman named William
Smith. Morgan was sitting in the kitchen of the hotel when Smith came in.
Morgan was holding a revolver and Smith asked to see it. Morgan said since
it was loaded he would not let it out of his hands. But Smith insisted, started
playing with it, and shot Morgan. The coroner's jury ruled it death from misadventure as Morgan had been speaking Welsh when he said it was loaded and
Smith did not speak Welsh.[152] Like their neighbors the Welsh associated guns

with Americans. When a labor leader at Swansea shot his wife, the newspaper noted that the man "had lived in the US and adopting a habit of many people of that country, always kept a loaded pistol in his house."[153]

HOMICIDE AND NATIONAL IDENTITY

Everywhere, the assumption was that homicides were committed by outsiders, with weapons imported by foreigners acting on instincts that were alien to the true national character. For the English, there were two crucial issues: first, that English civilization was such that violence was no longer necessary, and second, the English tradition of the fair fight. The two were in conflict, and as Wiener, Emsley, and Wood have argued, over the course of the nineteenth century the control of traditional violence was a major focus of the government. But killers also allowed the English to identify themselves. Englishmen who killed were not behaving like Englishmen—they were behaving like savages or Irishmen or Americans. Killing (except on the field of valor) was *not English*.

The Irish were willing to assume that most homicides were inadvertent so much so that killers were often worthy of as much sympathy as their victims. Most Irish homicide trials were for deaths in brawls and most did not involve a lethal weapon. Even when guns were used the courts were willing to assume there had been no lethal intent. Homicides might happen because of drink and passion, but murder was un-Irish. The Scots also failed to see their fellow citizens as murderers but Scottish courts insisted on atonement for sins. Scottish killers were the most likely to be convicted but the least likely to be executed. But the Scottish press was convinced that the only true murderers among them were the Irish immigrants. Homicide trials were so rare in Wales that generalizations are particularly difficult, but the Welsh, like their neighbors, were convinced that murders were committed by foreigners (though ironically the foreigners they most often had in mind were the English).

However, most homicide trials did not involve homicidal strangers or robbers or rapists. How do judges and jurors respond when the killer is not inherently Other but is a local man or woman responding to difficult but not unusual circumstances? The choices made reveal a great deal about underlying assumptions regarding gender, power, class, and the boundaries between public and personal responsibility.

CHAPTER 3

Class, Gender, and the Fair Fight

Unhappily law exists for the purpose of keeping what is
human and natural in check. (The *Times,* 3 August 1888,
10a)

He appealed to the jury to weigh the evidence without any
prejudice which might result from regarding the sex of the
deceased or the brutality of the crime which had been committed. (The *Times,* 28 January 1879, 11d)

CLASS AND JUSTICE IN ENGLAND

Though equality before the law is a basic tenet of British justice, British
courtrooms were not blind to social distinctions. Both class and gender influenced the outcomes of homicide trials, though their impact was neither as
clear-cut nor as significant as might be expected. The actions of Victorian
judges and juries did not always correspond to the prevailing discourse.
Though class in Victorian England is a complex topic to which huge tomes
have been and continue to be devoted,[1] there is no question that homicide
defendants from different points on the social scale were subject to very different expectations and reactions. In England the likelihood of execution rose
as the defendant's social status declined. Working-class homicide defendants
in England were nearly twice as likely to be executed as those from the middle or upper classes. On the other hand, the likelihood of a finding of insanity rose with the defendant's social status. Fifteen percent of upper-class
defendants were found insane.

Contemporaries were keenly aware of the impact of class distinctions on
justice. In 1872, after two prominent upper-class defendants who had been
convicted of murder were both granted respites on grounds of insanity, the
Spectator warned that "we have the greatest possible fear of a suspicion of

68

class-justice gaining ground with the English people."[2] In 1879 a group of working men met in London to discuss a case in which a laborer had been sentenced to death for strangling his mother although there was evidence of suicide. They passed a resolution noting that "[t]hey had ample proof lately that the law was not at all times infallible and they had as citizens a perfect right to protest against the carrying out of a sentence they believed to be against the weight of the evidence."[3]

Middle-class jurors were more concerned about respectability than mere wealth. A convicted murderer who claimed to have committed many crimes before his capture explained, "I made a point of dressing respectably as the police never think of suspecting any one who appears in good clothes. In this way I have thrown the police off their guard many times."[4] While income certainly was a factor in achieving respectability, it was by no means the only factor. Within the working class there was a sharp break between the respectable working classes—sober, hardworking men who by the last third of the nineteenth century were a significant part of the political and economic nation—and the roughs who had failed to internalize respectable behavior. Further, the mutual resentment between the respectable sober, skilled craftsman and the unskilled, rowdy laborer was often greater than that between the middle and working classes. In a famous case from Liverpool, a respectable working-class man was beaten to death by roughs who were incensed that his reply to a request for money for drinks was to ask them what they worked at.[5]

It was certainly easier to be respectable with a comfortable, steady income. Middle-class defendants were the most likely to be acquitted, in part because middle-class defendants could afford defense attorneys who appealed to the middle-class empathy for respectable families blighted by the conviction of a family black sheep. A London barrister whose client had deliberately shot and killed a neighbor asked the jury "for merciful consideration for the sake of his wife and children that they may be spared the cold pity of the world in having a near and dear relative convicted of murder."[6]

But still the poor but honest worker might be far more respectable than the wealthy wastrel. Though lower-class defendants were the most likely to be convicted, defendants described as "gentlemen" were a third less likely to be acquitted than middle-class ones. In 1879 Gerald Mainwaring— "described as a gentleman," and the son of a Staffordshire magistrate—was accused of murdering a police constable. After being arrested for reckless driving, he had pulled a revolver at the police station and fired three shots, killing one policeman and injuring another.[7] The solicitor general, who was "specially retained" to defend Mainwaring, argued, "The prisoner appeared to have conceived the wretched idea of having a 'spree' before going [to

America]. He therefore entered upon three days of reckless debauchery and purchased weapons which he meant to take with him to a foreign country, to which it could be wished such implements were confined."[8] After implying that America, alcohol, and firearms were really to blame, the attorney warned that if they found Mainwaring guilty, "then it must follow that no man can ever be so drunk as not to be responsible to the fullest extent for the consequences of his acts." He then attempted to paint the case as a tragedy for Mainwaring, who had inflicted "on himself and those to whom he is dear an irreparable injury." The presiding judge, Justice Lindley, complimented the solicitor general, "who was placed in a difficult position" but rejected the argument noting that the evidence "disclosed a story of sin and wickedness such as was rarely divulged even in a court of justice." After a three-hour deliberation, the jury found Mainwaring guilty of murder and Justice Lindley pronounced the death sentence.[9]

The case might have ended there. But ten days later the *Times* reported indignantly that the jury had not followed English legal requirements. According to the report, the jury had been divided, half of them "favouring a verdict of manslaughter in regard to a crime from which all deliberation or actual malice was absent" and half favoring murder. In order to reach a verdict, the jury members "agreed, quite contrary to their duties that the vote of the majority should determine the verdict and that the chairman should have a casting vote. There can be no doubt that the jury were guilty of grave misconduct." Though the *Times* insisted the issue was jury misconduct, the rhetoric suggested that the fact that a well-connected gentleman had been convicted of murder was also significant. Even though the death sentence was commuted, the *Times* was not satisfied: "The granting of a pardon does not obliterate the mischief of a verdict of guilt improperly obtained. The stigma sticks to the victim in spite of the royal Grace." Mainwaring, who had killed a policeman, was now described as "the victim."[10] The indignation is also interesting in light of the fact that Scottish murderers were executed on the basis of majority verdicts.

In the combination of drink and firearms, Mainwaring's crime was very representative of those of his class. Upper-class defendants like Mainwaring were nearly three times more likely to have used firearms in a homicide than working-class ones. This may be a partial explanation for the longer sentences given upper-class defendants. Another is that the sentences were influenced by the status of the victim.[11] In the vast majority of homicide trials the accused and the victim were from the same social class. Fewer than 2 percent of those tried for homicide in England had killed a social superior and only 4.5 percent had killed a subordinate or a social inferior.

In fact, only one English homicide between 1867 and 1892 seemed to be based specifically on class antagonism. In an extraordinary case in Winchester in 1887, John Henry Lush, a twenty-six-year-old laborer, shot a gentleman of independent means while he was walking on the Commons one afternoon. The men were complete strangers, but Lush said he did it because he had been out of work for eight months. In a less stable nation, the crime might have been seen as a dangerous symptom of class warfare, but a London jury found Lush insane and he was committed to an asylum.[12] Except for Lush, those who killed a social superior in England were motivated either by greed or personal animus. Over half were convicted of murder. For those convicted of the manslaughter of a social superior, the average sentence was thirteen years—more than twice the national average.

Only thirty-five English defendants were tried for killing a subordinate. Nearly half were acquitted and none were convicted of murder. But the manslaughter sentences in these cases were slightly higher than average. Justice Coleridge insisted that in England "the law throws its protection around human life so far as it can protect it, if it could be shown that the life of the veriest stranger and outcast had been taken, it would hold the man who took it quite as responsible as if his victim were the highest in the land."[13] Testing this hypothesis is difficult. In the 2 percent of English homicide trials in which the victim was from the under class (prostitutes, known criminals, tramps, gypsies), the verdicts and sentences were in line with general trends. But a great many such homicides went unsolved and even more were perhaps unrecorded.

BRAWLS IN ENGLAND AND WALES

That lower-class killers were given lighter sentences because their victims were also from the lower classes was demonstrated in reactions to the category of homicides most often associated with the working classes—brawls. Several scholars have traced the decline of tolerance for recreational violence in England over the eighteenth and nineteenth centuries.[14] By the last third of the nineteenth century over half of those accused of killing someone in a brawl were unskilled laborers. After hearing a trial involving a death in a brawl among workmen, Justice Willes noted that "[p]ersons better off at least restrained from personal violence, but the poor, who certainly had greater claim on the forbearance and sympathy of their fellows, seemed to act on the smallest provocation, with the greatest barbarity."[15] In another case, Justice Willes warned a London jury against acquitting on the grounds of self-defense: "[T]he result might be to encourage among a class of men who had very little control over their own passions when drunk—a practice which happily in this country had been exterminated among the higher classes—viz. the practice of dueling and they would have men resorting to knives on mere tiffs of passion."[16] The disdain for brawling, though strongest in the middle class, was not limited to the well off. Only 12 percent of skilled workers accused of homicide had killed someone in a brawl.

As the number and social status of participants in brawls in England declined, so did the punishments. Though the average sentence given in a manslaughter case in England increased slightly during the period, the average sentence for homicides in brawls fell nearly 15 percent between 1867 and 1892.[17] Many judges accepted that brawling was natural for the lower classes. Justice Brett told a laborer who was convicted of killing a man in a brawl: "I am never inclined to punish a man for infirmities of conduct, which are possibly excusable in persons of such a class as yourself. If the victim were foolish enough to challenge you to fight on Christmas Eve it is an infirmity to which one of your class is likely to succumb. You have done an illegal act, but I do not wish to place you in the class of criminals."[18]

The circumstances of such homicides were also changing. Though the number of homicide trials involving large drunken free-for-alls or one-on-one fights was declining, there was an 800 percent increase in gang-related homicide trials in England during the 1880s. At the March 1882 sitting of the Central Criminal Court, the grand jury heard that "[r]oughs and ruffians assembled together, armed themselves with weapons and on the Thames Embankment and other places riotously and tumultuously consorted themselves causing great public alarm. . . . [S]even dead bodies had been pulled out of the Thames at the Embankment; it was exceedingly difficult for the ordinary civilian forces to deal with such lawlessness."[19] Gang violence was also a growing problem in the cities of the industrial north.[20]

The change from random drunken brawls to gang fights made the divide between the respectable who increasingly forswore violence and the residuum who did not even more apparent. In 1888, when a young man was murdered by a gang in Regent's Park, the *Times* noted: "The public mind will dwell with painful interest on the revelation which the trial gives of the thick stratum of barbarism underlying our civilization. That the whole class of 'roughs' is a class which regards the police as its natural enemies, and is only kept from constant outbreaks of violence by fear, is a fact sufficiently familiar." The report compared the gang wars of London youth to "the tribal feuds of the Arabs and the Red Indians. Active feuds between one gang and another are in conflict with the system of life which we call civilized."[21] Law and civilization were designed to encourage higher standards of masculinity. Manhood was increasingly defined not by physical strength but by the ability to use reasoned self-control to avoid violent confrontation.[22]

Even though brawling was associated with the lowest classes, virtually every English judge expressed ambivalence about the criminality of brawling. England had a long tradition of the fair stand-up fight. In many ways the brawl represented an intersection of class and gender norms. No form of homicide is more closely associated with masculinity than deaths in brawls. The tradition of violent tests of manly honor is virtually universal, and the English had been particularly famous for it.[23] As the *Times* acknowledged in 1888, "There are codes of fellowship, unwritten laws, which have to be observed. It is all very human and natural."

The emphasis on reason over violence was not universally accepted, nor were judges convinced that such a change was possible or even necessary. Justice Brett explained in 1875, "I desire, for the sake of law and good government to draw a marked distinction between cases of unfairness or cowardice, and a quarrel and fair fight. . . . I do not think when men quarrel it is any great sin that they should fight out that quarrel if they would only fight fairly with their natural weapons,—their hands." Brett admired his countrymen's willingness to fight fairly and gamely. He said of a man who had beaten an opponent to death: "If he had given up when he saw that his opponent was weakened he would have been said to have been vanquished and human nature could not stand it; a man is very unwilling to give up when he is getting the better. He appears to have had courage, which I don't dislike to see in an Englishman—he declined to give up." Brett directed the jury to convict as this was "an offense against the law" but sentenced the killer to just one week.[24]

Justice Mellor shared the opinion that homicides in brawls were technically illegal but not seriously criminal. After hearing a case in which a man had beaten his challenger to death in a brawl, Justice Mellor instructed a Durham jury to convict him. "To his surprise the jury after a moment's consideration, returned a verdict of not guilty, on account of the provocation the prisoner had received. His Lordship expressed his astonishment at the verdict. However the justice of the case was not materially affected because the sentence he should have passed upon him would have been of the smallest description."[25] Justice Denman expressed similar sentiments in the case of a man who had died in a drunken fight. "It was clear that the man came by his death in consequence of unlawful violence, because men were not allowed to fight in that manner in the street . . . although the case was a very slight one with regard to gravity." The victim had issued a challenge and the accused had an excellent character. Denman said since there was "no foul play in the real sense of the word" he would sentence the man to just three days.[26] Justice Brett told a Lancaster jury that he "for one, would never punish a man if being provoked he had in a fair fight, had the misfortune to kill his opponent."[27] The average sentence given an Englishman convicted of killing someone in a brawl in which the victim had started the fight and no weapon had been used was just six months.

Some English judges even refused to condemn the man who threw the first punch. Justice Bramwell told a Liverpool jury, "A man was justified in defending himself if another was going to strike him and was not bound to wait to be struck first."[28] In a case from London, the deceased had pulled the killer's nose "than which no greater indignity could possibly be offered a man."[29] In another case involving a nose being pulled, Justice Thesiger told a jury that "he was no advocate of fighting, either with the fists or any other way; but there were cases in which an inoffensive man may be provoked beyond endurance."[30] English defense attorneys often tried to establish that the victim had "squared up"— the signal that the fight was on.[31]

Judges also accepted that in a fair fight to determine who was the "better man" there was no malice. Justice Lopes told a jury, "If death resulted from a mere trial of strength without anger the prisoner was not guilty of the charge."[32] Justice Manisty heard a case in which two men had met for a fight which "was in every way fairly contested," but the challenger had suffered fatal head injuries. The judge told the defendant who had pled guilty, "You did engage in that which was contrary to law but I think, taking into consideration your excellent character, which does you great credit, that this is a case in which I am justified in not sentencing you to be imprisoned." He released the man on £50 bond.[33] Another case in which a man died of a skull fracture in a fight which he had initiated was dismissed before it went to the jury. The victim had shaken his killer's hand before he died and told him that "he was the better man." Justice Lopes said that "even had the prisoner been found guilty the punishment would have been all but nominal."[34] In a case heard in London, Justice Willes told the jury that "the case disclosed what was more like an unfortunate accident than a crime. There appeared to be no previous ill-blood and the dispute seemed to have begun in play." The jury acquitted.[35]

Even judges who spoke against fighting gave light sentences. In a case from Liverpool in which coworkers drinking in a pub had agreed "to a fair fight with no kicking or foul play," Justice Stephen announced that "he wished everybody who heard him to know that a deliberate fight like this, even if conducted in a fair manner, was an illegal act. Under the circumstances, he must inflict upon the prisoner such a punishment as would mark the view the court takes of cases where human life is concerned." The sentence which was supposed to mark the seriousness of the case was only two months.[36]

However, if fair stand-up fights and drunken brawls were viewed with relative indifference, there was no sympathy for those who did not follow the rules. Englishmen took considerable pride in their sense of fair play.[37] In a case in which a man had kicked his opponent to death while he was down, Justice Brett said he "could scarcely believe that men could be so dastardly to fight as the prisoner had done. There was a time when Englishmen fought fairly but those times seem to have passed."[38] Kicking was a regional variation. In a case heard by Justice Lush in London, the victim had offered to fight in what he called "Lancashire fashion which was explained in court to mean the use of both feet and hands and to allow of a man being kicked when he was down." The accused had declined the challenge but "said that he should not mind a fair stand-up fight in the proper English fashion."[39]

Justice Grove's comments to a Welsh jury in 1880 were very like those being given to English juries. "If people would fight out their differences, they had better fight with fists, rather than deadly weapons, although he did not wish to commend fighting at all."[40] But the Welsh may have had different rules. David Rees and James Davies were tried for manslaughter at Carmarthen in 1875. They had beaten and kicked a man to death in a brawl. Witnesses testified that the participants had agreed to fight and had taken off their coats to do so, but Rees and Davies had kicked the victim while he was down. The victim's wife had tried to intervene but she had been pulled away as someone shouted "Fair play." The men had been friends and Rees had carried the victim home after the fight. After the jury heard that the victim had issued the initial challenge, the jury announced that there was no case and returned a verdict of not guilty.[41]

Though masculine honor was crucial in justifying brawls, the most commonly cited factor was alcohol. Over half of the defendants tried for homicides in brawls had been intoxicated at the time of the assault, as had over half of the victims. But drink was no mitigation. Though drink was mentioned as a factor in 57 percent of English brawl homicide trials, it was a factor in 77 percent of brawl homicide cases in which the jury convicted the accused of *murder* and in 79 percent of cases in which the killer was executed. When the verdict was manslaughter, the average sentence in English brawl homicides was 15 percent heavier if the accused had been drunk at the time.

Welsh juries were also more likely to return a murder conviction if alcohol was involved. Perhaps the most remarkable incidence of Welsh disapproval was a case from Swansea in which a puddler was charged with murder after a man died from being hit in the head with a stone during a drunken scuffle. Justice Keating carefully explained to the jurors the distinction between manslaughter and murder, clearly expecting the former. But the jury returned a murder conviction, adding that they "hoped the case would be a warning to persons indulging to excess in drinking habits."[42] This concern corresponds to a substantial increase in arrests for drunkenness in Wales. The Non-Conformist population of Wales may have been more heavily influenced by the temperance movement than their Anglican neighbors.[43]

But the Welsh shared the English ambivalence about the criminality of the fair fight. When a coroner's jury in Carmarthen heard a case in which a young man had killed a friend in a fight, the coroner spelled out the legal issues. Manslaughter was: "unlawfully and feloniously killing another without any malice, ill feeling or ill-will, but by accident when engaged in doing an unlawful act. There was no doubt the two boys fighting were doing an unlawful act. They had no right to fight and if death ensued in consequence, even by accident it was manslaughter." He explained that he had felt it necessary to "lay down the law as clearly as possible. . . . If they thought it was not a fight merely a frolic it would be quite different but in his opinion it would outrage every idea of sense and reason to suppose so."[44] The coroner's jury indicted the young man who was convicted and sentenced to three months for manslaughter. Whatever the law might say, late Victorian judges and juries in England and Wales were not terribly concerned about the deaths of working-class men in fair fights.

CLASS AND JUSTICE IN SCOTLAND

At least rhetorically the Scots viewed class issues differently than the English. The *Scotsman* delighted in making fun of the English obsession with class distinctions. In 1868 the paper reported that a Leeds clergyman had given "notice that 'the young ladies who were candidates for confirmation were to meet in the parsonage but that the 'young women' were to assemble in the schoolroom. We hope the church sticklers for social distinction will have influence enough to prevent the 'ladies' and the 'women' of his congregation getting mixed together in the upper world."[45] But the assumption that God was no respecter of persons might lead to the conclusion that those who remained in the lower classes did so from lack of initiative. The *Scotsman* insisted that class was a matter of merit and work rather than birth. "The working class in a country like this is not marked off from other classes by a sharp line. It is a class which merges by imperceptible degrees, into other classes, out of which the passage is easy to skill, talent and industry." While there was no shame in being born into the working class, staying there was a matter of choice. "It may be quite true that there are in the working-class many men of intelligence but there is nothing unkind in saying that as a general rule, that amount of intelligence would, if rightly exercised and unaccompanied by drawbacks have sufficed to take its possessors out of that class."[46]

In homicide trials the differences between the likelihood of conviction of upper- and lower-class defendants in Scotland were the same as those in England and Wales. Lower-class Scots were also more likely to be convicted of murder, though they were no more likely to be executed than upper-class defendants. But the difference in conviction rates was achieved in a different way in Scottish courtrooms. While in England and Wales upper-class defendants were more likely to be found insane, middle-class defendants in Scotland were nearly twice as likely to receive verdicts of not proven than were working-class ones. Scottish judges seem to be more concerned about controlling the lower classes. In nondomestic culpable homicide convictions, lower-class defendants received an average sentence of sixty months while the average sentence for middle- and upper-class defendants was just thirty-seven months.

The *Scotsman* insisted that in Scotland "the weakest may be sure that no one can take away from him what is justly his; this his life and property are secure, that any offence committed against him will be punished."[47] When a man was tried for killing a prostitute he claimed had robbed him, the judge insisted, "The woman killed was of a very bad character but the law held the life of every human being, bad or good in character, sacred and they could never allow character to influence judgment." Lord Ardmillan was as good as his word; her killer was sentenced to life in prison.[48] But this was not always the case. The conviction rate in Scotland did not vary according to the social status of the victim, but in 75 percent of the convictions in which the victim was a prostitute, tinker, or other member of what might be considered the lowest class, the sentence was less than two years. None of the fifteen Scots tried for killing a subordinate served more than two years.

Only five Scots were accused of killing social superiors, but two of the five were convicted of murder. Patrick Docherty, a nineteen-year-old Irishman in Lanarkshire, was part of a drunken group celebrating on a Saturday night when John Miller, a local shop owner's son, "was attracted to the street by the noise of a drunken rabble." Miller went out and began to laugh at Docherty and his friends. Docherty, apparently feeling insulted, struck Miller in the head with a pole. Miller died at the scene. Docherty was charged with murder and his attempt to offer a plea of culpable homicide was rejected. The defense attorney argued that "if it was murder it was the most useless, purposeless and aimless committed since the beginning of time." Nevertheless, the jury unanimously found him guilty of murder and he was sentenced to death. Even though Docherty had several character witnesses at the trial and the jury recommended mercy, he was executed. The newspapers wrote of Docherty's air of bewilderment, which must have been profound. In his native Ireland, even in the twenty-one cases in which an innocent bystander had been killed at a brawl, no one had been sentenced to more than ten years.[49] The fact that Docherty was an Irish miner and his victim the son of a Scottish merchant almost certainly influenced the outcome of the case.

A propensity for recreational violence is sometimes attributed to Celtic traditions. Certainly the ancient and early modern Scots had been a match for the Irish or nearly anyone else in terms of internecine warfare. James VI had written of his people, "[T]hey bang it out bravely, he and all his kin against him and all his."[50] By the 1860s the Scots were far less likely to kill each other in brawls, but some of the same rituals still applied. In a case from Dundee, a witness testified that "they had their coats off they called upon the best man to come forward and fight."[51] Like their English and Irish counterparts, Scottish juries seem to have been ambivalent about the criminality of such incidents. One Scottish jury made its problem with the law explicit. During a wake in Glasgow when Thomas Murray passed out from drink, his friend John Johnstone tied a ribbon around his head. When Murray woke up he challenged Johnstone to a fight. After one blow, the very drunk Murray fell and fatally fractured his skull. The jury found Johnstone guilty of culpable homicide but crossed the words "wickedly and feloniously" off the indictment. They explained that the action had not been wicked since no malice was involved, the victim had been drunk, the insult was imagined, and the victim fell after just one blow. If there had been no malicious intent, how could a death in a drunken brawl be considered wicked and felonious? In this case the prosecuting attorney responded to the jury's gesture by asking the judge not to impose a sentence.[52]

In Scotland, as in England, brawls were a lower-class activity. Sixty-four percent of those tried for killing someone in a brawl were laborers, miners, or soldiers for whom the Saturday night brawl was routine. The *Dundee Advertiser* reported the following exchange during a trial of a man accused of killing a coworker on a Saturday night in 1891.

WITNESS: On the night in question they were good enough friends. A fight in the neighborhood was a very common thing.

PROSECUTOR: A sort of Saturday night entertainment?

WITNESS: It is a general rule on a Saturday night. Both men wanted to fight and he fell down steps.

PROSECUTOR: Do you think it fighting for one man to stoop down and catch another and throw him down a stair?

WITNESS: I do not consider that would be exactly fair, but it is generally the way of a street fight.

After a ten-minute deliberation, the majority of the jurors voted that the accused was not guilty. The judge told the defendant the verdict was "very merciful and he hoped he would in future abstain from drink and street brawling and would live a respectable life."[53] But Scottish jurors may have accepted that certain groups would not live respectable lives.[54] Miners, who had actually been serfs in Scotland until the end of the eighteenth century, had a particularly low status. When a Lanarkshire miner was killed by a gang of fellow miners, a witness explained: "They were all the one kind and it would not do for us to interfere."[55] Only 36 percent of miners accused of killing a fellow miner in a brawl were convicted compared to 67 percent of all Scottish homicide defendants.

When a Scottish jury was allowed to render a verdict in a brawl homicide, they convicted less than half the time; however, in over a quarter of the Scottish cases involving brawl homicides the accused pled guilty. Fewer than 5 percent of defendants pled guilty in English and Irish cases of brawl homicides. Why such a high percentage of Scots pled guilty is unclear. Presumably they were hoping to avoid a murder conviction, but if so they may have been unduly concerned since fewer than 4 percent of Scottish trials for homicides in brawls ended with a murder conviction. Nor did a guilty plea mean the judge would be more lenient. The average sentence for a Scot who pled guilty to killing someone in a brawl was sixty-four months, if the accused had pled not guilty and been convicted by a jury the average sentence was fifty-seven months.

Though a guilty plea took the jury out of the case, in 1891 when a man pled guilty to killing a friend in a brawl, a Glasgow juror interrupted the proceedings, saying, "[I]t was only a drunken brawl." The presiding judge, Lord Young, angrily told the juryman he had no right to interrupt and explained that regardless of the circumstances, "The life of a Queen's subject by the law of the land as it now exists was not to be taken away by even fair but quite idle fighting and therefore when a life was lost by two men quite equally and

deliberately taking part in a fight the law said that loss of life was to be regarded as culpable homicide." But His Lordship's comments revealed more def-
erence to the law than concurrence with it. "That was the law of the land and
neither his lordship nor any juryman could express with propriety any opinion with respect to it. It was the law which must be enforced." Lord Young
then explained that "[t]he amount of punishment was a matter for the discretion of the courts . . . it had been his practice to take into very careful and
merciful consideration any circumstances which seemed to diminish the
guilt." He then sentenced the accused to fourteen days from the time of
arrest, which meant he was free to go.[56]

Drink was mentioned in 73 percent of the Scottish brawl homicide trials,
more than in any of the other nations though this may simply reflect more
scrupulous record keeping. In Scottish courtrooms the conviction rates and
sentences were the same in brawl homicides whether drink was cited or not.
As a judge pointed out, "[T]he defendant was so drunk as to not care what
he was doing, but that was neither in law nor in reason any excuse."[57] The
same might be said for brawling generally. There was no excuse in law or reason but still the Scottish courts did not demand much atonement.

CLASS AND JUSTICE IN IRELAND

Because class, religion, and history were heavily intertwined in Ireland, the
impact of class considerations in Irish courtrooms was distinctive. Most executions in Ireland involved land disputes, hence the farming class was disproportionately represented.[58] Manslaughter sentences were almost twice as
long for farmers and middle-class defendants as for working-class ones. Only
five Irish defendants were tried for killing a social superior. Three were convicted and the average sentence was nearly fifteen years. At least ten landlords
were murdered during the period, but no one was convicted in any of the
cases. Fifteen people were tried for killing an employee or other subordinate,
nine were convicted, but the average sentence was only twenty-two months.

Irish attitudes were also different regarding fighting. Brawling was both
more common and less class specific in Ireland than in Britain. Even though
the population of England and Wales was about five times that of Ireland,
there were more trials for homicides in brawls in Ireland than there were in
England and Wales. The Irish chief justice told one jury that such homicides
"will happen more or less to the end of time."[59] Forty-two percent of Irish
homicide trials were the result of brawls. In some quarters this was seen as a
positive. Brawling among friends and neighbors was preferable to political or

sectarian violence. In 1892 Justice Hannon was pleased to tell the Roscommon grand jury that the situation was very satisfactory despite an increase in assaults since that "was accounted for by the fact that the county was divided into parties, and they had been showing their discretion and intelligence by assaulting each other which was rather an Irish way of doing so."[60]

As in Britain, masculine codes of conduct called for an active response to a challenge. One assault victim assured an Irish judge that "he was always a manly man, ready to meet anyone singly in a fight."[61] Irish judges began trials by ascertaining whether either party had "wheeled"—the Irish custom of ritual challenge. If a challenge had been issued and no weapons used, Irish juries convicted in only 42 percent of cases and the average sentence was less than six months.

The notion that brawling was inappropriate for the respectable classes had not completely taken hold in Ireland. Though the majority of those accused of brawl homicides in Ireland were laborers, servants, or soldiers, 28 percent of defendants were farmers. One judge expressed his dismay that fights in Munster often involved "an exceedingly fine class of people physically fine and also intelligent, they were well dressed, apparently wealthy. It was melancholy to think that such people should be engaged in such a manner."[62] But Irish judges were apparently determined that such prosperous farmers improve their habits. Though farmers were only slightly more likely to be convicted than laborers, the average sentence for a laborer who killed someone in a brawl was seventeen months, for a farmer it was thirty-three months. It may be that in the late nineteenth century the Irish were gradually undergoing the same change in attitudes toward brawling that had earlier occurred in Britain. Irish juries were growing more likely to convict in brawl homicides and the sentences were getting heavier during the 1880s. The increase is relative however; the average sentence for a homicide in a brawl in Ireland was still less than half as long as the English average.[63]

Irish attorneys regularly offered drink as a defense. At one trial Irish Chief Justice Morris angrily complained: "[T]he case made for the defense was simply this: That any rowdy, drunken ruffian was to be let off scot-free simply because he made himself too drunk to understand what he was doing. It was insulting to the jury to tell them because a drunken ruffian had no particular spite to a person, he was to be at liberty to beat any person as he liked."[64] But Irish juries were 15 percent less likely to convict if the participants had been drunk.[65]

Everywhere judges and juries were ambivalent about the criminality of fair fights, but using the knife in a brawl was considered particularly reprehensible. Conviction rates were nearly 20 percent higher in England, Ireland, and Wales when a victim had been stabbed. Scottish juries were six times more likely to return a verdict of *murder*. In addition to the fact that killers who used knives in brawls were much more likely to be found guilty of murder and receive the mandatory death sentence, the sentences in manslaughter convictions where the knife had been used were at least 40 percent heavier everywhere throughout the United Kingdom. But the same discrepancies between Irish sentences and those in Britain continued. The average sentence for manslaughter in a brawl in which the knife had been used in England, Wales, and Scotland was between seven and ten years. In Ireland the average was just three years.

For example, William Erskine, a butcher in Edinburgh, was working when Joseph Leith came in and began to tease and taunt him. Three times Erskine walked away but eventually in his anger he struck Leith with a rope. Leith then drew a knife and stabbed at Erskine. During the scuffle Erskine got hold of the knife and Leith was fatally stabbed. Erskine pled guilty to culpable homicide. Lord Adam, the presiding judge, announced that "in consideration that accused was an inoffensive person and was so much provoked he passed sentence of five years penal servitude."[66] Lord Adam viewed the sentence as merciful; however, in Ireland it would have been exceptionally heavy given the circumstances. In a case from Galway, Patrick Dwyer confessed to killing Michael Mannion in a fight. "He challenged me to fight and I told him not to beat me and that he was superior to me and I told him several times not to raise a hand to me." But Mannion had insisted. "He went to the wall for a stone and ran after me and I am sure I pulled out a penknife and he was running very close to me and I thought he had a stone. I turned back and I must have stuck him with the penknife." Dwyer was sentenced to eighteen months, even though unlike Erskine, he was the one who drew the knife.[67] The rules for fair fights were enforced, but if men agreed to fight and someone died, especially if those involved were "all of one kind," the courts tended to view the homicide as a minor crime. On some level it was perhaps reassuring that despite the inroads of modern civilization, Britain still had a substratum of manly men ready to fight to prove themselves.

However much it might be preferred that men used reason rather than brute force, physical strength and the willingness to use violence were part of the essential definition of masculinity.

VIOLENCE AND GENDER

In 1884 an editorial in the *Times* argued that it was this capacity for violence that ultimately justified male control of the government. "Men will get the franchise for none of the fine-sounding reasons employed in political argument, but simply because they possess a large share of the physical force which however disguised is the ultimate basis and sanction of all law." Ultimately, the *Times* argued, might will demand and obtain civil rights. "The possessors of that force must have the right to make the laws when they seriously demand it no matter what may be thought of their intelligence because their worst mistakes cannot be so bad as their revolt." Having established that the threat of violence is the basis for enfranchisement, the editorial then argued that since women cannot maintain that threat, they cannot be enfranchised. "Women do not possess that physical force, and their admission to a share in law-making therefore defies the natural law of representation, no matter how it may be justified by superficial analogies." This natural law meant that the physically more powerful sex will dominate. "Some day and in some fashion the sexual distinction would assert itself, and laws imposed upon the physical masters by the vote of the other sex would be swept away by force, which it is the proper aim of all political institutions to regulate and keep in abeyance."[68]

This editorial illustrates a Victorian view of gender roles as absolute and essential. Further, it defined the capacity for violence as a masculine trait. Men were stronger and were meant to protect the weak, which might require the use of coercion against evildoers and subordinates. Victorian rhetoric in England often stressed women's emotional nature. Warning against giving the vote to women, the *Times* suggested, "It would be a dangerous experiment indeed to remove them [women]—we will not say raise them from the sphere of their present duty and happiness. The enfranchisement for which they ask has a direct tendency to change the character of our government; to dethrone calm judgment and to put sentiment and emotion in its place."[69] But the *Scotsman* claimed that a lack of faith in female reason was an English trait: "It has been and is a custom of legislation to deal with 'women and children' as persons standing on the same level, equally unable to take care of themselves. We have taken the liberty of protesting against this theory and practice, involving the fallacy that women acquire nothing by growing older, but continue as children to the end of their lives."[70] The *Scotsman* proudly insisted that the Scottish law recognized adult women's capabilities in ways that the English did not. "It was never law that a woman in Scotland lost her status because she chose to marry. There is no sinking of the *Rational* person by marriage."[71]

Much of the historiography of women and crime during this period has argued that violent women created a particularly difficult challenge for the courts and press as they so clearly violated these gender definitions. Feminist historians have suggested that women who killed had to be either demonized

or deemed insane—they must either be "mad or bad."[72] Following the logic
of their leading newspapers, one would expect Scottish women to be held
responsible for their actions whereas the English assumptions regarding the
emotional vulnerability of women might limit their culpability in homicides.
But in English homicide trials not involving spouses or minor children,
female defendants were no more likely to be found insane than were male
killers. On the other hand, Scottish women were almost twice as likely to be
found insane as men in the same circumstances. But in both countries fewer
than 10 percent of women accused of killing someone other than a spouse or
minor child were found insane.

Certainly homicide is a crime that in no way fits the conventional por-
trayal of the Victorian woman, and Victorian murderesses received enormous
attention from the press and public.[73] However, most women who killed were
not charged with murder but rather with manslaughter or culpable homicide,
and in many cases their crimes attracted very little attention. Historians who
focus on murderesses have overlooked the fact that sensational murder trials
involving respectable women were, by definition, exceptional. Records from
the United Kingdom between 1867 and 1892 include nearly three hundred
and fifty trials of women accused of killing someone other than a spouse or
minor child or stepchild. Only twenty-nine of these women were convicted
of murder. *English* men were more likely to be convicted of *murder* than were
English women, though in Ireland and Scotland the likelihood of a murder
conviction did not vary significantly according to gender. Even though
Englishmen were only 25 percent more likely than English women to be convicted of murder, once convicted men were over four times more likely to
actually be hanged. Only one woman was executed in Ireland and one in
Scotland between 1867 and 1892 and no women were executed in Wales.[74]

The courts were not indifferent to gender issues. The Irish judge who
complained that things had gone too far when the "women of the country
unsexed themselves and went and committed crime" would have probably
drawn nods of agreement from his colleagues on the benches of England and
Scotland. But overt attempts to offer womanhood as a defense usually failed.
For example, Kate Webster was accused of murdering her employer in 1879.
Her defense attorney pointed out that she "had a child of which she was
undoubtedly very fond. She was proved to have been a woman of motherly
and womanly interests. She went to see her child on every Sunday and holiday and her one object in life seemed to be to take care the child was properly looked after. Those did not seem to be the characteristics of a murderess." He went on to outline the references she had been given before taking
the job as servant to her victim and then asked, "Were not there things worth

considering before the jury sent a woman to the gallows." But the prosecution had anticipated the argument: "[I]t might be a question whether a woman, not a very old one, but not a very young one could have contrived such a ghastly plan as this but in the end they would come to the conclusion that this was a planned murder." The *Times* even admitted, "She has no characteristics of a criminal in her face, and though not handsome, is not ill-looking." Despite her looks and her child, the jury found her guilty and she was hanged.[75]

English women accused of homicides outside the nuclear family were slightly less likely to be convicted than English men. English women also received lighter sentences than English men. The average sentence for men convicted of manslaughter outside the nuclear family was seventy-eight months; for women it was sixty-eight. Clearly these women were not being demonized—but they were being held accountable for their actions. There is little evidence they were perceived as peculiarly mad or bad.

Scottish women had a higher conviction rate for homicides outside the nuclear family than either men or women in any other part of the United Kingdom. They were more than 20 percent more likely to be convicted than Scottish men. But judges also sympathized with their physical vulnerability. In Glasgow Jane Kelly, a respectable widow "of good character," was accused of killing Hugh Cook with a poker. Lord Young, the presiding judge, summarized the case: "[T]he prisoner appeared to have been the subject of an unprovoked assault by a man who struck her a violent blow in the face and knocked her down. . . . The crime was apparently not at all meditated by her." But even though the circumstances clearly indicated she had acted in self-defense, Kelly was convicted of culpable homicide. The judge explained, however, "If a woman was attacked by a man or struck violently and knocked down one would not be disposed to beat her again with many stripes because she had yielded to the impulse of passion. It was not excused but the pain of imprisonment which she had already suffered (four months) went well to atoning in the way of punishment for the guilt which she had committed." He sentenced her to one more month.[76] No matter how vulnerable they were, Scottish women were perceived as rational adults who must atone for their guilt. But Scottish judges were still harder on male killers. In cases outside the nuclear family, men convicted of culpable homicide received an average sentence of fifty-seven months, women only thirty-two months.

The sex of the accused had even less impact on Irish courtrooms. Irish women accused of homicides outside the nuclear family were convicted in 57 percent of trials, men in 64 percent. The average sentence for women was forty months, for men forty-one. This lack of distinction was particularly striking since women were the accused in fewer than 6 percent of the non-nuclear family homicides in Ireland as compared to 10 percent in England and Scotland.[77]

Violent Women

Ladies were still not supposed to be violent. In 1891 the SPCC brought charges against a builder's wife whose eighteen-year-old servant had died from abuse. "The court was filled. Most of those present being women." Justice Stephen ruled that there was no evidence of manslaughter and allowed the woman to plead guilty to assault but told her, "[N]o doubt you gave way to temper and were so far irritated as to strike the girl. That was very wrong. You were her mistress and entrusted with this girl and you had no right to strike her. Such conduct contrasts most unfavorably with what you are reputed to have said about being a lady." Ironically the judge went on to absolve her of the homicide despite her failure to meet class standards. "Though I do not believe you contributed to the girl's death, your conduct was very different from that of a lady, properly so called." To add injury to the insult he sentenced her to six months hard labor for assault.[78]

By the late nineteenth century the stereotype of the delicate submissive Victorian woman was sometimes mocked. In 1867 the *Gentleman's Magazine* noted that

> ladies do not faint nowadays, at least but rarely. If one can trust a perfect mass of evidence, oral and written, syncope, at the end of the last century and up to the 35th year of this, was a habit with ladies. A story without a swoon was impossible until lately. Let us thank heaven that our mothers, wives and daughters have given up the evil habit of becoming cataleptic at the occurrence of anything in the least degree surprising.[79]

Still, violent women did violate gender norms and were sometimes described as having masculine traits. When a single woman was arrested for murdering her servant girl, the *Times* reported that she was "of a somewhat masculine character and her neighbors were somewhat afraid of her."[80] The *Pall Mall Gazette* speculated that a French woman charged with murdering her mistress might actually be a man, citing "her harshness, her strength, her robust and masculine look both in face and figure . . . and it is a little remarkable that the murderer being a woman took away all the money she could find, but left the jewels."[81]

But they could also be figures of fun. In 1878 the *Scotsman,* under the headline "The Terror of a Mining Village," reported that a woman had been convicted of "striking her husband severely on the head with tongs to the effusion of blood and knocking down and striking her daughter-in-law. . . . The prisoner was said to be the terror of the whole village in which she lived."[82] The *Limerick Chronicle* reported with considerable glee an attempt by an estranged husband and his friends to retake the house his wife was living in. The man and his friends used hatchets and an iron-axle to try to gain possession of the house, but his wife and her female friends resisted and "presented a bold front to the invaders and like worthy amazons simultaneously rushed on the first man who entered (happening to be the unfortunate husband), felled him and prostrated themselves on his body, administering to him a sound thrashing." The husband and his friends were forced to retreat.[83] The light-hearted tone of the newspapers indicates that violence by working-class women did not inspire shock or horror. When two young women were tried for beating a man to death in Stafford, a male witness explained: "[H]e got the worst of it once before by interfering with women and thought it better therefore to have nothing to do with the matter."[84]

Their roles as wives and mothers did not render women incapable of violence. In 1867 Susan Bowen, a twenty-four-year-old married woman with a child in arms, was charged with stabbing Johanna Keefe, also married. They had been in a London pub when Bower "called her out and began abusing her." Bowen then drew a knife she had hidden in her infant's dress and inflicted several stab wounds.[85] At least one homicide in Scotland was over the killer's failure in the role of woman. Roseanne Simpson of Glasgow was charged with beating a female neighbor to death with a bellows because she had "taunted Simpson about having no children and used offensive language." Simpson admitted hitting her with the bellows. After witnesses testified to the great provocation, Simpson was found guilty of assault and sentenced to four months.[86] In Ireland after Eliza Burke was sentenced to one month for an assault with a hatchet, a debate began as to whether nursing infants could go to prison with their mothers. The clerk of the Kilkenny Court suggested that the child had to be formally named in the commitment, but the judge said it was a matter of course.[87]

Even though the fair stand-up fight was a test of manliness, the courts were not particularly hard on women who chose to participate. Throughout the United Kingdom at least eighty-nine women were charged with killing someone in a brawl. English women charged with killing someone in a brawl were 15 percent less likely to be convicted than men. The average sentence for women was only half as long as that of men. English women who killed in a brawl without the use of a weapon were convicted only 43 percent of the time and 84 percent of the convicted served less than two years. For Englishmen who killed in a brawl without using a weapon, the conviction rate was 65 percent and 74 percent served less than two years. Clearly the English courts assumed (correctly) that a blow or a kick from an unarmed man was more likely to be lethal.

Nevertheless, the reactions of English courts do not indicate that women who killed in brawls were seen as particularly deviant—either mentally or morally. English judges might even be impressed by women who took action in defense of others. A sixty-four-year-old woman was charged with murder for killing a neighbor during a brawl between two families. She had struck a man in the head with a "heavy iron instrument used for digging potatoes from the ground." The judge told the jury at the Wells Assize: "He was of the opinion that if the prisoner supposed on reasonable grounds that the victim was engaged in assaulting her husband, who was an elderly man and her son who was a cripple [,] that would reduce the crime to manslaughter. Nothing however could justify the use of such a weapon." She was convicted of manslaughter and he sentenced her to only nine months.[88] Amelie Prosser was tried at the Central Criminal Court for killing a woman who had made disparaging comments about her employer. The defense claimed that Prosser had beaten the victim to death because her employer told her to. Justice Channell said: "Should the jury have no doubt the violence resulting in the death had been caused by the prisoner and that violence was not inflicted with a view to the fair protection of her mistress it would be their duty to find her guilty." Drawing the implication that the action had been the fair defense of her employer, the jury acquitted her.[89] Justice Brett excused a woman who had sent threatening letters to jury members at her husband's murder trial, explaining that she was "excused for doing what she could for her husband."[90]

Even officials were fair game. Bridget McIntyre had killed a bailiff who was attempting to seize her baby's cradle while the child was lying in it. The presiding judge was shocked by the seizure: "Do you distrain cradles with babies in them: It was quite illegal." Since the seizure was illegal, the judge announced that the force used by the defendant was justified. The jury found her guilty but recommended mercy and the judge released her on her own recognizance.[91] But if women could respond to incitements to violence, they could also be held accountable for encouraging violence. Mary Ann Draper was charged with her son, Samuel, for murdering a neighbor. On Boxing Day Mary Ann allegedly told Samuel to have it out with the neighbor or he was no son of hers. Both Drapers were found guilty of homicide. Sam was sentenced to fifteen years and Mary Ann to ten years.[92]

In Ireland women who killed in brawls were 15 percent *more* likely to be convicted than men though their sentences were ten months shorter on average. A third of all Irish women tried for homicides outside the nuclear family had killed someone in a brawl, compared to 50 percent of Irish men. But still Irishwomen were the defendant in only 4 percent of brawl homicide trials. The case of Bridget and Catherine Kearney indicates that women did not necessarily shrink from fights. The two were charged with being part of a gang that beat a man to death in Limerick. On the day of his death the victim had testified against Catherine Kearney at petty session. He was beaten to death with stones on his way home from the courthouse. When the prosecution claimed that Catherine had shouted, "Kill him, kill him, don't you rise off him til you leave him cold," her defense attorney argued that she could not have used disgraceful language because at the time of the killing she "was engaged in fisticuffs in the road." While perhaps not the strongest possible defense, the Crown chose to adjourn Catherine's trial after the men involved were convicted.[93]

Scottish women were the defendants in 10 percent of brawl homicide trials—the highest percentage for the nations of the British Isles. Brawl homicides made up a third of nonnuclear family homicide trials for both men and women in Scotland. One defense attorney even suggested that Scottish women were more violent than men. His male client was charged with a particularly bloody robbery and murder. After detailing the crime, he argued that "it indicate a woman's hand because the ferocity . . . was totally unnecessary to accomplish robbery."[94] Scottish women accused of killing in brawls were more likely to be convicted, but served much lighter sentences. Scottish women accused of killing in brawls were 20 percent more likely to be convicted than Scottish men. However, the average sentence for Scottish women was two years lighter.

Scottish judges also sometimes expressed admiration for women warriors. Agnes McPhail and her husband were tried for killing a housemate. The McPhails had attacked a servant who told them it was too late to use the kitchen. When another lodger who felt it was unfair of the McPhails to gang up on the servant joined the fight, Agnes stabbed him in the chest with a kitchen knife. At their trial in Edinburgh, the presiding judge, Lord Young, was very impressed with Agnes. He told the jury that "when a blow was inflicted under such circumstances by a wife in defense of her husband it had not usually been considered proper to attach the name of murder to her wickedness and he suggested that if the jury were of the opinion that it was her hand which inflicted the blow they should return a verdict of culpable homicide." They did so and recommended her to mercy. In sentencing,

Justice Young said that "he took into consideration that she was rushing, although with very criminal and dangerous violence to the rescue of her husband, as she believed and that there was no premeditation. He took into consideration that she did not go to seek or even lift the weapon but had it in her hand using in the domestic occupation of cooking supper for herself and her husband." In addition to defending her husband and performing her domestic duties, Agnes McPhail had behaved honorably when the police came. "It was not without weight with him that at the time and upon the impulse of a woman and a wife, she said, according to the truth, 'Don't blame him it was me that did it.' He took that into account not unfavorably for her." Justice Young sentenced her to twelve months and announced that "the ends of justice would be satisfied."[95]

Even when the causes were not so noble, women who killed in anger were generally treated leniently by the courts. Women provoked by jealousy sometimes enjoyed support from judges. Margaret McDonald of Glasgow had killed a woman she believed was flirting with her husband. In "a frenzy of passion she had tortured her victim for an hour before killing her." But even though Justice Young said the crime was just short of murder, the sentence was far short of capital. He sentenced McDonald to ten years.[96] In a similar case in England, Justice Bovill directed the jury to acquit Ann Hitchins. "The women were in a humble state of life and it was suggested that the deceased was too intimate with the prisoner's husband. The woman quarreled and the prisoner struck the deceased several blows and caused her to fall." The victim died from a blow to the head, but since there was no proof that Hitchins had struck a blow to her head, the judge insisted she could not be convicted.[97]

Cases in which women were the killers might still make good copy even in the respectable press. When three women killed a neighbor in a brawl, the *Times* headlined the case "Murder by Women in Liverpool."[98] But the *Times* also acknowledged that femininity and homicide were not incompatible. After a woman was convicted of the murder of her lover's wife and child, an editorial noted that "the woman's character as known from her antecedents is at variance with such ferocity. But this perhaps is only one more proof that no one can tell of what a human being may be capable."[99]

Throughout the United Kingdom the courts accepted that women could and did kill for a variety of motives. If the crime was deliberate murder, the Scottish courts searched for mitigating circumstances, while Irish juries often chose to acquit regardless of the evidence. In England juries seemed to accept that murder was murder. Though defense attorneys sometimes insisted that their delicate clients could not be guilty, the argument was most often heard in a losing cause. The murder conviction rates for men and women in

England were identical. Regarding the lesser offenses involving killing in the heat of passion, throughout the United Kingdom it was generally accepted that women were subject to the same imperfections as men and light sentences could serve as atonement for their guilt.

Class and gender issues were certainly considered in determining whether the ends of justice were satisfied. The courts in Britain were not comfortable with murder convictions against middle- or upper-class defendants and such cases were rare. In England and Wales the courts used insanity verdicts to avoid executing the respectable. As Justice Martin pointed out, "[A] poor person was seldom afflicted with insanity but it was common to raise a defense of that kind when people of means were charged with the commission of a crime."[100] For the Scots, upper- and middle-class defendants could be granted the benefit of the doubt via a not proven verdict. Irish juries were less obviously influenced by class considerations. But everywhere murder convictions were relatively rare.

In manslaughter and culpable homicide trials where the death had been the outcome of uncontrolled anger or carelessness, the reactions were different. Middle-class defendants who had acted on impulse received heavier sentences than lower-class ones. Impulsive violence was natural, but the mark of respectability was rising above natural impulses. In England and Ireland middle- and upper-class defendants served longer sentences than lower-class ones, presumably because they should have been better able to control their violent impulses. Scotland did not follow this trend. In Scotland the heaviest sentences went to lower-class defendants, particularly Irish ones.

In Britain brawling was very much the province of lower-class roughs and at least in the last third of the nineteenth century so long as all the participants were from the same class, the courts do not seem to have viewed these homicides as a serious concern. In fact, judges often expressed ambivalence about whether homicides in brawls should even be considered criminal. Even though the ruffians who fought were compared to foreign savages in the press, judges might still take comfort in a fair fight as evidence of the national spirit. In Ireland where brawling was still a very popular pastime even among the prosperous farming class, the courts were beginning to take harsher actions against deaths in brawls—though the sentences were still lighter than those in Britain.

Not only did judges still harbor a certain respect for the tradition of the fair fight, they might even admire honorable fighting among women. Ladies, like gentlemen, were judged by a different standard and murderesses might inspire considerable horror, but generally working- class women who committed manslaughter were deemed neither bad nor mad. If they had been responding to provocation, their actions might even inspire a grudging admiration. However, women were also supposed to limit their violence to their own kind.

Gender-Victims and Killers

In 75 percent of the homicide trials in England and Scotland and over 80 percent in Ireland and Wales both the killer and the victim were male. Obviously the national conviction and sentencing averages were statistically determined by these cases. The patterns for cases involving women did not necessarily match the norm. English men tried for killing an adult other than a spouse were convicted of some form of homicide in 64 percent of cases regardless of the sex of the victim. However, if the victim was a woman, the likelihood of a conviction for the full offense of murder was twice as high as if the victim was male. Twenty-one percent of Englishmen tried for killing an adult female other than their wives were executed. Juries were far less likely to convict women of murder, but while English women who killed other women were convicted only 52 percent of the time, the likelihood of convictions rose by 25 percent if a woman killed an adult male.

One possible explanation for this is the fact that in order for a woman to kill a man, she would ordinarily have to use a lethal weapon. But even when a woman did not use a weapon, she was still more likely to be convicted if her victim was an adult male. In England women who killed adult men were considered both culpable and rational. Though 7 percent of men tried for killing women other then their wives were found insane, no woman tried in England for killing an adult male other than her husband was found insane. The average sentence for an English man convicted of the manslaughter of another adult was eighty-one months regardless of the sex of the victim. An English woman convicted of the manslaughter of another woman served fifty-eight months on average, but if her victim was an adult male, the average sentence rose to seventy-eight months.

Irish courts were less likely to convict if a woman was involved as victim or killer. Two-thirds of Irish men tried for killing an adult male were convicted, compared to only 50 percent of Irish men tried for killing an adult woman other than their wives. But a quarter of them were found insane. Nor were those who were convicted treated leniently. The average sentence for

Table 3.1. Homicide Trial Outcomes According to Sex of Killer and Victim

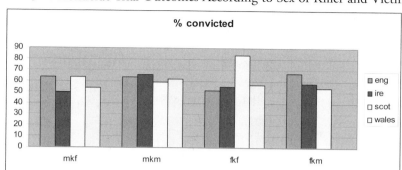

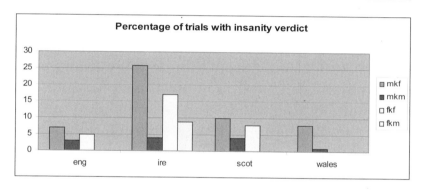

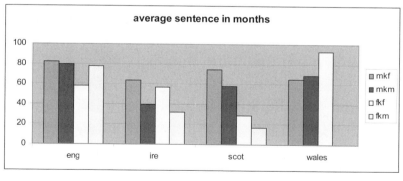

Irishmen convicted of killing an adult female other than their wives was two years longer than that for men who had killed men. The lightest sentences in manslaughter cases went to Irish women convicted of the manslaughter of adult males. Though Irish men who killed women were more likely to be insane, Irish women who killed men were treated very leniently.

The Scots had yet a different pattern. Eighty-four percent of Scottish women tried for killing an adult female were convicted compared to only 64 percent of men tried for killing women and fewer than 60 percent of those of either sex who killed men. But Scotsmen who killed women served a year and a half longer on average than those who killed men. Scottish women convicted of killing other women served only half as long as Scotsmen who killed men. Scottish women accused of killing adult males other than their husbands had the lowest average sentence—less than a year and a half.

The Welsh numbers are so small that conclusions are very hard to draw. Only seven Welsh women were tried for killing another adult—all of their victims were female.

In matters of class and gender the victim's status was at least as significant as that of the accused. The next chapter examines the way that gender and class issues influenced decisions in homicide trials involving family members and courting couples.

CHAPTER 4

Family and Courtship

For my poor deceased son, I was always very fond of him. He would have been the last person I should have thought of hurting in any way. I had no intention of injuring him. I merely wished to show him who was the master. (*The Times*, 26 March 1878, 4c)

SHOCKING FRATRICIDE AT SWANSEA. The deceased said to be a quiet hard-working man, and the author of his death a drunken dissolute fellow. (*Carmarthen Weekly Reporter*, 6 September 1873)

I intended to prevent Carty striking his wife, who is my sister and to prevent him doing so I struck him. . . . He struck me back I then left the kitchen. He followed me and threw me out the window. (*Glasgow Herald*, 29 December 1870)

There is this peculiarity in almost all the cases the parties are near relatives to the persons whom they are alleged to have murdered. (*Kilkenny Journal*, 28 February 1883)

Gender issues were highlighted in homicide trials involving relatives outside the nuclear family. In fact these cases revealed some of the most interesting differences among the nations regarding property, privacy, and class as well as gender. On the Island of Britain the overwhelming majority of family homicide trials involved spouses or parents killing their own minor children. Such cases accounted for over 83 percent of family homicide trials in England, Scotland, and Wales. In stark contrast, over half the family homicide trials in

Ireland did not involve spouses or minor children. The percentage of homicide trials that involved nonnuclear family members was more than twice as high in Ireland.

The high casualty rate among Irish relatives outside the nuclear family reflected economic and demographic trends. Inheritance patterns in Ireland changed during the nineteenth century. In order to maintain the integrity of the family farm, only one son could inherit and only one daughter could be dowered for marriage. However, since Ireland did not have a tradition of primogeniture, parents chose which of their children would receive the resources for an independent existence. Their siblings could either emigrate if they could raise the fare or stay on as unpaid servants to the chosen siblings.[1] In a rural economy where land was the key to economic survival, the situation was clearly ripe for violence. In a third of Irish homicide trials involving relatives other than spouses or minor children, the motive was a dispute over land or other inheritance. Such cases could often be summarized succinctly in the Outrage Reports:

> Francis Hanley, farmer's son, age 26, died from the effects of bullet wounds inflicted by his brother John. It was the intention of the father of these men to leave his farm to Francis the younger and more favored son, and this would appear to have excited the jealousy of his brother John, 30, who was arrested and sentenced to fourteen years penal servitude.[2]

The *Times* often expanded on the peculiarities of Irish society as in their account of the execution of Timothy O'Keefe, who had murdered his uncle in Cork. "The story of the crime which the unhappy youth expiated on the scaffold gives an insight into the bitterness which appears to rankle in the breasts of those who are parties to a family feud in this country, especially when the dispute has an agrarian origin." The moral that the *Times* correspondent drew seemed to be that the victim had been hated for his virtues. "The murdered man was a provident and careful person and managed by thrift and industry to lay aside some money. His brother was not so careful of his means and he got into difficulties." When the improvident brother lost his farm to bankruptcy, his thrifty brother bought it at the sheriff's auction. Initially Timothy's father was allowed to rent his former farm, but when he failed to pay his rent, his brother evicted him. "Then followed trespasses, assaults and appeals to the Petty Session. The members of the two families having engaged in bitter domestic strife. Thus matters stood until Sunday, the 30th of April, when John O'Keefe, while on his way home from mass, was waylaid and beaten to death."[3]

A petition to commute O'Keefe's death sentence had been rejected, which was not unusual for an Irish homicide involving land. Relatives who killed over land or inheritance issues were nearly twice as likely to be convicted of murder as were relatives who killed for other motives, and only one of the death sentences was commuted. Though such cases accounted for a third of all family homicide trials, three-quarters of the men hanged for killing a relative had killed in land or inheritance disputes.

In Britain, economic diversity and the long-established principles of primogeniture made inheritance issues less contentious. The British population was more mobile, less inbred, and less dependent on scarce agricultural resources. Land and inheritance were the motive in about 8 percent of English family homicide trials. But as in Ireland, family homicides over property were severely punished. Those convicted of killing relatives over land or inheritance were more than twice as likely to hang as other convicted English killers. No homicides over inheritance or land led to trials in either Scotland or Wales.

Thirty-one percent of Irish homicide trials involving blood kin were the result of drunken quarrels, some of which doubtless reflected other tensions. However, unless land or property issues were specifically mentioned, deaths in casual quarrels were dealt with lightly. The fact that the Irish so often killed relatives also reflected the small tightly knit communities in which so many of the Irish lived. In many Irish communities intermarriage meant that virtually everyone was somehow related to everyone else. So the fact that the victim in an Irish pub brawl was the second cousin of the killer may have been purely coincidental. Eighty percent of Irish defendants convicted of killing a relative during a brawl served less than two years and 60 percent of those arrested were not convicted at all.

Scottish police often expressed reluctance to get involved in family disputes, but if the conflict resulted in a homicide the conviction rates and sentences for those who killed a relative in a brawl were very similar to those for other brawl homicides. Sixteen-year-old Hugh Duffy had asked a police constable to help him get his drunken, belligerent older brother to come home with him, but the constable refused as it was not his place to interfere in a family quarrel. When charged with his brother's death, Hugh explained that after the constable left, his brother had begun beating him and Hugh had struck out "in a passion," forgetting he had a knife in his hand. Though the police had refused to interfere in the family quarrel, judicial authorities felt no qualms about sentencing Duffy to ten years penal servitude.[4]

Most homicide trials involving male relatives in England were the result of brawls, and fewer than half of the men convicted of killing a male relative served more than two years. Even when a lethal weapon was involved, family fights were rarely seen as serious crimes. For example, when his brother reached out and slapped some flowers Victor Wicks was carrying to a girl he was courting, he was so incensed that he stabbed him to death with the knife he had used to cut the flowers. After a London jury convicted him of manslaughter, Justice Day sentenced him to only six months.[5]

PATRICIDE

The outcomes were very different when the participants were father and son. Patricide was a very serious offense in England. More than 80 percent of men convicted of killing their fathers were sentence to penal servitude or death.[6] These figures are particularly striking since nearly half of the Englishmen tried for killing their fathers did so in order to defend their mother or another relative from the father's abuse. Despite their altruistic motives, more than 80 percent of them were convicted and 80 percent of the convictions led to heavy sentences, including one execution. English respect for patriarchy seemed to trump the virtue of defending one's mother. The lightest sentence in such cases went to Thomas Hartley, who went to his mother's aid when she screamed for help. His father then tried to strangle Thomas. The two men fell downstairs as they struggled. When the father was found dead the next day, Thomas was charged with manslaughter. Even though "the deceased was a very drunk and quarrelsome man who often attacked his son when he went to the protection of his mother," Thomas Hartley was sentenced to eighteen months for manslaughter.[7]

English courts were reluctant to pardon patricide even when the victim had been violent. The most remarkable case of the murder of an abusive father in England occurred near Crewe in 1890. The initial report was that Richard Davies, a fifty-one-year-old tailor, and his son had been ambushed on the road by two men who murdered Davies with a hatchet while his son had escaped. But two days later Richard Davies Jr., twenty, and George Davies, sixteen, were charged with his murder. At the coroner's inquest family members testified that Davies had been estranged from his older children but refused to discuss the reasons. Local authorities seemed to sympathize with the young men. The accused were not at the inquest because the chief constable at Crewe objected to "taking the prisoners through the streets and exposing them to the gaze of everybody about." The coroner angrily insisted that there was no evidence against the prisoners and the coroner's jury returned a verdict of murder by persons unknown.

But the police presented evidence before the local magistrates that the boys had confessed. Richard had told them, "It was because he was such a bad father not to me exactly but to George and the rest and a bad husband to my mother. For mother and them have been very nearly starved sometimes for he would neither buy them coal for the fire nor meat to eat when he was in a bad temper."[8]

Justice Willes presided over their murder trial. The boys' sister testified that even though Richard Davies had owned five shops, his sons worked for no wages and his family had only thirteen shillings a week for housekeeping expense. Neighbors verified Davies' brutality to his sons. Mrs. Davies, dressed in deep mourning, had insisted at the inquest that the family had lived happily together, but at the trial she testified that her husband "had pointed guns at me and threatened to shoot me. He frequently struck me in the presence of the children, No money was entrusted to me. He attempted to set fire to my bed. When he lost money as a bookmaker he was particularly violent, striking and knocking us all about without any cause." While Mrs. Davies had worked very hard to maintain her role as a proper Victorian wife, it was clear that the victim had not come close to the ideal patriarch. "He often prevented members of the family from going to places of worship. He often insisted upon the boys working on the farm on Sunday. Sometimes I sent my little children to chapel or school and was ill-treated for doing so." Finally she pointed to her son's role as her protector. "Some few weeks before my husband died he used serious personal violence towards me. Richard came down out of his bed and stood between us, to save me from my husband's violence. Richard has saved me many times from my husband's violence. Richard was a good son to me."[9]

Despite the evidence of habitual abuse, Justice Willes insisted that manslaughter was not an acceptable verdict as there had been no immediate provocation. The jury convicted the brothers of murder but recommended mercy. Over eleven thousand signatures were gathered in a petition for a reprieve for the brothers. When the Home Office announced that George, the younger son, would be reprieved but Richard would not, the decision drew heated objections. The Home Office received two thousand telegrams protesting the decision and the MP for Crewe gave a speech condemning the Home Office decision on the grounds "of the circumstances of their home life and the great provocation to which undoubtedly they had been subjected and the youth of the criminals."

A letter to the *Times* in response to the MP's speech offers a striking perspective on principles of justice, provocation, and defense. "Admitted that the murdered man was cruel and terribly tyrannical to his family and that therefore his sons becoming exasperated determined to murder him, such a man is the one who needs protection by the law." Instead of calling for the protection of the victims of abusive men, the correspondent insisted that "[a] harmless, inoffensive man is not likely to be murdered; he stands in no peril. One who irritates his fellows is in greater danger, and the fear of certain punishment is needed to protect him." The letter argued that the law's function was to protect those who might provoke long-term hatred. "The provocation of momentary anger producing uncontrollable action is recognized by law, but the provocation causing premeditated murder to be committed ought never to be regarded as an extenuating circumstance." Richard Davies was executed.[10]

Even when the victim was a tyrannical brute, patricide inspired horror. All but one of the English sons who killed abusive fathers was convicted. The one exception was a young man whose father was holding a knife to his mother's throat when he shot him. The first shot was fired as a warning, "but he would not leave go, so I shot him." Justice Lopes said it was justifiable homicide if the shot was fired "without deliberation, without vindictive feelings, honestly believing and having reasonable grounds for believing that his mother's life was in imminent peril and that the shot he fired was necessary to preserve life."[11]

The respect for patriarchy is reinforced by the reaction to cases in which other relatives were killed in defense of abused women or children. In 9 percent of English family homicide trials the killer had been acting to defend an abused female relative. When the killer was someone other than the biological son of the abuser, acquittals were twice as likely as in other homicide trials, and in the case of conviction, the sentences were twice as likely to be less than two years. In 1870 Phillip Rolph, a forty-year-old man, had struck his new wife in the face. When her twenty-three-year-old son heard about it, he went to his stepfather's workplace and beat him to death. Several persons were standing by but no one interfered. The young man, James Campkin, pled guilty to manslaughter. Before sentencing him, Justice Lush said that "manslaughter was a crime of every gradation. . . . The prisoner was no doubt exasperated at seeing his mother suffering from the recent violence of his stepfather. He did not at all wonder that he went in quest of the man." Since Campkin had already been in jail for a month, he was sentenced to just fourteen more days.[12]

The demands of filial respect were also considered when fathers were accused of killing adult sons. Chastisement was the motive in the majority of cases in which Englishmen killed their adult children. Robert Bull had thrown his son out of the house. When the son returned, a struggle ensued during which Bull punctured his son's femoral artery with a pair of scissors.

Because of Bull's excellent character, he was sentenced to only three days.[13] John Gooch fatally stabbed his son when they were both drunk. The defense argued that the son "had been a source of great trouble to him." Even though Gooch had tried to stab the arresting officer, Justice Hawkins sentenced him to only six months for manslaughter.[14]

Irish attitudes toward patriarchy were heavily influenced by land issues. Forty percent of patricides among Irish men were motivated by land and inheritance issues. As Christopher King, a Limerick's farmer son explained after poisoning his father: "He was a good father but had one failing, and that was the prevention of my starting in life; his intention being to continue on until his death. I was doing a servant's work for him and he would keep me there all his lifetime. Look at my age [thirty] now. What less could I do?" Despite this very incriminating statement, the young man was acquitted, prompting the presiding judge to express his astonishment at Limerick juries.[15] But the verdict in this case was not unusual. Only 41 percent of Irish men tried for killing fathers over land or money were convicted. Two different sets of Irish siblings had killed elderly drunken fathers for being "useless." No one was indicted in either case.

The reluctance to convict may have come from the sure knowledge that a conviction would mean a harsh punishment. A third of those convicted were executed and the others served long sentences. Ironically, some of those convicted would appear to have had more grounds for resentment than Christopher King. John Neel of Cork sent money home to his parents from America for fifteen years only to see his father give his land to his sister and her husband. After being disinherited, Neel entered his parents' home one night and shot his father in the head. Though his mother testified on his behalf, he was convicted of murder.[16]

A third of the recorded Irish patricides were the result of drunken quarrels. When Thomas Brennan was tried at Cork for killing his father, the paper noted that they were "people in humble life" and that witnesses had tried to stop the beating. One had warned him "not to go too far with the old man." While the remonstrances do indicate disapproval, the warning not to go "too far" would seem to imply that there was an acceptable amount of physical violence toward fathers. Eighty-six percent of those convicted in Ireland of killing a father in a drunken brawl served less than two years.[17]

The Irish were also more tolerant than the English of sons who killed to defend their mothers. Two Irishmen were tried for killing their biological fathers in defense of their mothers. One was acquitted outright and the other served six months. Irish courts rarely punished those who killed to revenge the abuse of a relative. In the five cases in which men in Ireland were tried for

killing an in-law for wife abuse, only three of the killers were convicted and
they all served six months or less. Most often such actions were accepted
without trial. A farmer who had come home drunk and, in front of the
neighbors, grabbed his wife by the hair, "threw her down and danced on her"
was shot to death while walking home. Though her relatives were suspected,
no one was ever charged with his death.[18]

Of the seven Scottish men killed by their sons, five died in drunken brawls
and in two other cases the sons were ruled insane. The sentences in such cases
paralleled those for brawls between nonrelatives. When Lord Young heard a
case in which a young man had stabbed his father who died a week later of
peritonitis, the prosecution accepted a plea of culpable homicide. The
defense attorney explained that "though he was charged with the murder of
his father there were circumstances in the case which took it entirely out of
the category of ordinary cases of parricide." The factors he cited, that is, that
both father and son were drunk and that the father was a violent brute, were
actually not unusual, but the defense claimed them as grounds for mercy.
Lord Young announced that "the extenuating circumstances must be very
strong indeed to reduce [the crime] to culpable homicide. It was a father
killed by his own son—killed with a knife, and his only doubt was where he
fully discharged his duty in imposing a penalty of five years."[19]

The heaviest sentence for patricide in Scotland between 1867 and 1892
was fourteen years. The defendant had killed his father with a spade during
a fight over money.[20] A young man who had beaten his father to death with
a poker was allowed to plead guilty to simple assault and served only six
months.[21] But one Scottish judge suggested that patricide had been taken
more seriously in the past. After hearing a case in which a man had stabbed
his son to death for striking him, the judge noted that "the provocation of
such a blow from a son to his father was aggravated and the offense was a
most serious one, and under an old law of Scotland, a capital offense."[22]

None of the Scots patricide cases involved the defense of an abused mother though one young man was charged with killing his father on the day of his
mother's funeral, but his motive had been that his father had failed to "return
with some drink which had been sent for." He pled guilty to culpable homicide and was sentenced to fifteen months.[23] The Scottish courts were lenient
with Walter Battison, who shot his stepfather when he found him kneeling on
his mother's chest, beating her face. He aimed at his stepfather's arms but the
bullet struck his lung. At his trial the judge accepted a petition signed by over
fourteen hundred people supporting his good character. Since the death was
apparently an accident, he was sentenced to only twelve months. However, in
England or Ireland he would probably have been acquitted outright.[24]

MATRICIDE

By the last third of the nineteenth century patriarchy carried considerably more weight in English courtrooms than in Irish or Scottish ones. There were also significant differences in attitudes toward matricide. More than twice as many Englishmen were tried for killing their mothers as for killing their fathers. Though only one patricide trial resulted in an insanity verdict, 36 percent of the Englishmen tried for killing their mothers were found insane, five times the rate for homicide trials generally. But the insanity verdict was not automatic. As with other homicides, when the killer was a particularly disreputable sort, the reactions were different. In 1873, under the headline "Shocking Murder," the *Times* reported that a man in Liverpool had beaten and kicked his mother because his dinner was not ready. "After leaping and dancing on the body he poured cold water on her and threw her down the stairs." The defense attorney argued that the "extraordinary brutality of the crime was evidence of insanity," but the jury found him guilty of murder and he was hanged.[25] On the other hand, when the son of a respectable innkeeper in Yorkshire killed his mother in front of the servants by kicking her for three hours, the defense explained that he had been drinking heavily, and he was found insane.[26]

In half of the English matricides the motive was chastisement. William Hughes, a laborer in London, hit his mother in the head with a hammer twelve times because his dinner was not ready. After the defense attorney successfully argued that his drunkenness made it impossible for him to have had murderous intent, he was convicted of manslaughter and sentenced to just five years.[27] The other men who beat their elderly mothers to death for such sins as drunkenness or selling boots served sentences of less than two years.[28]

The other common motive for English matricides was that the victim had become a burden. One couple was accused of killing the husband's mother as they dragged her to the workhouse. "She said she could not go. The prisoner said, 'no shirking back, you—you shall go' and he dragged her more than forty yards. She appeared to be resisting. After going a short distance they let the old woman fall down on the road and shortly after she died." A surgeon said she died of heart failure "accelerated by treatment she received. Her body was much emaciated." The son was found guilty of manslaughter but recommended to mercy for good character. The judge said "he was much indebted for evidence of his good character; still it was a bad offence." He sentenced the man to twelve months.[29] The average sentence for the manslaughter of a mother in England was less than half that of the average for the manslaughter of a father.

Fathers and sons in Ireland might engage in drunken quarrels or fight over land and inheritance issues, but killing one's mother, though not terribly unusual, was still considered a terrible crime. An insanity verdict in Irish matricide trials was nine times more likely than in homicide trials generally. Patricide trials in Ireland were nearly three times more likely to result in acquittals than were matricide cases. When a drunken vagrant who had lived off his impoverished elderly mother was convicted of killing her because she failed to provide money for drink, the judge "remarked if he had been found guilty of murder and hanged no one would have regretted it."[30]

The Scots were far less alarmed by matricide cases even though more than twice as many Scotsmen were tried for killing their mothers than for killing their fathers. Drink was a factor in two-thirds of the cases, though in different ways. Some of the killers had been provoked by the fact that the mother had been too drunk to attend to housekeeping duties—the same justification cited by several of the Scotsmen who killed their wives. One laborer who had beaten his mother to death was given a lighter sentence on account of his "excellent character" and the fact that the victim "was a woman so addicted to drink that she made his home not so comfortable."[31]

Other Scotsmen had killed their mothers during drunken family brawls. After hearing a case in which a seventeen-year-old was convicted of stabbing his mother to death in a drunken family melee on New Year's Day, the judge "said certainly no picture of domestic life could be more terrible than that presented in this case, and that it would be difficult for the imagination to shape a more sad and deplorable tragedy." When the jury returned a verdict of culpable homicide, the judges said it was a "very merciful view of the case" and sentenced him to ten years, adding that "[d]uring that time he had no doubt, the recollection of that dreadful night and the part he took in it would not depart from him.[32]

Even Irish immigrants might be forgiven for killing drunken mothers. In 1890 Patrick Quigley, a miner who had paid to have his mother and siblings brought over from Ireland, came by their house on New Year's Eve and found his mother drunk. He had flown into a screaming rage, throwing things and kicking furniture. When he returned the next day to find her drunk again and no food in the house, he beat and kicked her to death. The judge noted that "there was no more fatal weapon than a heavy pair of boots worn by a strong man." But the sentence was only seven years.[33]

Sometimes the only excuse offered by young Scotsmen who killed their mothers was their own drunkenness. Even then the crime was not treated as a particularly heinous one. Hugh Patterson, a young man whose "family occupied a respectable position," was a particularly disturbing example. To relieve the stress from studying for the excise exam, he had gone on a two-day drinking binge which culminated with a nosebleed that he treated by dousing a handkerchief with whisky and stuffing it up his nose. When he went home, his mother asked if he wanted some cheese. [H]e replied, "I'll cheese you," and shot her in the head. Patterson told police he could not remember why he shot her. He pled guilty to culpable homicide and was sentenced to ten years, the longest sentence given in any of the Scottish matricides.[34]

When a veteran of good character in Glasgow beat his mother to death, the presiding judge said, "The question to consider was whether it was possible, consistent with what was required for the vindication of the law to stop short of a sentence of penal servitude." He decided it was and sentenced the man to only eighteen months.[35] Three other Scotsmen who beat their mothers to death were allowed to plead guilty to assault because the victim had been in poor health, so the cause of death was unclear.

In-Laws

If British mothers might be viewed as ill-behaved burdens, mothers-in-law were even more suspect. Seventeen women in the United Kingdom were killed by their child's spouse. Seven of the cases were from Ireland and five each from Scotland and England. Two of the English cases indicate that quarrelsome mothers-in-law might be easy targets. At Winchester the bride and groom were attacked by the groom's mother as they left the church. She had not been invited to the wedding and in her anger threw a brickbat at the wedding party and ran at the bride with fists raised. The bride responded by knocking her down. The unhappy mother-in-law died five days later.[36] In 1890, when William Dixon was charged with the manslaughter of his father-in-law, the defense explained that he had been aiming the blow at his mother-in-law. Because Dixon was given a good character and the death had been unintentional, Justice Day released him for time served.[37]

Even when the verdict was guilty, the courtroom often reflected an assumption that the victim might have had it coming. In an Irish case the defense attorney actually told the court that "[i]t was in no spirit of levity that counsel reminded the jury that that member of the family was often regarded as a source of discord in the home."[38] The Irish outrage report of a case in which a man had beaten and kicked his mother-in-law to death noted that the victim "cause[d] dissension between husband and wife and induced the latter to leave home for a short time."[39] Another defendant explained, "[I]t was only my mother-in-law." Five years was the heaviest sentence given to an Irishman convicted of killing his mother-in-law.[40] One Scotsman was executed for killing his mother-in-law but he had also murdered his wife.

Homicide trials involving in-laws were rare in Britain—accounting for fewer than 5 percent of homicide trials in England, Wales, and Scotland. In England most of the homicide trials involving in-laws were the result of brawls and led to light sentences unless a lethal weapon was used. The only heavy sentences and executions were from the handful of cases in which the accused had either killed an in-law who was trying to protect a family member or had killed in an attempt to rob.

Only thirteen Scottish homicide trials involved relatives by marriage, less than a third of the number involving blood kin. The contradiction between the sanctity of family privacy and the state's insistence on personal accountability was a cruel bind for those caught in a violent household. John Curran had watched his brother–in-law Dennis McFayden abuse his sister, their children, and Curran's mother for seven years. He had sent for the police but they refused to intervene. After witnessing another round of brutality, Curran went home, got a knife, and stabbed McFayden in the neck. Curran, described as a quiet, sober man, had never been in trouble before, but because he had told the arresting officer that his "heart had been in it for seven years," the trial judge insisted that he was guilty of premeditated murder. He was convicted of murder and sentenced to death though the sentence was commuted to life in prison.[41] Curran's case again highlights one of the contradictions in Scottish attitudes. Even though the police were reluctant to interfere among family members, no quarter was given to someone who acted to protect a relative from domestic violence.[42]

The Scottish cases that did not involve defending or peacemaking stemmed from drunken brawls. In one case three sisters beat their brother's wife to death during a family picnic. Since no weapons were used, the women were allowed to plead guilty to assault and served less than twelve months.[43] But John Carty, whose brother–in-law fell out of a window during a drunken scuffle, was sentenced to eight years.[44]

In Wales, Harry Jones was tried at Caernarvonshire Assize for the manslaughter of his father-in-law, Owen Griffith. Jones was a miner working on the railway, which meant he was away from home for extended periods so his wife had her father living with her for company. Jones came home unexpectedly one night, very drunk, and immediately attacked his wife. He "seized her by the hair, shook her violently and otherwise ill-treated her. Her father attempted to protect her, upon which Jones kicked him so savagely that he died a few days later from the effects of the injuries he received."

When Jones was arrested, he told the police that "the old man had lived too long." Jones was convicted of manslaughter and sentenced to fifteen years, a heavy sentence for manslaughter, but the *Pall Mall Gazette* complained that Jones had gotten away with "a diabolical murder on rather favorable terms."[45]

Though homicide trials involving in-laws were rare in Britain, relatives by marriage accounted for 40 percent of Irish family homicide trials. Most of the homicide trials involving in-laws and step-relatives in Ireland were very similar to those involving blood relatives, but the Irish courts were less tolerant of those who killed in-laws. Relatives by marriage who killed over land or property were nearly three times more likely to be sentenced to penal servitude or death than were blood relatives in similar situations. Presumably it was easier to understand why an overlooked son might kill his brother than to excuse a greedy in-law. In 27 percent of Irish homicide trials involving in-laws the deaths were described as the result of casual quarrels. As usual, homicides in brawls were dealt with lightly. Only 21 percent of those convicted in these cases were sentenced to penal servitude.

FEMALE KILLERS

Women were the killers in fewer than 15 percent of homicide trials involving adult relatives in the United Kingdom, but the reactions varied among the nations. In England women who killed male relatives were likely to be punished severely. In Liverpool a family brawl led to manslaughter charges against two women. John McDermott, the victim, had poured a glass of beer, enraging his sister Elizabeth since the beer belonged to their mother, Eliza. When Elizabeth complained, John threw a basin at her which missed her and struck their father. Eliza than attacked John with a boot while Elizabeth struck him with a rolling pin. The women then dragged him outside where they were joined by the victim's brother, Thomas McDermott, who kicked John while the women continued to beat him. After John died of the cumulative effects, all three assailants were charged with manslaughter. The Liverpool jury found all three defendants guilty. Justice Kay sentenced the women to seven years each while Thomas was given just nine months.[46]

The fear of female assaults on patriarchy could also be seen in the only case in which an Englishwoman was charged with killing her father. Annie Costello had hit her father in the head with a rolling pin after he struck her first. The claim of self-defense held no weight with Justice Archibald: "You have been found guilty of causing the death of your own father by your own brutal violence. This is a most painful and miserable case and calls for a sentence which may be a warning to all others offending in the same manner." He sentenced her to ten years penal servitude.[47] But there were no others offending in the same manner. The only other case of patricide by a woman in the entire United Kingdom was a Scottish woman who was found insane.

No women in England, Wales, or Ireland were convicted of matricide, but one young Scotswoman was convicted. Jane Corrigan, a paper worker in Glasgow, was accused of murder for killing her mother "with a hatchet, delft and a kettle." Both the killer and victim were drunk at the time and the defense attorney pointed out that the room had been so dark that the prisoner had not been able to tell whether the items she was throwing at her mother were having an impact or not. She pled guilty to culpable homicide and was sentenced to ten months hard labor "so she could become sober and industrious."[48] Presumably her slovenly drunkenness was more of a concern than the death of her mother.

Nearly a quarter of the English women accused of killing a relative were charged with homicide through culpable neglect—a charge which assumes that women were responsible for the care of adults as well as children. While sentences for neglect of a child varied widely, neglect of a disabled adult was often taken very seriously. Maria Kershaw was charged with the manslaughter of her middle-aged sister-in-law. The *Times* said it was a "piteous case of cruelty towards a poor weak-minded creature." The victim had come to live with Kershaw and her husband when her mother died. The coroner found her body covered with bruises and emaciated. Justice Lopes said that "some persons seemed to think that poor helpless creatures might be subjected to any kind of maltreatment with impunity. Such persons must be taught that the laws of England were made for all and especially for the protection of the weak against the strong." Maria Kershaw was sentenced to ten years though it was not clear why Maria should have borne legal responsibility for the care of her sister-in-law.[49]

Only four Welsh women were charged with killing adult relatives, and in three of the cases the cause of death had been neglect. Two women were charged with manslaughter when the forty-three-year-old sister of one and daughter of the other died of starvation and neglect. When it was determined that the sister was married and had children of her own, charges against her were dropped. The seventy-year-old mother of the victim was convicted and sentenced to six months for manslaughter.[50] In another case a seventy-year-old woman was charged along with her son with the manslaughter of her daughter-in-law. The victim was bedridden and her husband worked thirteen hours a day, leaving his mother to care for his wife. "Rumors spread among the neighbors that she was neglected, ill-treated and not supplied with sufficient food and several of them went to see her and remonstrated with the mother-in-law." Other neighbors testified to seeing the accused throw filthy straw over the victim and beat her. The woman was found guilty and sentenced to twenty years.[51]

CHASTISING FEMALE RELATIVES

Assumptions about the domestic roles of women could be seen in cases where males killed female relatives. Forty percent of the Englishmen tried for killing female relatives other than their mothers explained that the violence had been punishment for lapses in behavior or housekeeping. Some brothers who killed sisters in England were reacting against female attempts to control. A young man who had beaten his sister to death with a hammer told police, "She might have been alive now if she had not 'nagged' me so. I hit her with the hammer. I don't know how many times I hit her when she was down for I had lost my temper." He was sentenced to ten years.[52] A "respectably connected" man who shot his sister to death left a note: "I have been treated so badly by that beast, my sister Constance that I must put an end to her life by shooting." He was found insane.[53]

The most common ground for English cases of the fatal chastisement of a female relative was her sexual behavior. In keeping with the respect for paternal authority, the courts sympathized with fathers who used lethal violence against a wayward daughter. When John Pattison beat his adult daughter to death with a brush, the presiding judge said, "[T]he prisoner was a sober, honest man, a good husband and a good father and had unfortunately caused the death of his daughter by striking her with a brush. No doubt she had provoked him very much and caused him considerable anxiety and when he struck her he could not have supposed that the blow would be attended with such an unfortunate result." He sentenced Pattison to only four months.[54] A chemist whose twenty-year-old daughter died of a ruptured kidney after being beaten for staying out late received the same judicial sympathy. "Though the prisoner gave way in a moment of anger, it was manslaughter of an excusable kind. It was a blow given in anger without any intention to do harm, under great provocation from his daughter, when he tried to prevent her going worse than she was." The judge sentenced the man to time served.[55]

The English courts only granted such authority to fathers, though brothers, uncles, and cousins sometimes tried to exercise it. A Yorkshire man who explained that he had cut his sister's throat because he "believed she was too good a girl for the man she intended to marry" was executed as were two other Englishmen who murdered female relatives whose romantic lives they disapproved of.[56]

Some Scotsmen also felt they should control the women in their household. When James Sandilands of Renfrew, Scotland, beat the woman he lived with to death because she did not have dinner ready when he got home, he was arrested and charged with killing his wife. Sandilands angrily responded that she was his sister. The exact nature of the relationship does not seem to have mattered to the court. Sandilands was sentenced to seven years for culpable homicide.[57] A widower in Glasgow, who cut his female cousin's throat, explained that he "had been provoked to do it because she was teaching the children bad."[58] In 1882 Agnes Smith was beaten to death by her father and brother. But the defense was able to fall back on respect for fatherhood, warning the jury not to convict a "[w]eak, old, sorely tired man who had made full atonement for the death of a favorite daughter." The Dundee jury convicted both father and brother of assault only and the father was released for time served.[59]

There were no cases where an Irishman killed a sister as a form of chastisement, but there was a case in which the roles were reversed. Mary Trophy, a young woman in Cork, murdered her eighteen-year-old brother with a hatchet. The two lived with another brother and Mary was housekeeper for the three of them. "Between her and the deceased a very bad feeling existed. She seemed to take pleasure in thwarting the unfortunate lad and frequent altercations ensued." After quarreling with him at dinner one night, Mary vowed she would have revenge. She slipped into the room where he was sleeping and killed him with a hatchet. She was sentenced to death though the sentence was commuted.[60]

REVENGE FOR SEDUCTION

Irish men were more likely to kill a female relative's lover than the woman. The Irish were the most inclined to use violence to avenge the rape or seduction of a female relative. There were sixteen cases in which an Irishwoman's relatives were tried for killing a man for seducing or taking liberties with her. Two cases in which the killer had shot the victim in cold blood before witnesses led to murder convictions, but half of those convicted of manslaughter served less than two years.

Three Englishmen killed men who had seduced female relatives. Again, fathers had more leeway. Henry William Pace, a foreman in a metal works, had allowed a young coworker to lodge in his home where the young man had seduced Pace's daughter but refused to marry her. During a discussion of the illegitimate grandchild, Pace killed the young man with a spanner. The defense argued that he had been suffering from "temporary derangement." Justice Coleridge sentenced him to eighteen months.[61]

In 1890 Walter Lyon, a young man in suburban London, stabbed an army sergeant he found in his mother's bedroom. The *Scotsman* reported the story as the tragic tale of a "fine, soldierly fellow" murdered the day before his wedding. However, within days the story became less clear-cut. The mother had been widowed for five months and the deceased was not the first man she had brought home. She had met the sergeant that afternoon, but when her son discovered them together she told him they were to be married the next day. Furious, the son had threatened to stab his mother saying, "I am going to do it mother I said I would if I caught you again." Stewart replied: "Don't stab your mother, stab me if you want to stab anyone." Lyon stabbed Stewart in the chest and then calmly went to the police to turn himself in. At the inquest a neighbor said he had heard the son calling his mother "opprobrious names." The coroner "pointed out that a man must not vindicate propriety at the point of a knife."[62]

After a London jury convicted Lyon of manslaughter, Justice Stephen said that "he could not deny that prisoner's act was most ferocious, most ungoverned and absolutely wanting in that moderate degree of self-control which it was the duty of every man to keep up. At the same time he could not but be impressed with the fact that the mother had misbehaved herself in a most disgraceful manner to incite him to the most violent passions." Lyon was sentenced to seven years penal servitude.[63]

Though Lyons killed his mother's lover rather than his mother, the case reveals some of the most frequent aspects of family homicide trials in England. Generally the English justice system was committed to preserving male dominance in the family, even if it meant allowing a son to chastise his mother. Women could not be trusted. Every woman charged with killing an adult male relative in England was convicted and all but one of them was sentenced to penal servitude or death.

GENDER AND FAMILY HOMICIDES

The English support of patriarchy was clear. Eighteen percent of men who killed female adult relatives were found insane. No English woman who killed an adult male relative was found insane. Women convicted of manslaughter for killing an adult male relative were more than twice as likely to be sentenced to penal servitude as the average English homicide defendant. Judges and jurors probably felt a particular sympathy for their fellow adult males. As Justice Channel explained to a jury in a case in which a woman was charged with stabbing the son of an alderman, "He did not think it was possible—he spoke for himself and was not laying down any judicial opinion—for anybody to divest himself of a prior sympathy in this case. A man, in the prime of life and in the possession of affluent means, had been suddenly called to his great account."[64]

But the need to protect women was also recognized. English males who killed female adult relatives were nearly twice as likely to hang as other male killers. Reactions to family homicides reinforced the ideal of the male as both the head of the family and its protector. Similarly women were to repay the protection with submission. Women who made a man's home "not so comfortable" regardless of the relationship were liable to chastisement. Women were also meant to be nurturers and were punished both in and outside the courtroom for failing to care for adult relatives or in-laws.

In the Irish courts the gender of the victim was crucial. Nearly half of the cases in which an adult woman was killed by a relative resulted in insanity verdicts. On the other hand, more than two-thirds of the convictions in which adult male relatives were the victims resulted in sentences of less than two years. Killing a female relative seemed so bizarre as to be evidence of insanity, however, one could have a variety of reasonable explanations for killing a male relative. The sex of the killer did not influence the outcome of these cases, however. The same was true of Irish homicide trials outside the nuclear family. Irish men and women accused of homicide were convicted at almost identical rates.

Scotland was the only nation where the number of family homicide trials involving female victims exceeded the number of trials involving male victims, specifically because of the very high number of matricides. Most of the men who killed female relatives felt that the woman's drunkenness justified their actions—the courts did not agree completely but no Scotsman was convicted of murdering an intoxicated woman. Though Scotland had a higher percentage of female homicide defendants than any other nation, Scottish women were selective in their choice of victim, and only seven Scottish women were tried for killing an adult relative. None served more than two years.

Only five Welsh homicide trials involved adult relatives and in every case both the killer and the victim were male.

COURTING COUPLES

The same idea that the women of a household were meant to be subservient to the men which was found in family homicides could also be found in cases in which men had killed women they were courting. Even if couples were not married or living together, some felt that the woman had become the possession of the man and should behave accordingly. As one woman explained, "We agreed that I am to be entirely with him—not to live with him altogether, but that I should belong to him."[65] But the courts were not inclined to agree. One area in which British courts were willing to grant women autonomy was in their right to refuse a suitor. At a trial in Dundee in which a man had attempted to murder his girlfriend, the young woman testified that "folk may go with folk and not mean to marry altogether." The defense attorney argued that the victim's conduct was "unendurable. He had courted her for nineteen months and she had broken it off at the whim of her sulky father." The judge interrupted to point out that "he thought in this country a woman could marry the man she liked."[66]

About 40 percent of Englishmen tried for killing their lovers were reacting to rejection. English courts clearly believed in a woman's right to refuse advances. More than half of the Englishmen tried for killing a woman who rejected them (either at first approach or by breaking up an existing relationship) were executed. The execution rate rose to 86 percent in cases in which the man had stalked a woman after she made her lack of interest clear. Even highly respectable men were executed. At Oxford the son of a well-to-do farmer murdered his fiancée with a revolver. "The youth and the position of the parties and their relations to each other combined to invest the trial with particular interest." After he shot her he claimed, "I had a right to do it." He told police he prayed with her before he killed her and hoped that the Lord would have mercy on her soul. Despite an insanity defense, he was convicted and executed.[67]

Insanity defenses rarely worked in these cases. Enoch Wadley, freshly released from an insane asylum, had tried to court a friend's sister. When the girl resisted, he threw her in a ditch and stabbed her thirty-eight times. He explained to police, "It is hard to love and not be loved." Several experts testified that Wadley was insane, but he was convicted and executed.[68] Only five Englishmen accused of killing women who had rejected them were found insane between 1867 and 1892, and thirty-three Englishmen who killed women who rejected them were executed.

Perhaps because Irish marriages were still usually arranged, such cases were rare in Ireland. Only four Irishmen were tried for killing women who rejected them. Three of them were found insane. Since marriage was usually about property in Ireland, apparently romantic passion could be ascribed to insanity. Ironically, the one exception was a case initially reported as "a strange occurrence which can only be explained by a supposition of lunacy." A young man walked into the hotel where his ex-fiancée worked and shot her in the head five times. After announcing that "he had come 112 miles to shoot her," he also tried to kill himself but failed. He was hanged for murder.[69]

To the Scots such behavior illustrated a lack of discipline. When a respectable young man in Dundee killed a woman because he discovered she had another sweetheart, the *Dundee Advertiser* explained, "The story of crime is one of ill-regulated lives . . . midnight debauchery is an indulgence as perilous as it is disgraceful."[70] In 1878, when a young man in the Highlands murdered a young girl, he explained "that it was the depth of his love for her that made him do it. He added he was never content unless she was near him or in his sight." When the defense offered a plea of insanity, a physician testified that he considered "him to be an ill-regulated, impressionable, emotional and unstable man." In other words, he was not insane, simply sinful. After the death sentence was pronounced, the prisoner "turning to the audience, said—'Take warning, then, for it was reading novels and drinking whiskey that brought me to this. I had a good moral training but I did not profit by it.'"[71]

Twenty-seven men in England, Ireland, and Wales were tried for killing women who had become pregnant or had gone to court to get an order for maintenance for an illegitimate child. The defense in these cases usually alluded to the sexual immorality of the victim. But most jurors did not blame the victim. At Bristol a "quiet, inoffensive" married man had fathered the child of a local "woman of rather an abandoned character, being frequently drunk and violent in her manner when interfered with." She had asked for more money to support the child and when he said he could not give her any more she threatened to take him to court. They struggled and he threw her off a bridge. She died of lung congestion. Despite the defense's argument that she was "a very low woman," that she might have been suicidal, and that the act was not premeditated, the jury convicted him of murder.[72]

Half of the Englishmen tried for killing pregnant girlfriends were middle-class men driven by fears of exposure and half of the men executed were middle class. In cases where a middle-class man had seduced a young woman from a lower class, the popular reaction was often particularly heated. A middle-class man who had cut his twenty-two-year-old pregnant girlfriend's throat after she reacted badly to being told that he "could not be bothered with her anymore" calmly showed the police the knife he killed her with and explained that they had fought. While he seemed unaffected, the neighbors were not. "The police had great difficulty protecting him from the mob." He was sentenced to life in prison.[73]

An Irish jury had a more difficult time with a case from Cavan. The daughter of a small farmer "was found dead in a shallow stream under circumstances that led to the presumption that she was murdered by a man named Hugh Fay, by whom she is said to have been pregnant, and in whose company she was seen immediately before the murder. His belt was found beside the body, and it is suspected that he killed her to evade fulfilling a promise of marriage." Because Fay was the son of a respectable local farmer, it took fifteen months and the implementation of heavy fines to force twelve men to serve on the jury. After trials at four consecutive Assizes failed to result in a verdict, Justice Keogh, lamenting that "the case was overwhelming," recognized that no local jury would be willing to convict and released the man with the understanding that he would immigrate. Within months of his arrival in America, Fay was murdered by the victim's cousin[74]—another example of the Irish preference for dealing with family issues outside the courtroom.

In Wales Cadwallader Jones, a married farmer, was accused of the murder and mutilation of a young woman who had been pregnant with his child. The defense argued that the victim already had two illegitimate children "and had already driven one man from his home, owing to her threatening to affiliate a child upon him. He [Jones] being recently married and desperate to maintain the happiness of his home and not to bring disgrace upon his wife and infant child entreated her not to go to his house." With such provocation "in a moment of fury, knowing that if the woman was to go to his house his happiness for life was ruined, he picked up a stone and threw it at her never imagining or intending that it should kill her." According to the defense, Jones had been so horrified when he realized she was dead that he left the body in the garden for six weeks before finally mutilating it and putting it in the river. Unfortunately for the defense, the postmortem revealed that she had been killed with an axe or billhook. It took weeks for all the body parts to be found. The defense failed. But as was often the case in Welsh courtrooms, the defendant had no means of assessing the effectiveness of his attorney. Jones was convicted and sentenced to death. "The sentence was then translated into Welsh for the information of the prisoner."[75]

FEMALE CRIMES OF PASSION

Only four English women were tried for killing their lovers. Three of the cases involved lower-class women and drew little attention, but in the fourth case the victim, Frederick Moon, the son of a London alderman, had been stabbed to death by his mistress, Flora Davy. The *Times* reported that Davy's husband had "separated from her owing to her bad conduct." In addition to being morally suspect, the *Times* reported that she did not have the appearance of a lady either. She "was rather tall for a woman inclined to stoutness, muscular and of a robust appearance."[76] Her defense counsel fully understood that she was not a sympathetic defendant. "When the news of the tragic incident broke there was but one universal feeling of sympathy for the family of the deceased gentleman especially his honoured and respected father. He was afraid that the sympathy did not extend itself to the prisoner." The defense attorney begged the jurors to reject the double standard. "If the relation of the prisoner to the deceased was an immoral one, he begged of them to remember that the sin of such a relation was not wholly on the side of the woman." He also attempted to establish that the relationship had been sincere. "If there could be degrees of immorality, he would say a less immoral one than such a relationship would ordinarily predicate." The prosecution was equally intent on painting a portrait of Davy: "There was no doubt that she was a woman of violent passions. Supposing it was true that the deceased threatened to throw a bottle at her head and that she took up the poultry carver, what a temper and state of mind did that exhibit? Was it not reasonable and probably that in a frenzy of vindictive passion she stabbed the man by whom she considered she had been insulted?" Davy was convicted of manslaughter. The judge said, "I entirely approve their verdict. . . . [T]he public safety will never be secured if in a quarrel of this kind one of the parties is to be allowed to resort to so deadly a weapon with impunity." He sentenced Davy to eight years.[77] But while Davy certainly suffered more negative press than women who killed less notable men, her sentence was considerably more lenient than that given any man who stabbed his lover, three-quarters of whom were executed.

Not a single woman in the Celtic nations was tried for killing a man she was romantically involved with other than a husband or a cohabiter. However, there was a case from Tipperary in which a justice of the peace was found shot dead. The outrage papers suggested discreetly that it might have been the result of a dalliance with his housekeeper.[78] The Irish preferred to take care of things privately and the courts often respected that decision. The issues were highlighted in an attempted murder case from Ireland. Like many cases in England and Wales, a married man found the happiness of his home threatened by an inconvenient woman, but in this case the assailant was the woman. "A young lady of attractive appearance" had made an appointment to see him in his home office. She began by asking for her letters back. When he told her he had burned them, she threw vitriol in his face. Her defense attorney suggested that the victim "had attempted to commit an outrage upon her and that he had repeatedly made similar attempts. She threw the contents of the bottle over him in defense of her honor." Despite the fact that she had made the appointment and arrived at the house with the vitriol, she was acquitted. "The verdict was received with cheers."[79] Rather than becoming modesty or the restraint of passion, the Irish jury celebrated a woman who did whatever it took to defend her honor.

The records for assaults and attempted murders suggest that Scottish women were also willing to take action, though the results were never fatal. When a young man called off the wedding after a two-year courtship and with the wedding date already set, the jilted bride responded by throwing sulfuric acid in his face. The acid destroyed one of his eyes but she expressed no remorse. While passing his house after her arrest, she shouted, "I've got revenge so far but I'm not content." The judge pronounced her actions "fiendish" and sentenced her to five years.[80] A factory worker in Dundee who threw acid on the man who seduced her received more sympathy. The defense produced a letter the victim had written to the accused which said, "If I have said or done any wrong I hope I will be forgiven by a higher power for I do not care for you so hope never to see you again on this earth." The letter outraged the judge: "The man did commit upon you the most grievous of all offenses that a man can commit upon a young female. You were courted by him lawfully and righteously but he betrays you, ruins you and then writes you that unfeeling I must say brutal letter. Under the provocation the letter naturally created in you, you were not in possession of your full mental rectitude." He sentenced her to just eight months.[81]

Almost twice as many English women killed a third party as a response to romantic difficulties as killed their lovers. Rather than blame the man, they sought to remove obstacles. Three women killed their lover's wife, one killed a lover's child, one killed her husband's lover, and in one of the strangest cases, one woman killed a total stranger in her romantic quest. Two of the women who had killed their lover's spouse were convicted of murder, but only one hanged and she had killed her lover's child as well.[82]

In the other case the jury apparently was won over by the appeal of "a bright, cheerful-looking young woman." Ellen Kittel, a twenty-one year old farmer's daughter, was charged with poisoning the wife of one of her father's agricultural laborers. The prisoner "was stated to be of a cheerful, kindly, affectionate disposition, with nothing vicious in her character or nature." However, she had told friends she intended to marry the man who was in his forties and had several children. She had purchased poison and she had taken food to the first Mrs. Kittel, who died of arsenic poisoning four days later. Within days of the death, she had moved in and taken over the Kittel household. She was also discovered to have been pregnant with Kittel's baby months before the death of the first Mrs. Kittel. In fact, her first murder trial had to be halted when she went into labor.[83]

For the *Times*, Ellen's mistakes were about class as well as morality. "The girl's father, being himself in a humble position, the family, who appeared uneducated, associated freely with the laborers and this man, being allowed to hang about the house, began to pay attention to the girl, his master's daughter." Despite the evidence, "Whether from consciousness of innocence or from strength of nerve, the prisoner never showed the least anxiety." The prosecuting attorney stressed that as she was pregnant, she had "the strongest possible motive that could influence a woman—the wish by speedy marriage to save herself from shame." The defense argued that the man was to blame: "The question was not whether the prisoner was innocent but was she alone culpable. Let them remember that she was yet a girl—hardly yet emerged into womanhood." After suggesting that nothing had proved her guilt, her attorney closed by noting that "[i]n the whole history of criminal justice, no prisoner had ever suffered so much as this poor girl had done. She had already endured the anguish of a trial for her life, while suffering the pains of childbirth."

Justice Martin specifically told the jury that they must "give the prisoner the benefit of the doubt," but added "that if the prisoner is innocent; she had brought all her sufferings upon herself by her own conduct." The jury acquitted her without leaving the box. "The verdict satisfied everyone who had followed the evidence and had indeed been confidently anticipated but it was not received with any expression of satisfaction."

After the verdict, "the girl, rose up and courtesied [*sic*] and thanked the jury and then as if suddenly remembering the severe comment made upon her conduct she flushed more deeply and sank down on her seat overcome with emotion."[84] As a young attractive woman of respectable parentage, Ellen Kittel received every benefit of the doubt despite evidence which might easily have convicted an older woman. The average age of a female poisoner convicted of murder was thirty-six, the average age of females tried for poisoning but acquitted was twenty-four.

A middle-aged spinster was the defendant in the most bizarre of the romantic murders by English women. Christiana Edmunds first set out to win the heart of the married man by poisoning his wife. The wife survived and she and her husband broke off contact with Edmunds who decided to deflect the suspicion by placing candy poisoned with strychnine in a local confectioner's shop. Edmunds also distributed poisoned candy in bags marked with the shop owner's name. When a four-year-old boy was killed by the poisoned candy she had planted in the shop, Edmunds volunteered to speak at the inquest in order to strengthen the case against the shop owner. Her eagerness aroused suspicion and further investigation produced damning evidence against her.

The *Times* described Edmunds as "lady-like in appearance," and the prosecutor acknowledged that the prisoner "had resided with her mother for some time at Brighton, with, as far as he knew, perfect respectability."[85] But the evidence against her was substantial as demonstrated by the desperation in the defense's summation. He argued that the mere fact that she had been passing out poisoned candy to children did not prove that she had poisoned the candy which killed the little boy. Having more or less admitted that she was guilty, the defense argued that "she was of impaired intellect. About twelve or fifteen months ago a great change came over her, and even now she had the idiotic vanity to deny her real age which instead of being thirty-four was forty-three." He suggested that the nature of her insanity "was the entire destruction of her moral sense." The presiding judge, Baron Martin, pointed out that "[h]e had heard a doctor say that all mankind were mad more or less but that had little to do with the case under consideration. . . . [E]very man [*sic*] must be responsible for his acts until it was shown to the contrary." After an hour's deliberation, the jury convicted Edmunds.[86]

But as the coverage in the *Times* made clear, Edmunds was not a man. She was a middle-aged lady from a respectable family. The *Times* suggested: "It must be admitted that a woman of the age of forty-three, with such a genealogy and history is precisely the kind of person who might be expected to go mad." The editorial did not say that such madness would only be likely in respectable women, but the implication was clear. An editorial noted that her behavior was ladylike:

> As sentence of death was pronounced her bearing was firm and betraying no visible emotion. It was also respectful and becoming. . . . Her countenance was slightly flushed and her eyes beamed with unwonted expression. In the few words of complaint she addressed to the judge she spoke with much modesty and propriety and afterwards heard the sentence with fortitude.[87]

Shortly after the trial, a panel of doctors determined that Edmunds was insane, the sentence was commuted, and she was sent to an asylum. The

Spectator was indignant. "Had Christina Edmunds been a servant she would have been hanged without more ado and we should never have heard a word about her latent insanity."[88]

HOMICIDE AND ROMANTIC MADNESS

In addition to the issue of class, Edmund's crime was interesting in its evocation of romantic madness. Even the *Scotsman* admitted that "neither the crime nor the criminal is of the common order. The criminal is not one of the vulgar sort . . . the story is almost romantic in some respects."[89] The notion of the killer as the victim of love seldom swayed juries, but it provided opportunities for the press to speculate on human nature. The press also found romantic interest in the trial of Miles Weatherill in Manchester. Weatherill had gone on a shooting rampage in the local vicarage after his sweetheart was dismissed from her job as a domestic servant and sent away. Though he was convicted and sentenced to death, the *Scotsman* editorialized: "It is plain that the man was madly, savagely, in fact, in love with the girl and seeing the calm, calculating way in which love nowadays is generally made and received there is something respectable in such thorough-going affection." However, the newspaper thoroughly approved of the guilty verdict: "We can only be thankful those steady-going jurymen have too little sympathy with ecstatic fondness for a lady-love to pronounce the erotic madness legal insanity." But still there was interest in the fact that Weatherill "was a pattern boy at school, and respected by all his neighbors as a well-behaved young man as he grew up." When he fell in love with the young girl, "He revealed the state of his mind to her master, who told him that it was very natural, complimented him on his openness, but ultimately refused to allow her to have him as a recognized follower. Thereupon Miles Weatherill courted her upon the sly—and there was certainly nothing very heinous in such conduct."

The defense had pled insanity but the *Scotsman* found useful instruction on human nature: "All revengeful anger is, of course, in a sense, a brief madness. If we give the reign to our passions, they may run away with us. But then we should not have so given the reins." This was a perfect illustration of the philosophy of Scottish courtrooms. We are all sinners, but we must atone when we cannot control our sinful natures. "Miles Weatherill is no madman, but a marvelous instance of the reckless excesses into which a morbid brooding over real or fancied wrongs, an inflamed exaggeration of one's own importance in the world, may hurry even the most decent seeming of men."[90]

The *Times* also found pathos in the case. After the charge was read, "an affecting scene took place between the prisoner and the witness Sarah Bell [the young woman he loved], who went up to him and embraced him"[91] Before pronouncing the death sentence, the judge said that his crime was "such as might rather be expected from a wild savage, than from one who had been brought up in a civilized country." But the *Times* cited an example of such a savage, contrasting Weatherill with a defendant from an uncivilized country who had beaten a woman to death "Not like Weatherill, an intelligent artisan, but an uneducated Irish laborer from Galway, Faherty was guilty of a murder both brutal and unprovoked. But he belonged to a class of men worked upon by mere animal passion."[92] Weatherill and Faherty both hanged, but they offered a useful illustration of the differences between an English artisan who was desperately in love and an Irish savage who was merely a brute.

Though the English press sometimes seized on cases for their romantic interest, the English courts were particularly unforgiving in homicides stemming from romantic difficulties. Eighty-six percent of men who killed someone for thwarting their romance were convicted and nearly 30 percent of them were executed.

Such cases were rare in Ireland, probably because the regulation of romantic life was largely carried on outside the courtroom. When a farm servant who had been "overly familiar" with his employer's wife was murdered in Kerry, an article from Dublin reported that the crime was "not altogether an act of violence but rather a vindication of the moral law by the virtuous young men of the district." Such vindications seldom led to formal charges. In another case in which a landlord had been murdered, it was reported that the crime had not been political but that the victim was known to have seduced several of the local young ladies.[93]

Trials in which third parties were involved in homicides related to courtship were also rare in Scotland. This may reflect the fact that most Scots, like the jurymen in the Weatherill case, had no tolerance for "erotic insanity." Certainly the motives in the two cases in which third parties were accused of killing young lovers indicate a pragmatic turn of mind. In one case, under the headline "Cruel Murder," the *Scotsman* reported that an elderly man shot at two young men who were coming to court his son's domestic servants. One of the men was fatally wounded, but the old man insisted, "I would do it again." He explained that the young men came too often and when they rapped on the girls' window, they disturbed his sleep. He was convicted of culpable homicide but "the Court having regard to his great age and to the extenuating circumstances imposed the mitigated sentence of four months." The sentence was met with "general applause."[94]

The courts were considerably less lenient in the other case in which three men were charged with culpable homicide for having chased a young woman off the side of Salisbury Craig. The men had accosted the young woman after telling her sweetheart that they were park guards and they would send her to meet him at the park gate. One of the accused turned state's evidence and explained that he and the others regularly went to the park with field glasses and "if they saw a man and a woman together they interrupted them for a piece of lark." But the larks sometimes included demanding money from the couple and/or sexually assaulting the young woman. They had been attempting to rape the young woman who fell to her death trying to escape. The presiding judge concluded, "[A] system of most abominable espionage had been practiced by a gang of ruthless men for a number of years in the Queen's park for purposes either of lewdness or of blackmail, which were equally disgusting to our common humanity." The men who were all gainfully employed married men in their thirties and forties were unanimously convicted of culpable homicide. The judge after saying that the "prisoners belonged to a class of men of whom it would require stronger language than he cared to make use of to express his abhorrence" sentenced them to seven years each, adding that a heavy sentence was "best for themselves as well as for the country."[95]

The differences in attitudes toward romantic homicides are reflected in the outcomes, incidence, and motives of such cases. In England where patriarchy was still largely enforced, the assumption of the need for male control seems to have been strong. Even though the courts punished men who killed women who rejected them, the rate of homicide trials in which men killed women they were courting was ten times higher than it was in Scotland or Wales and five times higher than in Ireland. This disproportion only reflects the actual number of trials. The *Times* reports at least twice as many cases in which there was no trial usually because the man committed suicide. Far more English suitors took "if I can't have you, no one can" to the ultimate conclusions than did their Celtic counterparts. The English courts punished these men severely—Englishmen who killed women they were courting were five times more likely to hang than men who killed their wives. Three-quarters of the Englishmen tried for killing their sweethearts were executed. But the fact remains that single women in England were at far greater risk of homicide from the men who loved them than women in Ireland, Scotland, and Wales.

The Irish courts were also hard on men convicted of killing their lovers, but such cases were extremely rare. Twice as many homicide trials in Ireland had to do with the enforcement of morality as with men killing their lovers. Only half of those accused of killing to enforce morality were convicted. Irish courts recognized the rights and capacity of the community to monitor sexual morality.

The *Scotsman's* suggestion that romantic passion was missing in the modern world was apparently accurate. Only ten Scottish homicide trials involved lovers or romantic rivals, and in four of the trials the defendant was a foreigner. Homicides stemming from "erotic insanity" were not a problem in Scotland.

Though women might be subject to violence from fathers and brothers, single women in Ireland, Scotland, and Wales were rarely killed by their suitors. Though the risk was greater in England, the courts punished such homicides severely. However, as we shall see in the next chapter, neither the courts nor reason offered the same protection to women once they married.

CHAPTER 5

Husbands and Wives

I am sorry to say that savage treatment by a husband towards his wife is not uncommon. There is a great deal too much of it generally attributable to that poison called whiskey. There is a great deal too much of it and the way in which these poor women are treated would wring the heart of any man that has a spark of humanity in him. (*Scotsman*, 22 April 1875)

A husband is charged with assaulting his wife; I don't think that indicates a very disorganized state as regards the peace of the country; although it does affect the condition of the society. The prisoner did what he would characterize as an unmanly act upon the occasion having pushed her down and he should not have acted so towards a woman no matter what the circumstances. (*Kilkenny Journal*, 13 June 1885)

Under provocation he had been seized by a sudden frenzy which would sometimes even assail a good man . . . he struck his wife with a stick only, not intending to do more than administer some chastisement. For there was no sign of blood upon the poker. (The *Times*, 27 March 1868, 12c)

"Wife Beaten to Death by Her Husband at Cardiff: Strong Drink Is the Cause." (*Carmarthen Weekly Reporter*, 31 October 1884)

On the Isle of Britain, 20 percent of the men tried for homicide were accused of killing a spouse. This caused considerable alarm in England.[1] In an article discussing the criminal statistics for 1872, the *Times* noted with dismay that

124

ten of fourteen executions in England had been for the murder of wives and that twelve of twenty murder convictions were for the murders of wives or lovers.[2] As Justice Hawkins put it, "[I]t seems to me that there is no class of persons in the community who require or deserve the protection of the law from the violence of persons of a brutal character more than women, who too often are obliged to submit to great violence from those who ought to be their natural protectors and defenders."[3] Scottish judges shared the concern. Lord Craighill complained that "wife-killing through wife-beating is unfortunately of too frequent occurrence."[4]

Wives also made up 20 percent of Welsh homicide victims, but given the size of the Welsh population this still meant an average of fewer than two such cases per year. In 1884 the *Carmarthen Weekly Reporter* described the murder of a wife as "one of the most shocking tragedies which had been recorded in the annals of the town of Swansea." In fact, the case bore many characteristics that would have been familiar to authorities throughout Great Britain. A man who had been habitually abusive to his wife when drunk had beaten her to death. For the Welsh, such cases were infrequent enough to still cause shock.[5]

While the British may have seen the number of spousal homicides as a source of national shame, the relative rarity of such crimes in Ireland was a source of pride. Only 7 percent of the men charged with homicide in Ireland had killed their wives. On the eve of a trial for domestic homicide in Kilkenny, a newspaper noted: "The scene presented to the public in the county courthouse is happily one of rare occurrence in this country, no matter what other crimes unfortunately occur from time to time, that of wife murder seldom or ever finds place in the dread category."[6] As one Irish judge told a grand jury: "A husband is charged with assaulting his wife. It is an unusual case in this country and it was all their pride that very few such cases of the kind happened in Ireland no matter what might occur in other countries."[7] The "other countries" clearly referred to England. When an English politician suggested that the relationship between England and Ireland should be like that between a husband and wife, the *Limerick Chronicle* noted that "his matrimonial analogy unfortunately reminds us that Englishmen are only too well known for their unamiable propensity to beat their wives."[8] The distinction between the Irish who were kind to women and the English who beat their wives was a useful one. It reinforced the idea of the English as bullies and the Irish as noble and long-suffering victims.

In Britain men accused of killing their wives or female cohabiters were more likely to be convicted than other male killers and they were likely to receive heavier sentences. English courts grew less tolerant of spousal homicides throughout the nineteenth century.[9] Between 1867 and 1892 the English conviction rate for men accused of killing their wives rose by nearly 20 percent, the murder conviction rate rose by 40 percent, and the average sentence for men convicted of manslaughter for killing their wives rose by more than a year. At the same time the incidence of English men tried for killing their wives fell by 40 percent.

In Ireland the incidence of wife killing increased by nearly 30 percent, with the bulk of the increase coming in the late 1880s. Though the Irish rate of trials for wife killing was the lowest in the United Kingdom in 1867, by 1892 it was the highest. Perhaps in response to the increase, the courts began to treat these cases more severely. Between 1884 and 1892 the conviction rate rose by nearly 30 percent. The *murder* conviction rate for spousal homicides in Ireland more than doubled during the same period and the average manslaughter sentence rose by three years. The average sentence given an Irish man convicted of the manslaughter of his wife was nearly twice as long as the average Irish sentence for manslaughter. But again the increase was relative. English juries were still nearly 25 percent more likely to convict than Irish juries were, and the average English sentence was nearly four years longer. An Englishman tried for killing his wife was also four times more likely to hang for his crime than an Irish husband.

The Scottish pattern was different from either of the other two. First, the Scots had the highest rate of men tried for killing their wives—nearly twice that of the Irish and 50 percent higher than the English. But throughout this period both the number of cases and the conviction rate declined. The average sentence for a Scottish husband convicted of manslaughter also declined during this period. Further, Scottish husbands were the least likely to be convicted of *murdering* their wives.

To put it more simply, the number of Englishmen killing their wives was declining at the same time the likelihood of conviction and the severity of punishment increased. In Ireland the incidence of men tried for killing their wives was increasing as were the likelihood of conviction and the length of sentences. In Scotland the number of spousal homicide trials, the conviction rate, and the length of sentences were all declining. The responses to spousal homicide also parallel larger trends. The English regarded it as a social problem to be addressed by state action. The Irish traditionally viewed family violence as a private matter that did not require greater state intervention—though they were beginning to reassess that position.

Since the number of cases was declining, the Scots presumably saw no need for greater deterrence. There is also evidence that at least some Scots thought that the problem was a very limited one. In an editorial in 1878, the

Scotsman assured its readers that "brutality to wives is a survival to be found only to the lowest classes of the population." Therefore, solutions should be focused on the lower classes: "What is wanted is to rouse and quicken in the class prone to wife-beating the sense of shame and disgrace already attendant in all round public opinion. These feelings of shame in respect of attacks by husband upon their wives are non-existent in the class from which the brutal wife-beaters come."[10]

A WORKING-CLASS VICE?

Working-class Scots who killed their wives were nearly 20 percent more likely to be convicted than men from the middle or upper classes. However, once convicted, working-class wife killers received slightly lighter sentences. There are two possible explanations for this. One is that the lives of working-class women were considered less valuable. But another and perhaps more likely explanation is that judges made allowances for working-class failings and hoped through encouragement to elevate them. When a common laborer in Glasgow was tried for beating and kicking his wife to death, the presiding judge, Lord Deas, offered sympathy for the defendant: "It was a single, reckless act attended probably with consequences which the prisoner never anticipated and which were not so palpable at the time as to lead one to suppose that death would be the result." The judge intended to send a message to the working classes that by mastering their impulses they could improve their lot. He concluded by noting that "there were no more respectable people in the country than the working men if they behave themselves as they ought." He sentenced the man to only eighteen months.[11]

English judges also spoke of wife abuse as a lower-class habit. Justice Bramwell explained to a laborer convicted of killing his wife, "[I]n one sense I am really sorry for you because it appears that you have been an honest hard-working man. But it is necessary that people in your class should be taught—what I fear they don't understand—that they have no right to beat their wives."[12] Justice Grantham complained in 1886 that "[t]here seemed to be an idea prevalent among people of the prisoner's class that they might ill-treat and kick their wives; he intended to do all in his power to show them that it was not so."[13] Lord Chief Justice Coleridge shared the concern "in some classes of society a wife seemed to be regarded as a kind of inferior dog or horse."[14]

English judges and juries worked to correct this opinion. Working-class men accused of killing their wives were nearly 30 percent more likely to be convicted, ten times more likely to be executed, and when convicted of manslaughter their sentences were three years longer on average than those of middle-class wife killers. At least one defense attorney tried to counter the prejudice by arguing in defense of a man who had kicked his pregnant wife in the stomach: "[A] good deal was said in these times about the brutality of the working classes, but in this case the prisoner had not even had his boots on." The argument failed. The man was convicted and sentenced to fifteen years.[15]

In Britain there was little question that this "class from which brutal wife-beaters come" was centered in particular regions and that a disproportionate number of Irish immigrants were involved. Though Ireland had the lowest rate of spousal homicide trials in the United Kingdom for much of the period, Irish immigrants in Britain were tried for killing their wives at a higher rate. In Ireland priests arranged marital separations and extended families offered shelter to women who left abusive husbands, as well as retaliation against the abusers.[16]

REGIONAL VARIATIONS AND IRISH IMMIGRANTS

In the slums of industrial Britain, Irish wives were far more vulnerable. More than 40 percent of spousal homicide trials in England occurred in the Midlands and the North. An editorial in the *Scotsman* complained that "[t]he very brute beasts do not treat their mates with the savagery practiced by the so-called Christian men in the Black Country."[17] The *Times* began a report on a drunken Irish laborer who had killed his wife by knocking her down and kicking her in the stomach, "There seems to be a homicidal mania among a certain portion of the Irish population in the county of Durham." The report revealed the Otherness of the Irish. "Some neighbors and an Irishman" came up and pulled the man off his wife. The husband "ill-used the Irishman who attempted to protect the wretched woman, who was then lying in a pool of blood, and blackened one of his eyes." While the "Irishman" had taken direct action to stop the attack, "the English residents of the neighborhood having brought the police he was taken into custody." Though the newspaper did not comment on the different reactions, the fact that the Irishman was singled out as fighting the husband while the "English residents" sent for the police points to an important difference in attitudes toward domestic violence. In Ireland most domestic violence ended when relatives or friends of the couple intervened. The relatively low rate of spousal homicide trials in Ireland may indicate that these interventions came sooner rather than later.

In England by the late nineteenth century, the correct procedure was to notify the police, though this approach often failed to save the victim.[18]

The same tone could be found in the Welsh press regarding wife murders by working-class Irish immigrants. In 1874 the *Carmarthen Weekly Reporter* noted, "The lists of sensational events which have recently taken place in Cardiff and its immediate neighborhood has [*sic*] just been augmented by one. Patrick Riley, Irishman [,] had reported to police that his wife had died from excessive drinking." The police went to investigate and found: "In one miserably furnished room Riley, his wife and four sons with the wife lying on the bed with evidence of considerable violence to her head and face." Riley had come home drunk and beaten and kicked her to death.[19] At Riley's first trial the jury failed to reach a verdict. At the second trial the defense suggested that the multiple head wounds and broken ribs might have come from a fall and that there was no proof that her death was a result of the beating and kicking she experienced on the night she died. The jury acquitted Riley.[20] Another man accused of beating his wife to death was described as "one of the most pitiable exhibitions of the depth of degradation man sinks to by indulgence in drink. But for the intelligence and some remnant of moral conscience displayed when he spoke, he might have been taken for a wild beast."[21]

Regional variations in verdicts and sentencing were striking in Ireland. Only 10 percent of persons tried for killing their wives in Munster were convicted of the full offense of murder. Sentencing patterns also varied considerably. Seventy percent of the men convicted of killing their wives in Munster served fewer than two years. In the other provinces only about a third of convicted wife killers received such light sentences. This is particularly surprising since the sentences in manslaughter cases were determined by the judges who worked on circuit, so the sentences given in Munster were being given by the same judges as those in the other provinces. The most likely explanation is the fact that in 49 percent of the Munster cases no weapon had been used— in Leinster and Connaught less than a quarter of the accused men had not used a weapon. This raises an interesting question. Either Munster husbands were twice as likely to kill their wives with their bare hands or the authorities in Munster were more willing to bring homicide charges in such cases than were their counterparts in other provinces.

Half of the trials for the killing of a wife in Scotland were heard in the southwest, and as with most sorts of violent crime in the area, the Irish were overrepresented. The conviction rate for Irish husbands accused of killing their wives in Scotland was 100 percent. Only one was convicted of murder, however, and nearly half of them were sentenced to two years or less. Irish immigrants accused of killing someone outside the immediate family were three times more likely to be executed than were native Scots. Presumably Scottish judges felt that the lives of Irish women were not particularly valuable. The coverage of a case in Glasgow in 1875 demonstrated a level of weary resignation to such barbarity in their midst. Under the headline "Alleged Wife Murder in Glasgow," the *Scotsman* reported, "[T]o the long list of murders resulting from assaults by husbands on their wives another case was added at Glasgow yesterday evening." About the couple, the newspaper said: "[T]hey are both of Irish extraction . . . both seem to have been greatly addicted to drink . . . it was difficult to say whether the man or the woman drank hardest. . . . They found the woman still lying in the close, none of the neighbors evidently having put themselves to the trouble to try any restorative means."[22]

A Private Matter

Relying on the police and the courts may have been the preferred course in Britain, but it was no guarantee that violence would end. When the neighbors of a Liverpool couple brought in a policeman, the wife asked that her husband be arrested. "The officer, hearing they were husband and wife, advised them to 'settle it' and himself went away whereupon the neighbor explained that it was 'a shame for a policeman to see a woman ill-used by a man in that way, with her face covered with blood and not take the man in charge.'" The woman died later that same evening.[23] In Glasgow when a witness reported that a neighbor was beating his wife with a hammer, the policeman replied that "it wasn't his beat."[24] In Northern Wales, the son of a woman who was being beaten by her husband went to the police station. The policeman said, "Something similar to what had occurred before I suppose?" When the policeman forced his way into the house, the abusive husband kicked him in the stomach at which point the policeman left even though the woman was lying unconscious on the floor. The woman died within hours. The policeman told the coroner's jury that the wife "had complained to police several times of her husband's abuse."[25]

Calling in the authorities could also be dangerous. At least six Englishmen killed their wives as a direct response to the wife bringing charges for assault.[26] One man told his wife when she signed a complaint against him, "You might as well sign your death warrant."[27] A woman in London lodged a complaint against her husband for assaulting her but "on the evidence of witnesses who said he was a peaceable man and was worried by the deceased, the summons was dismissed. The next phase of their married life seems to have been the murder of the deceased to which the prisoner has unreservedly confessed."[28]

Even in England the extent to which family violence was a public issue was subject to debate. In an attempted murder case in which the victim had testified that she was still willing to marry the attacker, Justice Bramwell told the jury, "The fact that the victim was willing to take him for better or for worse could not in the least benefit him for the trial was instituted on public grounds in order that other women might not be similarly ill-treated and injured."[29] On the other hand, the *Times* correspondent for the Home Counties reported that the only murder case at the Maidstone Assize was "one of those cases of beating and ill-usage of a wife, which are unhappily, so common among the lower classes. And it was not a case to excite any particular interest."[30]

Many people, including some magistrates and policemen, still saw domestic violence as a private matter. When a London magistrate heard the case of an eight-year-old boy who had been sent out to beg because his stepfather was in jail for beating his mother, he blamed the mother. "It was most disgraceful of the wife to publicly expose the fact that her husband had been imprisoned, particularly as she had been the cause of it. Most wives would have endeavored to keep the occurrence secret." Because of her "disgraceful" behavior the magistrate granted custody of the boy to the stepfather.[31] Disgrace as well as finances influenced the decision in an Edinburgh sheriff's court. The woman and her mother both testified that the husband had struck and kicked his wife and the man pled guilty. The sheriff said it was "much against his inclination not to pass sentence of imprisonment. But the wife appeared a most respectable person and to do so would be to punish her."[32] He released the man with a fine though the fact that the wife had brought charges suggests she was willing to see him imprisoned.

Irish courts were particularly sensitive to the gap between those things which might be outside the written law and those actions which were truly immoral. An Irish judge seemed to allude to this distinction when he remarked that wife beating "was not only criminal in the eyes of the law but lamentable in every way."[33] Irish judges were also willing to leave severe punishment to heaven in cases where a heavy sentence would create practical problems. When an Irish farmer whose wife died after a severe beating was found guilty, the presiding judge explained: "He had undoubtedly killed his wife. The poor woman only complained to the police when his misconduct became intolerable, and on the way home from the police barrack the prisoner kicked and beat her . . . upon his soul rested the guilt of that act." But whatever his moral guilt the man was sentenced to just nine months since the couple's two children needed at least one parent.[34]

Private citizens who intervened in domestic violence were liable to assault themselves. A Scottish minister testified that he had heard a woman screaming on the night a tinker murdered his wife. He explained that he thought the woman was merely tipsy and that he had not interfered because he was afraid of the tinker.[35] In an Irish courtroom a witness to the murder of a farmer's daughter explained that he had not interfered because "he thought it might be a struggle between a man and a woman of ill-fame, in which it would not be well for him to interfere."[36] A Norfolk jury acquitted a husband who had fatally stabbed a man who had rescued his wife from a beating.[37]

Even though interference was risky, in most domestic homicide cases it was the neighbors who finally sent for the police, and their testimony was usually vital in determining the trial outcome.[38] Sometimes they voiced their opinions before the trial. A man who killed his wife in Sheffield was "hooted by a mob as he was driven through the streets."[39] When charged with the attempted murder of his wife, Samuel Dickens explained that "my wife has always been very good to me and would lay down her life for me until neighbor women played the part of IAGO against me."[40] The comment is remarkable not only in the man's confidence that were it not for a cabal of women his wife would have gone on being "good" without protest, but the allusion to Shakespeare suggests that wife beaters were not always ignorant brutes.

Sometimes neighbors testified on behalf of the husband. When a Salford man was tried for murdering his wife, neighbors testified that they had looked after the children "during the neglect of their mother." The *Times* concluded that while the case demonstrated the "extreme misery of the home of a working man whose wife had given way to the habits of drunkenness . . . on the brighter side, it was an example of the unostentatious and unrecompensed kindness which are exhibited by the poorer classes in our larger towns to their neighbors in difficulty or distress."[41] But in another case "the woman was allowed to remain without medical assistance until the following day. This shows a state of mind among the lower order that is sufficiently ominous."[42]

British juries usually acquitted civilians who killed to stop a wife beating. One successful defense attorney argued that the "prisoner would have been unworthy of the name of man if he had not interposed to prevent a man killing his wife."[43] Similarly three young Welshmen who had beaten a neighbor to death were acquitted after the defense explained that "all the prisoners did was to interfere to prevent the deceased using violence towards his wife."[44]

WIFE BEATING AND WIFE KILLING

Knowing when to intervene was difficult since very few spousal homicides were premeditated. Most followed the pattern outlined by Justice Cleasby:

"drinking, drunkenness, violence, blows to a wife in a state of weakness, exhaustion and death."[45] In a report from Stafford the *Times* wrote: "This was another case of death occasioned by a blow from a man's fist. He was drunk and struck her on the head without provocation. She died the next day but at the time of the blow the occurrence seemed not to be sufficiently uncommon to call for any reply."[46] When husbands were tried for killing their wives, habitual abuse was reported in 55 percent of Scottish cases, 13 percent of English cases, 12 percent of Irish cases and 26 percent of Welsh cases though the actual incidence was probably much higher. A Liverpool man charged with killing his wife had thirty-one previous convictions for abusing her.[47] Everywhere when habitual abuse was established, the likelihood of conviction went up, a higher percentage of the convictions were for murder, and the sentences for manslaughter were longer.

Still, defense attorneys were eager to distinguish between murder and the "accidental" death that might follow a beating. In a case in which a man had kicked his pregnant wife in the stomach, the defense argued that "he had no intention to do her any harm . . . it could not be murder resulting from an act which he never could have intended as anything else than a gesture of command or intimidation."[48] A Manchester defense attorney contended that though his client had beaten his wife with a fire iron and then kicked her in the face five times as she lay dying, his only intention was to "give her a brutal beating and not to inflict grievous bodily harm in which case their verdict should be manslaughter only."[49] Even victims suggested that physical chastisement was sometimes acceptable. An Englishwoman who had been beaten to death by her husband said in a dying deposition: "He has beaten me before many a time. Sometimes I have given him cause; but he had no cause to beat me that night."[50] Justice Brett told a jury, "If the man was only brutally ill-using his wife without any intent to inflict serious injury and only doing what might or might not cause such injury, then it would be only manslaughter."[51] Despite the campaign against wife beating, fewer than 10 percent of the Englishmen tried for beating their wives to death were convicted of murder and a third of those convicted of manslaughter served fewer than two years.

Irish defense attorneys also suggested that chastising a wife was a right which had nothing to do with criminal homicide. When some Limerick men were prosecuted for assaulting their brother-in-law in retaliation for abusing their sister, the prosecuting attorney indignantly asking the jury, "Was this a way a man was to be treated in a free country and under a free form of government because he had beaten his wife?"[52] Patrick Butler of Galway told neighbors who tried to stop him beating his wife that "he married her, she was his wife and he could do what he liked with her."[53] Sixty-five percent of the Irish men convicted of beating their wives to death served fewer than two years. The attitude of many judges corresponded to that of the one who heard a case in which a physician testified that a woman had died of internal hemorrhage two hours after her husband beat and kicked her. He was convicted of manslaughter but the judge "considered that when he threw her down he had no intention of causing her death." Since the man had been in prison fourteen weeks awaiting trial, he sentenced him to just one additional week in prison.[54]

A Scottish defense attorney argued vehemently that wife beaters were a breed entirely apart from murderers: "Were the jury to be led to the ridiculous and absurd conclusion that because a man struck his wife once or twice, and called her once or twice a bad name, therefore he was a man who had that malice, who was so fiendish in his heart, as to entertain the idea of taking away that woman's life?"[55] Only one of the fifty-five Scotsmen accused of beating their wives to death was convicted of murder and his death sentence was commuted. A series of articles in the *Scotsman* suggested that violence against women might be understandable. "The criminal at the bar has often been goaded into his crime by provocations of domestic misery caused by his wife's faults." The editorial suggested that men who resorted to violence against wives who were drunks or scolds were not really criminal. "It is only after putting aside cases like these that the devilry of brutes given over to drink and all evil passions is reached."[56] Some letters to the editor echoed the sentiment: "[W]hat about the working man whose wife through acquired habits of drinking, has made herself fit to pawn his clothes so that he cannot appear respectably in public; or when he goes home to his meals she meets him with an empty dish and an evil tongue or perhaps with the weight of a chair?"[57]

CHASTISEMENT

The idealized gender roles of the mid-Victorians meant that both husbands and wives had very specific roles and duties. Men were meant to protect women. After sentencing a man to fourteen years for assaulting his wife, Justice Stephen said: "He had sworn to love, cherish and protect this woman, instead of which he had treated her like a slave and abused her in a most brutal manner."[58] An Irish judge complained, "[T]he wife was dependant on the husband, she had no other protection and when the husband neglects his duty and not only does so but flies into fits of uncontrolled passion against his wife, he must be prepared to meet the consequences of his guilt."[59] The Scottish judge Lord Young told a man convicted of killing his wife that it was a judge's duty "to protect innocent life and weak and feeble women from having their lives sacrificed by such ruffianly hands as yours."[60]

But what constituted "innocent life" and which husbands were ruffians were both still open to debate in the press and among the public. Though violence was by no means part of the Victorian ideal of domesticity, violence could easily erupt when either party failed in their duty. The notion of marriage as a contract in which both parties have specific duties and expectations is useful in understanding nineteenth-century domestic homicides. Most men who killed their wives were not driven by romantic passion or sexual jealousy but by frustration at not having their daily expectations met. The testimony in these cases deals far more often with wives failing to provide meals and keep the home comfortable than it does with infidelity or rejection.

Judges and jurors sometimes offered sympathy. In a case in which "a quiet, steady man" killed his "drunken, violent, jealous" wife after he came home to find her drunk and no supper prepared, neighbors testified that the victim had gone into the yard and said "she was ready to fight her husband like a man." When he threatened her with a poker, she dared him to throw it. He did and the poker penetrated her temple. Before sentencing him to fifteen years for manslaughter, Justice Coleridge "offered great sympathy."[61] John Crowe of Durham explained the circumstances in which he had fatally stabbed his wife:

> When I came home to dinner there was no dinner ready for me. She was drunk at the time. She took a knife to me. When I came home at night there still was no tea ready for me. I took the knife. I am sorry for it. It is a bad job. It can't be helped. I had better be dead than in such misery.

The jury found him guilty of manslaughter but recommended mercy. Justice Willes sentenced him to five years but apologized for disregarding the recommendation to mercy, saying that "to protect the lives of women under such circumstances he felt bound to pass a severe sentence."[62] Justice Willes's sentiments appear to have been shared by most of his colleagues. The average sentence for a husband convicted of manslaughter for killing a wife who was a bad housekeeper was just five months.

In Scotland judges were sympathetic toward frustrated husbands if not indulgent. Though none of the Scottish men who had killed a wife for poor housekeeping were convicted of murder, all were convicted of culpable homicide and the average sentence was eight years. Lord Deas told a man who had kicked his wife to death, "Your violence was called forth by very provoking circumstances. Your wife came home drunk and nothing was prepared for you in the house as you had every reason to expect."[63] The man was sentenced to five years, which the judge pointed out was the lowest possible term of penal servitude.

Only two men in Ireland and one in Wales cited poor housekeeping as a motive though the outcomes suggest it might have been a good defensive strategy. All three were convicted but none served more than nine months. In Tipperary John Croghan's neighbor heard him shouting, "What a nice house-keeper you are! I found a hen up the road!" and later heard sounds of violence. When the police arrived and found his wife dead from a head injury, Croghan said, "She is dead, I killed her, what about it?" He was sentenced to just four months.[64]

Gender roles involved more than housekeeping. Judges tried to stress that violence against women was unmanly. But some men cited the need to maintain their position as the "man of the house" as a motive for killing their wives. Robert Plampton, who had stabbed his wife for pawning a blanket, explained, "I always was a man. I don't deny it."[65] Edwin Davis explained that he had beaten his wife to death because "he would not be mastered by a woman."[66] Another man had met his wife in the street "and pulled off his coat to fight her like a man."[67] Often the unspoken corollary to the assumption that men were meant to protect women was the assumption that the women would be submissive. One English man who had killed his wife explained to the police that "she annoyed him and he paid her. He settled her because she would not do what he wanted. They had been happily married for forty-one years and if she had done what he told her he would not have killed her."[68]

In many quarters there were lingering doubts as to how often the husbands were really to blame. As the *Scotsman* insisted, "There are such creatures as bad wives and bad mothers—women who make their homes places of torture to the husband and misery to the children."[69] Protecting innocent women was one thing, protecting slatternly drunken scolds was something else, especially if the killer was a good man. While "goodness" and "badness" are highly subjective and the testimony in many trials was highly inconsistent, an analysis of those cases in which some consensus about the character of the killer and the victim seems to have been reached reveal some interesting differences.

English conviction rates were identical whether the victim was of good character or bad, however the likelihood of a *murder* conviction nearly doubled if the victim was shown to have been of good character. In the interest of public safety English judges and jurors were sometimes willing to return murder verdicts against good men with bad wives, though the strain was sometimes apparent. The Home Circuit correspondent for the *Times* wrote a heartrending account of "an honest, hard-working and industrious laborer" who was charged with murdering his wife. "The case was one of the most painful that have [*sic*] ever been heard in a court of justice." The couple had been happy until the wife's mother moved in with them, which began a "marked deterioration in the young wife's character and conduct. She became dirty, untidy, and unthrifty and neglected her household duties. She got her husband into debt and left the children in a dirty and untended state." Despite earning good wages, the husband came home from work one day "to find his little all seized for rent and he himself literally out of his house. It was too much for the unfortunate young man to bear." The couple walked off together and an hour later he returned and announced that he had killed her. The jury returned a murder verdict as instructed. However, while Justice Martin was pronouncing sentence of death, "he fairly broke down and burst into tears; and it was with the utmost difficulty that he could command his voice sufficiently to utter the concluding words, overcome as he was with emotions in which everyone in the court shared."[70] The sentence was commuted.

The Irish were also sympathetic toward men who killed "bad" wives. A case heard in Dublin in 1883 "disclosed a deplorable condition of domestic life among the working-classes." The accused, Edward Cowan, "was a man of exemplary character, respectably employed as the clerk of works at Trinity College: employment which only men of a superior class can obtain." But Cowan "had the misfortune to be linked for life to a drunken, ill-tempered, ill-tongued woman, whose habits were a constant cause of annoyance to him, which he bore with patience until the day of her violent death." He told his employer that "in a fit of anger he had flung the scissors at her." A neighbor described him "as one of the best of husbands, whom she had known to give wages to his wife, even when she was drunk." Though he was found guilty of manslaughter, the jury requested mercy.[71] Irish jurors, like their English counterparts, convicted in wife killings at the same rate regardless of the character of the accused and the victim. However, the average sentence for men who killed "bad" women like Mrs. Cowan was only half that of the overall average for Irish wife killers.

The Scots seem to have been keenly aware of the problem of "bad wives," especially those who spent their husband's wages on drink. Generally, in Scotland a woman's failure to meet the standards for a good wife—that is, obedience, housekeeping, and sobriety—was expected to mitigate the penalty for violence by the husband. When a laborer in Glasgow threw a paraffin

lamp at his wife during a drunken fight, the lamp ignited and burned the
woman to death. She had crawled under a bed to escape his blows and he
used the lamp to look for her and then threw it at her. He had made no
attempt to extinguish the fire or to rescue his wife. Nevertheless, after hearing evidence that the deceased "was hardly a pattern woman," the judge sentenced the man to only eighteen months, explaining that he preferred "to err
on the side of leniency and was assuming that he had picked up the lamp
with no intention of burning her. The lamp was simply the handiest object
to throw."[72] More than a third of the men tried for killing bad wives in
Scotland were not convicted at all. The average sentence given a Scotsman
who killed a good wife was twelve years, for a bad wife it fell to seven years.

VIOLENCE AND DRINK

Trials in which husbands killed wives in a fight in which both were partici-
pating were a challenge to the notion of men protecting "feeble women."
Englishmen who killed their wives in a fight during which both spouses used
violence were no less likely to be convicted than other wife killers, but sentences were lighter. Even a woman in the advanced stage of pregnancy could
be considered to blame for violence. George Osborne's wife was nine months
pregnant when he beat her to death. Nevertheless the coroner's jury indicted
only for manslaughter as he claimed that she hit him first. At the trial neighbors said that his wife had boasted to neighbors that in fights she "bested" her
husband. He told police that when he came home and dinner was not ready,
he said it ought to be and she "grinned at him and picked up a stick." He
admitted that during a scuffle he had kicked her, but said he "had done it in
a passion." Justice Denman told the jury that the crime was manslaughter if
the husband and wife "were evenly matched and he inflicted the injury in hot
blood." Her advanced pregnancy did not figure in the equation. He was
found guilty of manslaughter and sentenced to five years.[73]

Fighting was a regular part of life for some Welsh couples as well. David
Beddoes, a shoemaker, was tried for killing his wife, Annie, at Cardiff. They
were both drunk and quarreled when he refused to read the newspaper aloud.
When she threw his spectacles under the fire grate, he threw the poker at her,
which struck her in the throat. He was sentenced to six months.[74]

Irish courts treated fights between husbands and wives with the same tol-
erance they extended to brawls. A man in County Carlow explained:
"[M]yself and the old woman often had a row and I often beat her more than
I did yesterday evening. She fell inside the threshold and remained there. I

stepped over her about half past one and came back and stepped over her again and left her lying there. I did not think she was dead." Though the medical evidence was that she had not died from the fall, he was acquitted.[75] Eighty-two percent of Irishmen convicted of killing their wife in a fight served fewer than two years.

In Scotland men tried for killing their wives during fights were convicted and sentenced at the same level as other men tried for killing their wives. When a "respectable looking" engineer in Glasgow beat his wife to death during a fight on the day after Christmas, the judge pronounced his action inexcusable. "Anything more atrocious more cruel and unmanly could not well be conceived."[76] But domestic violence was still normal for some. When a Lanarkshire miner was accused of murdering his wife with a poker, their daughter testified that "it occurred to her it was just one of the usual little quarrels. . . . She did not think it would be serious."[77] The mother of one homicide victim testified that the accused "was a quiet, decent man who always brought home wages and never spent them. She struck him on the head first. He just pushed her on the bed and took her by the hair of the head and did her no hurt to cause her death."[78]

Provocation could be nothing more than irritating comments. The *Scotsman* warned of "scolds, who contrive to produce perpetual worry by the constant use of a bad tongue. The slatternly scold is often the terror of her neighbors and if her husband is a dull heavy fellow, his hands do for him what his head is unable to accomplish."[79] In Ireland and Scotland a man who killed a sharp-tongued wife was less likely to be acquitted but also less likely to be convicted of murder.

Irish and Scottish courts both convicted three-quarters of men who had killed their wives in a moment of anger. However, only 10 percent of Irishmen and only 7 percent of Scots who killed wives after being provoked were convicted of *murder*. But while the Scots and the Irish were both unlikely to see passionate killings as murders, the average sentence for a Scottish man convicted of culpable homicide for killing his wife in anger was two years longer than those given men who had not acted in a passion. On the other hand, the Irish courts took pity on those who lost their temper. The average sentence of an Irishman convicted of killing his wife when provoked was three years fewer than that of other Irish husbands convicted of manslaughter.

English courts were less willing to accept verbal provocation as a justification. Justice Bovill told a jury: "There was scarcely any grounds for suggesting that language, however provoking or long continued would justify taking a life."[80] In a case in which a man had kicked his wife to death after a quarrel, the *Times* reporter complained: "We are sorry to say that the Jury found this ruffian guilty only of manslaughter on the ground, it would seem that the hasty expressions of a bruised and bleeding wife are some excuse for a husband killing her outright."[81] An angry judge told a defendant who had killed his wife for nagging him, "The evidence had shown him to be a drunken, cruel and profligate husband, which justified the many angry reproaches of his wife."[82] English men who killed their wives in response to mere words were more likely to be convicted and 41 percent of those convicted were sentenced to death, though their sentences were more than twice as likely to be commuted as those of other condemned wife killers.

The culpability of a drunken woman or a drunken husband was also subject to debate. The English were keenly aware of the role of alcohol in domestic violence. the husband, the wife, or both had been intoxicated in at least a third of the wife killings that came to trial. In half of those cases both parties were drunk. *The Pall Mall Gazette* noted wryly that "[n]o greater provocation can present itself to an intoxicated man than the discovery that his wife is intoxicated also."[83] When only one of the partners had been intoxicated, the reactions were very different. In England the average sentence given a sober man convicted of killing a drunken wife was three years fewer than the overall average for wife killers and seven years fewer than the average sentence given a man convicted of manslaughter for killing his wife when he had been drunk and she was sober. The rhetoric sometimes clashed with the sentencing. Justice Lopes told a man who had beaten his drunken wife to death that "he could not give effect to recommendation to mercy from the jury as it must not be supposed that a man might ill-treat his wife because she was a drunkard." But the sentence was only twelve months.[84]

Nor were English judges impressed with insanity pleas on behalf of drunken husbands. When a defense attorney tried to argue that his client had been in a state of drunken insanity when he beat his wife's head in with a hammer and then cut her throat, Justice Hawkins said that "all that they showed was that the prisoner was passionate, quarrelsome and ill-tempered and moreover that he was given to drinking."[85] Like nearly 50 percent of English men who had been drunk when they killed a sober wife, the man was convicted of murder and sentenced to death.

Though Irish judges gave the same sentences regardless of whether either party had been intoxicated, Irish jurors were much more likely to blame the drink rather than the drinker. They were also likely to see drunken women as more in need of protection than sober ones. Sober men who killed drunken wives were almost twice as likely to be convicted as drunken men who killed sober wives—a reversal of the English situation. Thirty percent of Irishmen who had killed their wives while intoxicated were found insane.

In more than 78 percent of Scottish spousal homicide trials either the killer or victim or both were drunk. This was much higher than the reported incidence in England, Wales, and Ireland but may simply indicate that the Scots were more scrupulous as record keepers and more appalled by drunken women.[86] According to the *Scotsman,* "Nobody who has not actually seen it will believe the perfectly reckless and insatiate craving which a woman exhibits for liquor who has once abandoned herself to it. Her husband is only too likely, in some moment of sudden exasperation over his wife's misconduct, to be led into acts of violence."[87] A Glasgow jury was highly sympathetic towards a commercial traveler who was sober when he killed his drunken wife. Even though a physician testified that she died from a series of violent blows, the defense attorney's summation was met with cheers and the jury voted unanimously to acquit. Lord Deas, the presiding judge, cleared the courtroom and rebuked the jury that "no man was entitled to murder his wife because she was drunk; on the contrary he was bound to exercise all possible care in watching over her." But the verdict stood.[88] Only one Scotsman was convicted of killing a drunken wife when he had been sober.

Even when the husband had also been intoxicated, a bad woman might be blamed. In a well-publicized case, John Young, a coal merchant who been married to "a notorious drunkard" for twenty-five years, was tried for killing his wife. He had "tried to wean her but she went from bad to worse, neglected her family and sold everything of her husband's property to buy drink." One day he found her in "a small dark room in a house of bad moral reputation in company of a man who was the prisoner's own servant." Young, who "was naturally irritated," proceeded to beat his wife to death. Young had plenty of character witnesses; however, the prosecution pointed out that he had also been intoxicated and that he had beaten his wife about the head and face for twenty minutes.

The presiding judge sympathized with the prisoner. "She was in such a place being frequented by a woman would naturally arouse the wrath of her husband and almost to deprive him for the moment of reason and that you should have struck her in those circumstances is not really greatly to be wondered at." As was usually the case in a Scottish courtroom some atonement was required but it was heavily tempered with mercy. "You did give way to passion . . . therefore you must suffer punishment although the punishment which you have suffered at her hands and must have suffered since her death is greater." He was sentenced to six months.[89] The case was influenced not only by the disgraceful conduct of the wife but also by the highly respectable status of her husband even though he had also been drunk at the time.

In a precedent-setting case in 1867, Lord Deas heard the case of Alexander

Dingwall, a well-connected man who had retired from the Indian navy. Dingwall and his wife were both "of dissipated habits" and though his estate had an income of nearly £600 a year, neither of them were allowed to handle money. On New Year's Eve, Dingwall had gone out and in the spirit of the holiday was able to obtain alcohol. The landlord heard screams and when he reached their rooms, Dingwall announced quite calmly: "I have murdered Mrs. Dingwall." When the police came, Dingwall told them he had been provoked because his wife had hidden the whiskey bottle and laughed when he asked for it. Since there was no question he had killed her, his defense rested on the issue of insanity. In his charge to the jury Lord Deas argued that Dingwall could not be found insane; however, his intoxicated state could be an indication of diminished responsibility. Dingwall was convicted of culpable homicide and sentenced to ten years. The case is cited for establishing that drink might legally be considered as a factor in reducing murder to culpable homicide.[90] But in Scotland diminished responsibility seemed to be available primarily to the well-connected. Despite the Dingwall precedent, men in Scotland who had been drunk when they killed their wives were more than three times more likely to be convicted of *murder* than those who had been sober. However, as the Dingwall case also illustrates, the social status of the accused was an important factor in determining trial outcomes.

The social status of the victim could also be critical. The role of class distinctions in English cases was particularly evident in cases of neglect. Throughout the United Kingdom killing a sick wife was usually punished much less severely than killing a healthy one, presumably because the death was less likely to have been intentional. An Englishman convicted of killing a sick wife was more than two and a half times more likely to serve fewer than two years than a man whose wife had been healthy. Charles Brett's wife died of broken ribs from a beating, but since she had been terminally ill with consumption and "in consideration of his abstaining from using the stick," he was sentenced to only four months for manslaughter.[91] When John Royle's wife died of peritonitis five days after a brutal beating, Justice Huddleston said he was "perfectly satisfied that it was by the prisoner's violence that the unhappy woman came to the death and the medical evidence certainly did not agree with the suggestion that the death was the result of disease. When violence of that description had taken place the least he could do was sentence the prisoner to six months hard labor."[92]

Scotsmen accused of killing ill wives were no less likely to be convicted than those whose victims had been healthy, but judges were far more lenient in sentencing. Two-thirds of the men convicted of killing an ill wife in Scotland were sentenced to fewer than two years. The light sentences are in part a reflection of the fact that when the victim was in ill health, the courts often gave the accused the option of pleading guilty to assault since the cause of death might be in doubt. In fact, judges seemed to think this was a right. A Glasgow man whose wife had died of asphyxia while her husband held her by the throat was initially charged with murder. But the defense argued that she had been subject to fits, which might cause asphyxia. He was found guilty of assault and the judge ordered him released immediately as he had spent three months in prison awaiting trial and the "charge ought not to have been brought as murder."[93]

LADIES

However, in England simply failing to provide proper care for a lady was punished far more severely than beating a sick working-class woman to death. That ladies deserved special care was demonstrated in the case of Harriet Staunton, an heiress who had married against her family's wishes and had starved to death in an isolated farmhouse. Though no restraints had been used, her husband, his mistress, and the husband's brother and sister-in-law who had lived in the house with Harriet were all charged with murder.

Justice Hawkins left little doubt as to his preferred verdict. According to the *Times:* "[T]he concluding part of the narrative he gave with great pathos and feeling to which the crowded court listened with intense interest." Hawkins stressed the motive rather than the issue of legal responsibility. Most of his charge to the jury was devoted to the illicit connection between the husband and Alice Rhodes. "The wife gone, the husband would have made Alice Rhodes his lawful wife and her offspring his legitimate child. This, he said, might be a motive for a most atrocious murder. . . . [T]he learned Judge also alluded to the cold, hard-hearted indifference with which all witnessed the poor woman lingering to death." The jury found all four of the defendants guilty of murder though they recommended mercy for the women. Clearly pleased with the verdict, Justice Hawkins told the convicted murderers: "[Y]ou have been found guilty of a crime so black and hideous that I believe in all the records of crime it would be difficult to find its parallel. With a barbarity almost incredible you plotted together to take away by cruel torture the life of a poor innocent, helpless and outraged woman."[94]

However, the verdict inspired a good deal of unease. The *Times* showed no sympathy for the Stauntons but noted "in the actual process of doing Harriet Staunton to death Alice Rhodes had hardly any participation . . . the jury was influenced by supposed strength of interest she had in the death." In other

words, if Alice Rhodes was Louis Staunton's motive for killing his wife, she
was guilty of murder—a highly dubious legal position. Six hundred medical
men signed petitions to have the verdict overturned and the *Lancet* insisted
that the crime was at worse merely criminal neglect. The Home Office commuted the sentences of the Stauntons to life in prison and Alice Rhodes was
given a free pardon. The *Times* concluded that the jury (and by implication
the judge) had been unduly influenced by the wish to punish immorality.[95]

Even after the death sentences were commuted, the question remained as
to why the in-laws bore legal responsibility for her death. The sentences stood
in stark contrast to cases in which the victim had not been an heiress. When
Thomas Gillett, a man who "had money in the bank," was convicted of
allowing his paralytic wife to starve to death, Justice Hawkins sentenced him
to three months for manslaughter.[96] In a case in which the bedridden wife of
a laborer had died of starvation, Justice Grove said there was no case to go to
the jury as no restraint had been used. Presumably it was not her husband's
fault she was bedridden.[97]

Two and a half years after the Staunton case, James Louis Paine, a fifty-
year-old commercial traveler, described by the prosecution as a man "of
depraved habits and unscrupulous character," was charged with the murder
of his wife, Annie Jane Fanny McLean Paine. Like Harriet Staunton the victim was a "lady"—the daughter of a lieutenant colonel. Annie McLean Paine
had died of liver disease brought on by alcohol poisoning. The charge of
murder was brought against her husband on the grounds that "if he had
taken proper care of the lady in his charge, he would not have allowed her to
have such a large quantity of drink." Given that working-class men who
actively killed drunken wives usually received the sympathy of the courts, it
was remarkable that Paine was held legally responsible for failing to stop his
wife's drinking. The prosecution argued: "It was prisoner's duty having her
under his protection to defend her against herself. . . . If he did not administer the spirits himself but abstained from preventing her from having spirits,
knowing that the result would be her death then he was guilty of murder."[98]

Like Louis Staunton, Paine's greatest sins of commission were greed and
adultery. Before her death Annie had signed her entire fortune over to Paine,
who was having an affair with her nineteen-year-old maidservant. Paine's
defense attorney admitted that his client was a scoundrel but argued that did
not make him a murderer. The victim had asked for alcohol and had often
refused food. The evidence showed that Annie McLean had a drinking problem before she met Paine and that they both drank to excess. Shortly before
her death Paine had brought her to London for medical advice. There was
contradicting evidence on whether Paine had continued to give her alcohol,

but the innkeeper testified that Paine had told him, "if anything was given to her it must be some milk."

Nevertheless, in his charge to the jury Justice Hawkins left no doubt about Paine's guilt. "If he allowed her to commit acts which would produce death, with the intent that she should die, that would be murder; and if he simply allowed such acts recklessly and negligently without intending her death, that would be manslaughter. It is for you to say by your verdict to which of these offenses you consider the prisoner guilty." The jury found Paine guilty of manslaughter. It appears that in Hawkins's view Paine's worst crime did not involve alcohol. "You took her in her miserable plight, unable to move and unable to speak to a lodging-house in Seymour-place—respectable enough I know but at the same time it is not the place in which the daughter of Colonel MacLean should have been placed. . . . You left her alone. . . . I cannot dwell with moderation upon your inhuman conduct." The innkeeper said that after ordering that Annie only be given milk, Paine had looked at his drunken wife and said that "it was a sin to preserve such a life." This comment had been the last straw for Justice Hawkins: "I can conceive of nothing more atrocious than the exclamation you made on the last morning on which the poor creature saw the light of day. . . . You have, in my judgment been guilty of a crime next in enormity to the crime of murder." He sentenced Paine to life in prison.[99]

The *Times* also argued that the victim's status as a lady worsened the crime:

> Criminals of the sordid stamp of Paine are common and are quickly forgotten. But the memory of the poor cripple who had lived among gentlefolk falling into the clutches of a ruffian whom she loved, being dragged from one depth of misery to another and finally dying among strangers in a lucid moment of a drunken stupor will haunt for some time those who had read the reports of the trial.

Annie Paine was not like other victims: "The tragedies of great cities of which this is the latest, have rarely any mystical or poetic elements. Their ghastly vulgar details are usually but the foul exhalations from underlying corruption and squalor." However, Paine's death was memorable for its emotional resonance. "A story such as this has its own vein of pathos, and the spectacle of this poor deformed creature, clinging half in terror, half in love, to her deceiver and destroyer and somewhat trustful to the last, will touch those who might be unmoved by grander and more imposing sorrow." In fact, the *Times* implied that Annie Paine was no more responsible for her condition than a sick child. Paine was guilty because "it is clear that he took no pain to prevent her drinking to excess. It was a duty which the law imposes whenever any one assumes the control of one who is dependent and helpless—an obligation of an ill-defined character created for the protection of the weak who are at the mercy of the strong."[100]

Whether such a duty existed in the case of competent adults seemed largely to depend on the relative status of the victim and her protector. Drunken neglect on the part of a husband was only a crime when the wife was an heiress. Six months after Paine was sentenced to life in prison, Justice Hawkins heard the case of a baker whose wife had accidentally set herself on fire when she knocked over a lamp. During the twenty-four hours she lay dying of severe burns, her husband never sent for medical aid or did anything to help her. His defense attorney successfully argued that he had no duty to provide medical care.[101] In another case a drunk man had refused to send for medical aid or allow neighbors to help when his wife went into labor. Instead he had grabbed his wife by the throat and demanded whiskey. When she died he was charged with manslaughter, but Justice Stephen said that while there was "no doubt the prisoner's conduct was very dreadful, to convict him of causing his wife's death it must be far more serious. Supposing any drunken husband were charged with such offenses it would be carrying the criminal law too far." The jury returned a directed verdict of not guilty.[102]

It was also significant that Paine and Staunton were guilty of marrying above their class in order to enrich themselves. The situation was slightly more complicated when a respectable Englishman killed his equally respectable wife. In 1891, Justice Hawkins heard a case in which a wealthy man, Charles Wood, and his daughter were charged with the manslaughter of his wife. Medical experts testified that the woman had died of exhaustion from chronic alcoholism and want of food and her death had been accelerated by violence. Witnesses testified that Wood had dragged her home and tied her up. Though he was clearly guilty of greater violence than Paine, Justice Hawkins directed the jury to acquit.[103]

That respectable men were not brutal to their wives would seem to be a given, yet the idea that the death of a respectable middle-class lady should go unpunished was also a problem. One obvious solution was to find that middle-class wife killers were not responsible for their actions. In England middle-class men accused of killing their wives were more than twice as likely to be found insane, and even when juries convicted, the Home Office might intervene. In 1871 John Selby Watson, a sixty-seven-year-old former Latin teacher and headmaster, murdered his wife. In the initial report of the crime the *Times* described him as a "man of great learning and classical talents." The report implied that the victim must be to blame: "Those who are acquainted with the deceased lady concur in saying that she had a bad temper. . . . It is quite evident that a quarrel must have suddenly arisen in which probably some observation was made by the deceased, which goaded her husband to madness."[104]

But bad-tempered or not, she was a lady, as Watson himself admitted in a note he wrote before a botched suicide attempt: "I hope she will be buried as becomes a lady of birth and position. She is an Irish lady and her name is Anne." In the note Watson also explained that "often and often she provoked me, and I have endeavored to restrain myself but rage overcame me and I struck her." In fact, he had struck her six times in the head with the butt of his pistol. He had then locked her body in the library and told a servant that the bloodstains were from spilling port wine. Her body was not discovered until the day after the murder.[105]

Watson's status insured that the "trial excited much interest." The Lord Mayor, several aldermen, and the sheriff attended. Even the prosecution described Watson as "a man of education and culture." However, as the trial progressed, his status seemed to diminish. In the initial report the *Times* had described Watson as the author of five books; now the newspaper pointed out that all but one of the works had been self-published. One physician offered as evidence of insanity the fact that Watson "said he was entitled to some consideration for what he had done in the past. That seemed to the witness to be extremely irrational seeing that he had only been a schoolmaster."[106]

The defense argued for insanity, suggesting that "the nature of the crime, its atrocity and ghastly details went to establish insanity." The prisoner, his attorney claimed, was a victim of "the demon of depression."[107] The jury found Watson guilty of murder though they recommended mercy "on account of his advanced age and previous good character." In pronouncing the death sentence, Justice Byles told Watson: "Nobody who heard this trial can regard your case otherwise than with the deepest compassion."[108] Within days the grand jurors and a number of medical men were complaining about the verdict. Two weeks later Watson's death sentence was commuted on the grounds of insanity.

The commutation prompted the *Spectator* to muse on the significance of class in court: "No one can help feeling a certain amount of pity for Mr. Watson; but we have a nervous feeling that a very different measure of justice has been dealt out to him and to certain criminals of a lower class, whose reprieves have been steadfastly, we do not say unjustly, refused." The suspicions were well-founded and the working classes were increasingly well-informed. Three years later when a boot maker was convicted of murdering his sweetheart, he told the judge that "if he was to be sentenced to death then the law had been unequally administered in the case, among others of the Rev. Mr. Watson for the murder of his wife." Though his point was valid, the man was executed.[109]

The *Spectator* also complained about the public reaction to Watson's case: "The correspondence produced by Mr. Watson's case and the sickly sympathy expressed for him, have not been creditable to English moral feeling. A former headmaster of Stockwell Grammar school calls him 'the unhappy and ill-used Mr. Watson' [he does not refer to the unhappy and ill-used Mrs. Watson]."[110] The *Spectator's* position was closer to that found in Irish courts where middle-class men who killed their wives were more likely to be convicted and executed than working-class wife killers. In keeping with the claim that the Irish were particularly chivalrous, judges often insisted that the code of Irish masculinity made assaulting women unthinkable and the more comfortable the man's social and economic position the more heinous the offense. After prosecuting a man accused of habitual wife beating, the attorney noted that "the defendant being a respectable man I would ask you to inflict the severest penalty on him."[111]

The contempt shown toward upper-class Irishmen who abused their wives was demonstrated in County Cork in 1887. Dr. Phillip Henry Eustace Cross, a "gentleman of means," was accused of poisoning his wife. The Crosses and their five children "lived in a comfortable position, receiving and visiting the surrounding gentry." However, in the autumn of 1886, a young governess at a neighboring estate caught Dr. Cross's eye. By the spring of 1887, the two of them were checking into Dublin hotels as husband and wife and Mrs. Cross was beginning to show "the well known symptoms of chronic arsenic poisoning," though her husband insisted it was heart disease. When his wife died in early June, Cross had her buried immediately, signed a death certificate saying the cause of death was typhoid fever, and married the young governess a few days later. His haste prompted questions that led to the exhumation of the body and the discovery that the first Mrs. Cross had been poisoned with both arsenic and strychnine.[112]

The prosecuting attorney told the special jury, which had been assembled to guarantee Cross a trial by his peers, that the case was unprecedented in Ireland: "[A] husband murdering his wife in his own house in order to fly back to a woman whom he had seduced, and to place her in the position of the wife who had been poisoned." Cross's defense attorney attempted to use his unseemly behavior as evidence of innocence. Cross's quick remarriage, while indefensible from "a moral or delicate point of view was the thing above all others a criminal would have avoided."[113]

While both attorneys were making the arguments that might be expected in such cases, the presiding judge, James Murphy, a Protestant (as was Cross), made it clear in his charge to the jury that he had no sympathy for the accused. Justice Murphy seemed to be most offended by the lack of respect:

> Was it right to leave the mistress of the house to the casual attendance of servants who were up or down or in or out as they liked? It had been said and rightly that they were not trying the prisoner for neglect or disregard of his wife during her illness. No; they were not; but they were bound to see whether or not Christian acts were omitted from disregard or from dislike.

According to Murphy, Cross's very emotions were to be considered: "If he was not a loving husband he had no right to be there: foul adultery, heartless and callous indifference on the occasion of her death, that after the very scant funeral rites were performed he left to join that creature again, he hurried with wicked speed to replace the faithful wife then in her grave—all this had been proved without doubt." The judge's charge was more damning than the prosecution's summation:

> Was there an anxiety to get rid of Mary Laura Cross? Was there a substitute provided? That a substitute was so provided had been proved; that a cause existed no question of doubt could be raised. Let them ask themselves these questions and ask themselves whether deceased was done to death by poison. If they believed she was, then they must find the prisoner guilty.

They did so and Murphy sentenced him to death. It was the status of the victim rather than the social status of the accused which weighed most heavily with Justice Murphy. While much of the treatment Laura Cross received was probably far superior to that experienced by most wives, Justice Murphy was clearly bent on avenging the loss of her rights as a lady. Nor was his reaction unique to his class. "When the prisoner was being removed from the court-house to the gaol he was hooted by the assembled crowd."[114]

While English and Irish juries were willing to avenge the deaths of ladies, no native Scot of the middle class or above was convicted of murdering his wife during the period. Sometimes Scottish juries went to extraordinary lengths to avoid doing so. One of the most remarkable cases involved a locked-room mystery. John Lang, "a respectable well-to-do farmer," and his wife had retired to their bedroom one night with the door and windows locked. The next morning the wife was discovered to have been brutally mutilated. In that only the farmer and his wife had been in the room and physicians determined her wounds could not have been self-inflicted, the husband was certainly the obvious suspect. Two knives were found on his person when the body was discovered and his clothes were spattered with his wife's blood. He told police he did not remember what had happened but added, "I did not attack and assault my wife to my knowledge." The *Scotsman* noted that "the Langs were hitherto considered a respectable family and the occurrence has caused great consternation among the quiet villagers where no crime approaching the present atrocity was ever committed."[115]

The crime was a particularly grisly one. According to the medical report, "all the pieces of intestines were cut off by an instrument of moderate sharpness."[116] The woman lingered in considerable agony for a week, all the time insisting that her husband had "always been very kind to her." The prosecution insisted that the fact that the victim had not wanted her husband blamed was not reliable: "[T]hey must remember that she was the mother of a family, whose good name would be gone if their father was branded as a murderer. He could not think it improbable or unnatural that suffering, mutilated, dying as she was she should have endeavored to screen from the consequences of his guilty act this unhappy man." Further, there was no other logical explanation for the crime. "It was impossible from the circumstances that the injuries could have been self-inflicted." The defense attorney presented a number of character witnesses and argued that the couple had long been happily married and there was therefore no motive. Suggesting that the woman's death was destined to always be a mystery, he reminded the jury of their obligation to give the accused the benefit of the doubt and he asked for a verdict of not proven—"a verdict wherein justice and mercy would embrace each other." The judge said that it was hard to understand why the accused could not explain what happened, but a man of good character deserved the benefit of the doubt. After a ten-minute deliberation the jury returned a unanimous verdict of "not proven." The verdict was a popular one. "On leaving the court the public outside gave the accused another hearty cheer."[117]

Even more than by social status, Scottish courts were influenced by xenophobia. In Scotland 23 percent of the men tried for killing their wives were non-Scots. Half of the men who were executed for killing their wives were of foreign birth. Two very similar cases from Edinburgh demonstrated the prejudices. In 1878 Eugene Chantrelle, a Frenchman who taught at a girls' school in Edinburgh, was accused of murdering his wife. She had been his seventeen-year-old student when they married and had given birth to their first child two months after the wedding. After several years of a very unhappy marriage, Mrs. Chantrelle had died of severe gastric distress that the prosecution claimed was the result of opium poisoning. In addition to the murder charge, Chantrelle was indicted for "having evinced towards her malice and ill-will, with having falsely accused her of monstrous immoralities and with having threatened to shoot and to poison her."[118] One hundred and ninety-eight pieces of evidence were offered and the prosecution produced one hundred and fifteen witnesses. The most significant was arguably an insurance company executive who testified that the defendant had purchased a £1000 life insurance policy on his wife, the first the company had ever issued on a married woman. Most of the other witnesses testified to Chantrelle's infidelities, coldness, and general hostility toward his wife.[119]

While the prosecution clearly established that Chantrelle was not much of a husband, the only physical evidence directly linking Chantrelle to his wife's death was the fact that opium had been found on her pillowcase several days after her death. No poison was found in her body. Chantrelle argued, plausibly, that the opium had been planted to implicate him after his wife died from natural causes. During the summing up the defense attorney once again tried to distinguish between Chantrelle's shortcomings as a husband and the accusation of murder: "Was it not as ridiculous an inference as could possibly be fancied that because a man was unfaithful to his wife and frequented bad company that they were to come to the conclusion that he was guilty of a murderous intention? Was the suggestion reasonable, was it manly, was it fair?"

Perhaps the appeal to fair play was a sign of desperation because the judge was clearly on the side of the prosecution. In his charge to the jury the judge argued that Chantrelle's prior behavior was indeed relevant.

> Not that a man that lived on bad terms with his wife, or a man that lived a loose life, was likely on that account to kill her, but that where all domestic affection had apparently been rooted out, or at least had been so largely impaired—the accused was in a different position from one that had been always affectionate with his wife and gave her no cause of complaint.[120]

He directed the jury to "give the prisoner the benefit of every reasonable doubt that had been suggested but on the other hand if they had no doubt they would do their duty." After deliberating for an hour the jury returned a unanimous guilty verdict. Chantrelle was sentenced to death.[121]

In a report of Chantrelle's execution, the *Scotsman* outlined the unique features of the case. "A man widely known in the city as an accomplished teacher, and who in social life had come much into contact with not the least influential . . . Chantrelle's case is the only one in which a man of education has been executed in Edinburgh during the last fifty years for a crime committed in the city." In the same editorial the newspaper compared Chantrelle's case to a wife murder in Paris.[122]

The French connection appears to have been crucial as evidenced by a very similar case heard a few years later in which the accused was a respectable Scot. In the summer of 1890 John Webster, an innkeeper, was accused of poisoning his wife. Unlike Mrs. Chantrelle, whose body contained no remnants of poison, the body of Mrs. Webster was full of arsenic. There was no question about the cause of death, though Webster had told his in-laws that his wife died from cholera. Like Chantrelle, Webster had purchased a £1000 insurance policy on his wife. There was also evidence of marital discord. The victim's sister testified that she had heard Webster threaten to blow his wife's brains out. Shortly before the trial, an employee from the inn who was to have been a key prosecution witness committed suicide to avoid testifying.[123] At the Chantrelle trial much had been made of the fact that Chantrelle had taken his meals away from his wife and children, in what was referred to as "the French manner," yet testimony revealed that Webster had also taken his meals away from home and that, like Chantrelle, he slept in a different bedroom from his wife.

Webster's defense initially relied largely on character witnesses. A former employer testified that "he always found him most trustworthy and satisfactory, gave him a high character for straightforwardness, attention to business and strict soberness and honesty." Another neighbor said he had always found Webster "a very straightforward, persevering and hard-working man." But the crucial argument was the suggestion that "the deceased had been suffering from an unpleasant internal affliction for which arsenic was a frequently employed remedy." Though neither husband nor wife seemed particularly sympathetic, once the defense had been able to raise the possibility of Mrs. Webster having had a venereal disease, her status as a victim plummeted. "The jury were absent only for about ten minutes and returned a unanimous verdict of not guilty. The verdict was received with loud cheers, which the officers of the Court endeavored without effect to silence. Webster was then liberated, and on leaving the Court he was cordially congratulated by relatives and friends."[124] Despite Mrs. Webster's "internal affliction," the case against Chantrelle had been weaker than that against Webster. The actual cause of death was better established in the Webster case. Nevertheless the two juries reached unanimous and opposing verdicts. The immoral Frenchman was guilty; the "straight-forward, hard-working" Scot was not.

The Scots were not alone in their suspicions of foreigners. Every European who was tried for killing his wife in England was convicted and half of them were executed.

INFIDELITY

The rejection of European morals could also be seen in cases involving adultery, which was cited as a motive in the United Kingdom far less frequently than more mundane irritations. The *Times* noted with some surprise that of twelve spousal murders in 1872 "in only three of the cases does infidelity or the suspicion of it appear to have come into play."[125] Husbands tried for killing their wives cited jealousy or suspicion of infidelity as their motive in only 15 percent of English cases, 13 percent of Irish cases, and 10 percent of Scottish cases.

One of the classic definitions of the distinction between murder and manslaughter is the notion that finding one's wife with another man would reduce homicide to manslaughter since the passion involved would mitigate the circumstances. But men who counted on this provision were often disappointed. English men who killed their wives out of jealousy were more than twice as likely to be convicted of murder as other men who had killed their wives. In defending a man who had killed the woman he lived with when she returned from London with another man, an attorney referred to "old theory of our law that if a man found his wife in the act of adultery with another man, he was justified in killing the adulterers on the spot." Justice Byles interrupted to ask, "Where is that to be found?" The lawyer replied that he had always thought it was so. Justice Byles said, "No, if he is not guilty of murder, he is not guilty of anything. You said he was 'justified' or I should not have interfered with so startling a proposition." Somewhat chastened, the attorney explained that he meant to say "that it was not murder, though it might be homicide, for which a day's imprisonment might satisfy the requirements of the law." Justice Byles told the jury it was his duty to tell them uncontrollable passion "was no defense, nor was it so far a defense that could mitigate the crime to manslaughter; for unprotected, indeed should we be if a man might take the lives of any of us and say it was done under an uncontrollable fit of passion." He had not caught them in the act and there was no proof of infidelity. "The question for the jury was narrowed to the issue: Did the prisoner kill the woman? If he did it was a case of murder if he did not he should be acquitted there was no middle ground."[126] The man was convicted and executed.

Even when the jealousy was based on solid evidence, there was no guarantee of sympathy. In English cases where the victim had clearly been guilty of infidelity, the conviction rate was 95 percent and 42 percent of the men were convicted of murder. When the situation was more ambiguous as to the wife's conduct, the conviction rate for murder rose to 66 percent and the number of sentences fewer than two years fell to 13 percent. But when the jealousy was clearly unfounded, the overall conviction rates actually fell since nearly 20 percent of the men who killed wives out of jealousy for which there was clearly no basis were ruled insane. But if convicted, in 70 percent of these cases the jury convicted for murder with the mandatory death sentence.

In England men who killed their wives for being sexually unfaithful were more likely to be convicted of murder than men who killed their wives for failing to have supper ready. The severe penalties partially reflect the fact that husbands who killed out of jealousy were nearly 40 percent more likely to use a lethal weapon than husbands acting from other motives. But even correcting for differences in method, jealous husbands who used lethal weapons were nearly 20 percent more likely to be convicted of murder than husbands with other motives who used lethal weapons. Husbands who beat their wives to death out of jealousy were nearly 60 percent more likely to be convicted of murder than husbands who beat their wives to death for other reasons.

Scotsmen who killed out of jealousy were more than twice as likely to be found guilty of murder as husbands who killed for other motives, and they received heavier sentences when convicted of manslaughter. In 1880 William Alexander, a laborer in Greenock, entered a neighbor's apartment to find his wife passed out drunk on a bed with a seaman standing by the bed. Furious, Alexander began beating his wife. When the sailor tried to intervene, Alexander threw him down the stairs. The judge pronounced it the "most unprovoked assault he had ever seen" and sentenced Alexander to ten years.[127]

Over half of the Irishmen who killed their wives over jealousy that was unfounded were found insane. But Irishmen who killed a wife over jealousy for which there may have been some basis were convicted at about the same rates as other men who killed their wives, but their sentences tended to be heavier. Deaths in brawls over minor insults or wheels may have been tolerated but not when the issue was sexual jealousy. A man who returned to Ireland after two years in England and found his wife had an infant angrily demanded to know who the father was. When his wife refused to tell him, he stabbed her. At his trial the judge ruled that the paternity of the child was irrelevant to his defense.[128]

Four Welsh husbands were tried for killing a wife out of jealousy. Three were convicted of murder; the fourth was sentenced to twenty years. In one case the killer told police: "A man next door kept looking through a hole in the wall and making faces at my wife. I have cautioned her about it often, and she knew my temper well." But there was no hole in the wall and doctors determined that the man was suffering from delirium tremens. Even though he was clearly delusional, the jury convicted him of murder. When the death sentence was commuted, it "was a surprise since the murder was atrocious and little or no sympathy has been expressed in favor of the murderer."[129]

Part of the reason for the official lack of sympathy for husbands who killed out of jealousy was the fact that such crimes were linked with Europeans. The *Scotsman* reported that "[a] Paris banker has been fatally stabbed by his wife under circumstances of a peculiarly French Character. She found out her husband had spent the night with his mistress [;] went to place where they were staying and stabbed him."[130] Britons were expected to have better self-control. Justice Field said that "he hoped it would be long before English juries adopted a system, which he believed was largely prevalent in some other countries of appending to their verdict a recommendation to mercy on the mere suggestion of infidelity unsupported by evidence."[131] In 1878 the *Times* devoted a column and a half to "A Roman Murder" in which an Italian had murdered his wife out of jealousy. The *Times* explained, "[T]here is this difference in the final treatment of these cases, that while in England the law as it stands is sure to be carried out and a just homage paid to the value of human life, in Italy *circostanze attenante* may really nullify the law and show the slight value which is set on life."[132] Justice Grove echoed the sentiment in a case in which a man had murdered a woman who threatened to leave him. Grove said, "[H]e had no doubt the real motive was the feeling of jealousy. If the law did not regard such acts as murder there would be no safety for human life and human society could not exist. Men were not to be allowed under the influence of the feelings of jealousy, to sacrifice the lives of others."[133]

Like jealousy, abandonment was not accepted as a justification for violence. When a woman separated from her husband, her legal protection seemed to have increased. Sixty percent of men who had killed their estranged wives were executed in England and 40 percent in Ireland. Only one Scotsman was executed in these circumstances, but the average sentence was more than fifteen years. Though divorces were difficult to obtain, informal separations were not unusual. When a woman's body was discovered in Westminster, the police advertised in hopes of reaching identification. When hundreds of people turned up, the *Times* commented on the "remarkable feature of the number of missing wives brought to the notice of authorities." The victim was never identified.[134]

COHABITATION

Of course, not all couples were legally married. While cohabitation was not unusual among working-class Victorians, judges sometimes found such relationships particularly suspect. After a young woman in London died from injuries inflicted by the man she lived with, Justice Brett took the opportunity to point out that

> he was living with her in a state which almost uniformly resulted in brutality on the part of the man. He had the power seeing they were unmarried of casting her on the world at any moment and an unmarried man when he had that power unless he exerted considerable control over himself, was prone to use it with considerable violence.[135]

In May of 1881 Justice Coleridge heard two cases at the Old Bailey in which men had kicked to death the women they lived with. In the first case, a man had kicked his wife to death in front of witnesses because she had kicked his dog. Justice Coleridge announced that "he must pass upon the prisoner a sentence to show that human life was a precious thing in the eyes of the law and could not be taken without punishment." But he sentenced the man to only six weeks. In the other case the couple had not been married. The man had thrown the woman to the ground and kicked her because she had been drunk and failed to prepare his tea. She died two days later of shock and blood poisoning. In this case Justice Coleridge said that "it was the duty of persons in his situation to mark with a strong hand their opinion of brutal crimes, especially when they were perpetuated upon women." He sentenced the man to five years penal servitude.[136]

The *Scotsman* explained, "[I]n many cases of brutal assaults upon women by their so-called husbands, there is no legal marriage for the law to dissolve."[137] When an itinerant pot seller was charged with the murder of an Irish woman with whom he had cohabited for several years, "[w]itnesses testified to having heard him telling her that as she was not his wife she had no claim upon him."[138] Whether women who were not legally married to the men they were living with were more vulnerable physically is impossible to gauge. The fact that the man and woman were not married was mentioned in 19 percent of English trials, 6 percent of Irish trials, 9 percent of Scottish trials, and 12 percent of Welsh trials in which women were domestic homicide victims. The likelihood of conviction was not affected by whether the couple had been legally married, but judges in both England and Scotland gave substantially heavier sentences when the couple had been living together without marriage. Such an arrangement might make a woman more vulnerable physically, but in the event of her death the courts would exact greater retribution. Women without husbands merited more legal protection, even if the biggest threat to married women was their own husbands.

In examining the explanations offered for wife killing the similarities are telling and speak to the common assumption that masculinity depended on control of the wife, that female provocation might be beyond endurance but that good women should be protected, and even those who were not "pattern women" deserved protection from lethal attacks. In England, middle- and upper-class men who killed their wives were more likely to be found insane. Men who married above their station were considered particularly reprehensible, and if they caused or allowed the death of their wives they received no quarter from judges. For the Scots, domestic homicide was a social problem that threatened their perception of themselves. It was the sort of thing that foreigners or drunken workers might do. But it was not credible that a respectable Scot might be guilty of killing his wife. The only exceptions were for husbands driven to distraction by drunken women. But the Irish, who also saw domestic homicide as alien to their national character, thought of domestic homicide as a very rare occurrence and therefore not a particular threat to society at large. Unlike the Scots, they were particularly sympathetic to both killers and victims who had been intoxicated. Working men might be forgiven a regrettable impulse but wealthy men who plotted to rid themselves of a bothersome wife were given no quarter. Rather than refusing to believe that a respectable Irishman could do such a thing, the courts punished him severely because as an Irishman he should have known better.

WIVES KILLING HUSBANDS

Almost all public commentary on spousal homicide referred to husbands killing their wives, which happened about ten times more often than the reverse. Wives accused of killing their husbands were more likely to be convicted than husbands killing wives in Ireland, less likely to be convicted in England, and roughly equally likely in Scotland. Only one woman in the United Kingdom who killed her husband was found insane. Killing a husband rarely seemed irrational. Five Englishwomen were hanged for killing their husbands. Though no women in Ireland, Scotland, or Wales were executed for killing their spouses, everywhere women who killed their husbands were more likely to be convicted of murder than women who chose other victims. The figures were influenced by the fact that wives were more likely to use lethal weapons to kill their husbands than the reverse, which usually meant heavier sentences. Of course it would be unlikely that a woman could kill a man without a weapon of some sort. On the other hand, in over half of the English cases, a third of the Irish cases, and a quarter of the Scottish cases in which husbands killed wives, no weapon was involved.

There was also a particular horror in the idea that a man might be made vulnerable to an attack by his wife. One of the English wives convicted of murder had cut his throat while he slept—demonstrating the kind of treachery that was most threatening to patriarchy. Six of the convicted murderesses had used poison. The *Times* suggested the female poisoner had a special fascination: "Almost always there is a strange attraction to poisoning cases . . . implying some domestic treason, for it is only a member of a man's own household, or an intimate friend, that has the opportunities of close intercourse which a case of poisoning commonly implies. Hence, the special and tragic interest in such cases."[139] Nearly half of the women hanged in England had poisoned their victims.

In two of the cases in which Englishwomen killed their husbands, the wife had been the physically stronger spouse. Catherine Churchill, the only non-poisoner to hang for killing her husband, was more than thirty years younger than her husband. She claimed that the eighty-three-year-old man had died from a fall. But the police found a bloody billhook on the scene. After evidence was presented that the victim had been about to change his will, she was convicted of murder and hanged.[140] Rose Brown beat her elderly, crippled husband with an iron bar. In her defense Brown argued that he had used provocative language. Justice Lindley said, "[N]o language would have justified her conduct." Brown's defense also pointed out that the beating itself had not killed the man. He died of erysipelas. The average English husband whose wife died from disease or infection that stemmed from a beating served five years, but Justice Lindley insisted this was murder. "He was unable to think what amount of provocation in point of law would justify the prisoner's conduct. He was a quiet, inoffensive and very old man and she ought to have treated him with every kindness." She was convicted of murder, though the death sentence was commuted.[141] Englishwomen who killed husbands for financial reasons or to pursue another relationship also did not fare well. Eighty percent of such cases ended in murder convictions.

But when the homicide occurred during a fight in which the husband might have been expected to hold his own, the courts were more sympathetic. Nearly half the Englishwomen accused of killing their husbands during a violent struggle were acquitted, and of those convicted nearly half served fewer than two years. English judges recognized that wives might sometimes need to strike back. When a woman "of most respectable appearance" was charged with killing her husband by hitting him in the head with a poker after he struck her in the face, Justice Huddleston told the jury the "law makes excuses for the imperfections of human nature and if a person suffering from a blow strikes back in hot blood and kills his opponent the crime is manslaughter only." He sentenced her to twelve months.[142] In a similar case from Hereford, the daughter of the verger of St. Alban's was charged with stabbing her drunk and abusive husband. Justice Blackburn told the jury the act could not be considered self-defense but the jury acquitted her any way and "the verdict evidently met the approval of everyone in the court."[143]

The general sympathy for women who struck back could be seen in the public reaction to a case from Kent in which the judge did not display leniency. When Justice Brett sentenced a schoolmaster's wife to ten years for killing her husband, "[t]he case excited a very deep and painful interest in the town. . . . [T]he sentence seemed to make a very painful impression on the crowded audience and there is an impression in the town that a less severe sentence might have sufficed." The woman had thrown a knife at her husband during a fight at the dinner table and the knife had struck him in the throat. The coroner's jury had ruled the death an accident and, as the newspaper pointed out, a case of manslaughter in a pub brawl at the same session resulted in a sentence of only two months.[144]

The fact that Irish women who killed their husbands were more likely to be convicted and received harsher sentences than Irish husbands who killed their wives in part reflects some of the peculiarities of Irish marriage as well as the extremely small numbers of women involved. Only eighteen Irish women were reported to have killed their husbands and only fourteen of them stood trial. Irish women who killed drunken and abusive husbands during fights were usually given very light sentences. The only woman in Ireland who served more than six months for killing her husband during a fight had set her husband on fire with a paraffin lamp. The five women who had joined with other family members to hasten inheritance by killing a husband who was deemed old and useless received heavy sentences. Cruelty to the weak and greed were both punished severely.

Three other Irishwomen had never hidden their animosity toward husbands their families chose for them, and here the courts were more ambivalent. Judges and jurors often expressed their disapproval of arranged marriages especially when young women had been forced to marry older men to secure property for their families. Twenty-five-year-old Margaret Brosnan was charged with murdering the fifty-year-old man she had been forced to marry in return for her new husband's paying off her father's debt. Margaret never even pretended that she found the marriage anything but painful. "When going to the chapel on day of the marriage she gave expression to her feelings of disgust and said she wished to God either he or she would be dead before they reached the place." There was little doubt about her guilt. She had smashed her husband's head in with an axe in front of witnesses. But the Kerry jury convicted her only of manslaughter. After the verdict, the judge told the prisoner, "[Y]ou have been made a victim by that selfish old father of yours by coercing you to marry a man against whom you had such a dreadful animosity." He seemed to genuinely regret having to sentence her to twenty years.[145]

In a similar case from Galway, a teenaged girl had been taken out of convent school to marry a man twice her age. Within a year she was accused of poisoning her husband. The circumstantial evidence looked highly damning: the young woman had written love letters to her brother-in-law, had told friends that she would soon be free of the husband she despised, and had deliberately kicked over a bowl in order to prevent the chemical analysis of its contents. Nevertheless, before the defense even presented its case the foreman of the jury announced that the jury had decided to acquit. As she walked home from the courtroom she "was cheered through the streets." In addition to inspiring the sympathy of the jurors, the young woman also apparently won the affections of the local police as the case was not reported with other homicides in the official return of outrages.[146] In the third case, the jury decided the wife had merely cleaned up the mess after her father killed her husband. She was also acquitted.

All of the cases in which Scottish women were convicted of killing their husbands involved violent struggles and only one resulted in a murder conviction. Isabella Grant, described as a "frail-looking elderly woman," had stabbed her husband to death. The *Scotsman* noted that the couple's domestic life had been "extremely wretched." Four months earlier she had been punished for hitting her husband on the head with a pot. "After stabbing him she refused to offer any aid." The presiding judge charged for murder and the jury voted nine to six to convict her of the full offense. However, the jurymen immediately signed a petition for mercy and her sentence was commuted.[147] The weapon was crucial. The only Scottish women who were sentenced to penal servitude for killing their husbands had used a pickaxe, a knife, and a paraffin lamp. In the remaining cases involving women who had struck violent husbands in the head with tongs, clothesline poles, chairs, or other household items, the sentences were less than a year and in some cases the women were allowed to plead guilty to assault.

Only three Welsh women were accused of killing their husbands and one of them committed suicide before trial. The only one convicted was a fifty-nine-year-old woman who had killed her seventy-five-year-old husband after previously serving jail time for assaulting him. Though she claimed her husband had died from a fall, neighbors claimed to have heard shouts of "murder," a bloodstained hammer was found at the scene, and smears of blood covered the kitchen wall. Like other women who killed vulnerable husbands, she was convicted of murder but was recommended to mercy on account of her age and sex.[148]

The other Welsh case serves as a reminder that jury decisions, especially in Wales, are an imperfect representation of public opinion, especially in cases where the crime had occurred in a small town but the trial was held at the assize in a large city. Sarah Matthews of Llannelly told neighbors her husband had passed out from drink but the neighbors discovered he was dead from a wound to the back of the head and that there were bloodstains on the poker. When the coroner's jury indicted her for willful murder, she maintained a "stolid and indifferent demeanor."[149] At the assize at Swansea, after her attorney pointed out that the Matthewses were regular chapel goers and had been happily married for thirty-eight years, she was acquitted. While the Swansea jury may have felt the case was not proven, the Llannelly neighbors were convinced she was guilty. When she arrived back in Llannelly, an angry mob met her train shouting "if they could only get at her."[150]

Wives in the United Kingdom rarely killed their husbands, but when they did the criteria were fairly consistent. The offense was heightened if the crime was premeditated, if the victim had been particularly vulnerable, or if greed were part of the motivation. On the other hand, women who struck back in self-defense, although usually convicted, rarely served long sentences. In England the average sentence for men convicted of killing their wives was twice as long as the average sentence for women convicted of killing their husbands. In Scotland husbands served two and a half years longer on average. But in Ireland wives who killed husbands served an average sentence of nine years; husbands who killed wives served only six and a half. Irish husbands usually killed during a drunken fight; Irish women were more likely to kill for a reason.

Nevertheless, women rarely killed their husbands. Instead, when wives turned homicidal, it was in their role as mothers.

CHAPTER 6

Children

I don't think the prisoner did any wrong, only she neglected to nurse the child. She was very poor. (*North Wales
Chronicle*, 22 January 1887)

No plan could be devised by which to train up children to
become afterwards untractable and even dangerous, than
by cruel treatment, harsh treatment and semi-starvation
and other forms of cruelty in their youth. Neglect of that
kind left its impress on the body and on the minds of children which was never lost, and which bore evil fruits when
they grew up. (*Scotsman*, 21 February 1891)

A woman named Benstead took a hatchet to her five year
old daughter. When arrested she told police the child was
disobedient and she thought she would kill it. (*The Times*,
7 September 1872, 8b)

Happily in all ranks and classes in Ireland there were not to
be found many hardhearted mothers. It was always found
that mothers loved their offsprings and looked after them
with gentleness and care. The life of the youngest child was
as sacred to the law as was that of its parents. (The *Times*,
5 April 1892, 10b)

The contradictions in Victorian society were perhaps strongest when the
issue was children. Sentimental portraits of children in art and literature were
enormously popular. Nineteenth-century reformers arguably made more
progress in stopping cruelty to children than had been done for centuries.[1]
Certainly the middle-class press frequently celebrated the great progress they

had made. But even the *Times* seemed to waver between sentimentality and a detachment bordering on the callous. In an 1870 editorial the *Times* noted that

> there is something peculiarly though painfully interesting in the suffer-
> ings of sick children. The utter helplessness of the little patients and their
> touching recognition of every act of kindness towards them are circum-
> stances which add immensely to the melancholy satisfaction which any
> one with a heart must feel when brought in contact with these children.[2]

The comment was part of a piece praising donations to the great Ormond Street hospital for children, but the image of deriving "melancholy satisfaction" from contact with seriously ill children is reminiscent of the tears shed for Little Nell. Even more striking was a report on the trial of a couple whose eight-year-old daughter had died of abuse and neglect. "Some amusement was caused by the prisoners mutually accusing each other in the dock. The male prisoner said she was a dirty woman and would not even wash his shirt. She said he starved her, beat her and swore at her."[3] For all their reforms, it is startling that Victorians could calmly evaluate the entertainment value of the suffering and deaths of children.

In keeping with this objectification of children, in accounts of child homi-cides the victim was routinely referred to as "it." Even with children of school age this was the practice in the press, among officials, and even in testimony given by parents. Children might be "peculiarly interesting," but they were rarely considered as individual human beings. In fact, rather than being thought of as adults in miniature as some scholars have suggested about chil-dren in earlier periods,[4] in late Victorian homicide trials children were often perceived more like animals—entertaining, amusing, sometimes useful, and even loveable, but never as autonomous human beings.

Exactly how many children were homicide victims in the Victorian United Kingdom is particularly hard to determine. In the trial records children between the ages of twenty-four hours and fifteen years were the victim in 22 percent of English homicide trials, 15 percent of Welsh, 14 percent of Scottish, and only 8 percent of Irish. However, these numbers are probably more indica-tive of official attitudes than the real number of child homicides.[5] Arrests, pros-ecutions, convictions, and sentences were all influenced by the fact that physi-cally it was far easier to kill a child than an adult. Blows or neglect which might not seriously harm an adult could kill a young child, and authorities were often particularly scrupulous about not being too hard on those who killed a child without clearly intending to do so. But though children were more physically

vulnerable, the courts often concluded that psychologically it was more difficult to kill a child. People who killed children were more likely to be found
insane—nearly five times more in England and Wales, nearly four times more
in Scotland, and almost twice as likely in Ireland.

Throughout the United Kingdom, public interest in and the official reactions to child homicides varied enormously. Some child homicides attracted
very little notice and other cases became sensations. For example, when an
Englishwoman who had lost her job beat her four-year-old to death with a
poker, the *Times* described it as a "murder of frightening character."[6] But in
another case from the same area, the *Times* concluded that a case in which a
woman was charged with starving her two-year-old "was of no public interest."[7] The differences in the cause of death might be the explanation for the
variations in coverage, but in two cases from Wales the reactions were
reversed. When a Welsh cattle drover cut the throat of his seven-year-old
daughter, the local newspaper noted that "[h]is trial drew no crowds and little excitement."[8] But when a child starved to death in the same area as a result
of the mother's negligence, the newspaper reported that "public indignation
and excitement have been painfully aroused."[9]

In Victorian England the balance between the responsibilities and privi-
leges of the state and those of the family were a focus of considerable debate.[10]
Interfering between parent and child was not only a violation of the sanctity
of the home—it could also mean an additional financial burden on the rate
payer. In 1870 the *Times* suggested that the English were unique among the
nations of Britain in their belief in the autonomy of parents. "Our social
practice is not so ambitious as that of Presbyterian Scotland or Catholic
Ireland. We permit people to take their own courses and to go their own
ways." In return for this lack of supervision, parents bore full responsibility
for their children. "We insist on every child being duly cared for by those
who have brought it into the world. Whatever the cost or the shame this
must be done." The *Times* argued that this insistence was because the English
placed a greater value on each human life than did other people and believed
that no one would care for a child more effectively than its biological parents.
"Because [England] intends better than other states, therefore the rebels do
worse than other rebels. . . . But then comes the necessary correction."[11] In
other words, the state would intervene only after the fact. The *Times* implied
that though English authorities were slower to intervene between parent and
child than in other countries, they would punish parents who failed more
severely.

But the homicide records do not completely bear out the claim that the
English were uniquely concerned about the life of each child. Parents were

the accused killers in two-thirds of the child homicides in England between 1867 and 1892. But English juries were less likely to convict parents accused of killing their own children than people accused of killing adults or nonrelated children. English parents who killed minor children were also more likely to receive sentences of fewer than than two years and much less likely to be executed. Even though eighty-nine English parents (20 percent of those tried) were convicted of murder, only fourteen were executed. Accused parents were also far more likely than other killers to be found insane. Even though the laws regarding children were being debated and changed during the 1870s and 1880s, there was no significant change in the conviction rate or sentencing patterns for child homicides in England between 1867 and 1892. Most often variations in trial outcomes seemed to reflect the alternating urges of sympathy for the parents and the hope to deter others by making an example of the accused.

While the English debated public versus private responsibility, in Scotland child abuse, and by extension child homicides, were very much public issues. As with other homicides, the Scottish courts were inclined to require atonement for the sin regardless of the circumstances. The conviction rate for parents accused of killing their children was the same as for people accused of killing adults. People accused of killing a nonrelated child were 20 percent more likely to be convicted. Parents who killed children were subject to the same sentences as those who killed adults. The only difference was that parents who killed children were four times more likely to be found insane than other killers. The Scots also grew increasingly less tolerant of child homicide. Unlike England, where the conviction rate in child homicides remained constant over the period, in Scotland the likelihood of a conviction for culpable homicide in child homicides rose by nearly 50 percent between 1867 and 1892, and the sentences got heavier. However, no Scottish parent was convicted of *murdering* his or her own child. The heaviest sentence given to any parent was twenty years.

In Wales the concern was public but still largely based in community rather than state control. The Welsh press tended to use sensational headlines in reporting child homicides and often stressed the need for community intervention. However, the implication was that neighbors should intervene directly rather than simply wait for the state to play a role. After a coroner's jury returned a verdict of "murder by persons unknown" in a case in which a child's body had been discovered, the *Carmarthen Weekly Reporter* noted that "[i]t is a startling thing that in a civilized country a child can be disposed of by throwing its body into a roadside ditch and no trace found of the inhuman parent."[12] Welsh juries were less likely to convict when the victim was a child than when the victim was an adult. But in child homicides, parents were more likely to be convicted than nonrelatives.

The Irish took great pride in the belief that unlike their British neighbors, the Irish were kind to children. A young woman who tried to establish a branch of the Society for the Prevention of Cruelty to Children (SPCC) in Limerick was chided by the local press which explained that while she came from "England where the newspapers are crowded with horrible details of appalling cruelties to and murders of children, such crimes are unknown to the darkest records of our country." Not only was the SPCC unnecessary, the bishop of Limerick believed that "it must do more harm than good" to have a volunteer society "intruding into the houses of the poor, raising questions between parents and children."[13] But it may also be that Irish authorities in keeping with the bishop's sentiments on intrusion were less willing to prosecute parents for the deaths of their own children. A comparison of the homicides which appear in Irish court records or newspapers with those in the official outrage reports reveals that child homicides were ten times less likely to be included in the Irish outrage papers than adult homicides.[14]

Though the differences in reporting criteria make rate comparisons problematic, the rate of parents tried for killing a biological child between one day and fifteen years old per one hundred thousand population was .69 for Scotland, .65 for England and Wales, and only .43 for Ireland. However, when hearing child homicide cases, Irish juries had conviction rates very close to those of English juries and followed the same pattern of convicting parents at a lower rate than people who killed adults or nonrelated children.

NEWBORNS

The age of a child homicide victim was critical to the disposition of cases. The deaths of newborns fell under different legal and psychological criteria. As Justice Stephen had explained, neonaticide "is less serious than other kinds of murder. You cannot estimate the loss to the child itself; you know nothing about it at all. It creates no alarm to the public."[15] The actual number of neonaticide cases is extremely difficult to gauge. The number of neonaticides that failed to reach the courts at all was probably far higher than for other types of homicide. They were also less likely to be reported in the press. The *Times* correspondent for the Home Circuit declined to report neonaticide cases, insisting that they "did not present any feature of public interest."[16] No neonaticides were included among the homicide reports in the Irish outrage papers (though infanticide numbers were included in the statistical tables).

On the other hand, the Scottish records included indictments for the murder of newborns, so the sources make it seem that Scottish mothers were particularly lethal when the likelihood is that Scottish authorities were simply more likely to prosecute and record such cases.

However, the outcome of such cases can reveal a great deal about attitudes toward sexuality, public responsibility for children, and the role of the law. The history of the treatment of neonaticides is long and complex.[17] In Victorian Britain these cases were usually dealt with far more leniently than other homicides. The laws of the United Kingdom provided alternative charges in cases in which a mother killed a newborn infant immediately after birth, which recognized the distinctiveness of such acts. The charges of concealment of birth in England, Ireland, and Wales and concealment of pregnancy in Scotland did not require that the jury actually find the woman guilty of killing her child.[18]

In England, Ireland, and Wales, even when the evidence suggested that a mother had deliberately killed her newborn, she was usually only convicted of concealment of birth, which carried a maximum penalty of two years. As Justice Wills said of a young woman convicted of concealment of birth even though her newborn was discovered with its throat cut, "[N]o doubt but that the prisoner in every sense except the legal sense had murdered the child."[19] In an Irish case the presiding judge told the jury there was no doubt that the newborn had been murdered, but directed them to return a verdict of concealment of birth and then sentenced the young woman to the two-year maximum sentence for concealment.[20] After a Welsh coroner's jury had returned a murder indictment for the death of a newborn, the Crown attorney declined to offer any evidence and the judge directed for an acquittal. The young woman then pled guilty to concealment of birth. Justice Stephen, noting that "her crime bore a disagreeable resemblance to murder," sentenced her to nine months.[21]

Because there was no legal distinction between killing a newborn and killing any other victim, courts were often caught between maintaining a legal fiction—that is, that the infant had been born dead and the corpse hidden, or convicting the mother of murder, which carried an automatic death sentence. Only three Englishwomen were convicted of murdering newborns between 1867 and 1892. Why these three women were singled out is difficult to determine. One of the murder convictions came in a case in which the death may actually have been accidental. Fanny Gant, a domestic servant, was arrested after the body of a newborn infant was found. The police reported that the "prisoner said of her own accord that child was hers and that she had made away with it." The death had been the result of strangulation and the corpse had tape around its neck. After Gant was convicted of murder and sentenced to death, "before being removed from the dock she stated that she had tied the tape round the child's neck to assist her delivery; that she fainted and on recovering found the child dead on the floor." Ironically her version of events would meet the classic definition of concealment of birth.[22]

The three women convicted of murder were domestic servants as were nearly 80 percent of the Englishwomen charged with neonaticide. This is not particularly surprising since domestic workers made up the largest group of working women. Further, a pregnant domestic servant was in an impossible situation. She could not keep her job if she had to look after a child and her wages were too low to pay for childcare. As a defense attorney for a servant who had decapitated her newborn said, "[I]t was one of a very sad class of cases."[23] These domestic servants showed remarkable physical stamina as well as a gift for denial. Most gave birth alone, immediately went back to work, and simply tried to ignore the existence of the child.

One of the murder convictions was just such a case. Letitia Dordy, a general servant in Liverpool, was accused of murdering her newborn child in 1867. Her mistress testified that she had been suspicious but that Dordy had denied "being in the family way." On 21 February, "a loud cry was heard through the house and when the prisoner was called by her mistress into the parlor she was some time in making her appearance." When she did appear, Dordy explained that the cry had been the cat. The next morning blood was found on the kitchen floor. Since Dordy "was going about her duties that morning as usual, her mistress sent her for some beer." While Dordy was out, the mistress searched her room and found the child's corpse between the bed and the mattress. The infant was "covered with coal dust . . . and there was a red mark encircling its throat. On her return and after being taxed with it prisoner . . . soon admitted it and said that the child had been born dead in the coal cellar and the red marks were from falling on the coals." However, a doctor testified that the child had been strangled with a ligature. Dordy, who was undefended at her trial, was convicted of murder and sentenced to death. Though her sentence was commuted, no one seemed to notice the remarkable fact that within minutes of giving birth Letitia had reported to her mistress and that the day after she had "been going about her duties as usual."[24]

In two of the murder cases the victim had been strangled and in the third drowned. This reflects the general pattern in English neonaticides where cases resulting from suffocation were likely to lead to the heaviest sentences. The lowest average sentence in English neonaticides was for cases in which the newborn had died from a cut or stab. In these cases the average sentence was just twelve months. The difference reflects the fact that when no weapon had been used, it was possible to reach a verdict of manslaughter. If a knife was used, however, the choices in English courts were reduced to murder or concealment since the knife implied intent. All eight English manslaughter convictions involved strangling, neglect, or beating. In six of the manslaughter convictions the sentence was longer than the two-year maximum allowed for concealment.

The logic of these manslaughter cases was demonstrated in a case heard at the Oxford Assize in 1874. Emma Handley had given birth alone and told no one. Nine days later the child's body was discovered in a box under the bed. "It was proved that no preparations had been made by the prisoner and that the birth had been kept secret from her father and mother." In other words, the birth had truly been concealed. Further, "there were no signs of violence to be found on the body, but in the opinion of the medical men the child was full born, was born alive, and from the inflated condition of the lungs, had lived for an hour or more." Justice Brett directed the jury to acquit on the murder charge. The defense then argued that while it was impossible to deny concealment, simply failing to provide for the child did not constitute manslaughter. Justice Brett disagreed, arguing that regardless of intent "if she allowed the child to die from her wicked negligence that would make her guilty of manslaughter." After she was convicted of manslaughter, Justice Brett told Handley that "he was about to make her a sad and terrible example. The crime of which she had been found guilty was far too prevalent, and that though under his direction the jury had acquitted her of willful murder, yet, morally speaking, there was little doubt that it was that which she had intended." He sentenced her to ten years penal servitude.[25] Handley was particularly unfortunate—not only in that she was chosen to be the example but also in that the method of death made a manslaughter verdict feasible. The longest sentence given to any of the nine Englishwomen accused of using a lethal weapon to kill their newborn was two years.

What is most remarkable about the murder and manslaughter convictions in England is that though the verdicts were exceptional, the circumstances were not. It may be that jurors who encountered such cases less often found the deaths of newborns more horrifying. All of the murder convictions for neonaticide in England and nearly two-thirds of the manslaughter convictions were from the north and west even though only 17 percent of the trials were heard in those regions.

In keeping with this geographic trend, of the five murder convictions for neonaticide in the United Kingdom, two were in Wales, the site of only 5 percent of the trials. Wales also appears to have had the highest overall conviction rates for neonaticide cases (87 percent compared to 73 percent for

England). Welsh officials often made a determined effort to identify the parents of dead infants. In 1869, when an infant was found floating in a pond, a reward of £35 was offered for information along with a free pardon to "anyone giving information, who was not the actual perpetrator of the foul and disgraceful deed."[26] When a coroner's jury in Carmarthen left an open verdict in the case of a newborn infant found in a ditch, the local newspapers complained that "the baby seems to have been regarded much as people regard a superfluous kitten. . . . [I]t is a horrible reflection that an infant, which may possibly have been murdered, can be flung into a ditch without leaving any traces of the murderess."[27] Under the headline "Dreadful Child Murder Near Cardiff," the *Carmarthen Weekly Reporter* explained that an eighteen-year-old domestic servant had driven a pickaxe into the skull of her newborn infant. She was convicted of murder at the winter assize in December and "was then carried from the dock shrieking loudly."[28] In the other murder case a charwoman was found guilty of murder for drowning her newborn. A watchman in Cardiff had seen her throw the child into a canal and rescued it. The child later died at the workhouse.[29] Because the child was alive when taken from the canal, it was impossible to argue for concealment of birth.

The Scottish courts offered the greatest flexibility in the deaths of newborns. Though Scottish women accused of neonaticide were only half as likely to be acquitted as their English counterparts, no Scottish woman was convicted of *murdering* her newborn. Even when the methods used implied intent, the Scottish courts invoked the concept of diminished responsibility. For example, when Elizabeth Fraser was tried for stabbing the second-born of twins, the judge suggested that in light of her "excited state" a plea of guilty to culpable homicide would be acceptable.[30] Over a third of those tried for neonaticide in Scotland were convicted of culpable homicide and sixteen of them (nearly a third of the culpable homicide convictions) were sentenced to penal servitude.

Because Scottish jurors were more willing to find women who killed newborns guilty of a lesser form of homicide, the courts could be harder on women who had used weapons against newborns. In Scotland the average sentence in cases where a cutting implement had been used in a neonaticide was three times heavier than if the child had been strangled or beaten. The longest sentence (twenty years) was given to a young woman whose child's death "was caused by forcible strangulation and was hastened by a wound on the neck." A bloodstained knife was also presented in evidence. After the medical testimony, the prisoner pled guilty to culpable homicide.[31]

Officials in the Irish church as well as the government took great pride in the fact that Ireland had a lower illegitimacy rate than Britain and that Irish laws made life even more difficult for unwed mothers. As one priest put it, Ireland's status as "an island of saints" depended on maintaining the current policy: "At present the Irish girl knows that she has nothing to gain but disgrace if she outsteps the bounds of morality, and they should be cautious before they place any temptation in her way."[32] Perhaps out of sympathy for the harsh policy, Irish juries were reluctant to convict in neonaticides and Irish judges gave the lowest average sentences in the United Kingdom for the crime of concealment.

Throughout the United Kingdom, the deaths of newborns often inspired judges to couple harsh rhetoric with light punishment. When a twenty-seven-year-old servant in Wales pled guilty to concealment of birth, Justice Kelly sternly announced that

> she had been suspected of the greatest crime it was possible that man or woman could commit. Under these circumstances he was afraid that that was not the first time with which she had to reproach herself with a great deal of immorality and improper conduct and therefore he must visit her offense with some severe punishment.

He then sentenced her to four months—one of the lightest sentences given for concealment of birth anywhere in the United Kingdom.[33]

Of course the fact that almost all neonaticides involved illegitimate children meant that the accused was always guilty of sexual immorality if nothing more, and hiding her shame was in keeping with prevailing ideas about female modesty. English Justice Quain acknowledged that "that sense of shame which is part of the very essence of every woman is working against the law in these matters."[34] When sentencing a twenty-three-year-old domestic servant for concealment of birth, another English judge announced: "It should be known that when a woman is placed in such circumstances as yours her duty is to discover her shame. For far greater shame will be caused by concealment."[35]

In Ireland Justice Barry blamed infanticide cases on a growing concern with propriety: "The rude, ignorant man or woman, and even the wild beast, will have a particular tendency to protect their offspring, but in this age of civilization, this crime was on the rise." With civilization came a sense of shame, "because the more enlightened people are getting the more inclined they are to conceal their feelings."[36] The case of Eliza McNamara illustrated this desperate need for secrecy. When she was arrested for infanticide, McNamara told police she would sooner die than have her father know she had given birth to an illegitimate child. Even though she lived with her father, he had never suspected she was pregnant. The child had died about an hour after she gave birth in an abandoned shed. She said in her deposition that when she told a friend of the baby's death, he said, "I was the luckiest he ever knew." A Limerick jury acquitted her of concealment of birth.[37]

A Scottish defense attorney asked, "Could it be wondered at that suffering severe agony both of body and of mind, tortured by the heartless betrayal of her seducer, the loss of her situation, and the knowledge that she had outraged the feelings of her father and friends, and her own shame she was almost beside herself, scarcely accountable for her own actions and was driven to this rash deed?"[38] After another Scottish woman was convicted of culpable homicide, the presiding judge stressed that two sorts of immorality were involved. Lord Young told the defendant: "I am not going to address you upon the impropriety of your conduct as a young unmarried woman having an illegitimate child. Other girls have fallen before you, with more or less excuse, so that one would make allowance for their transgression. It is not for immorality of that kind that I have got to sentence you; it is for being an unnatural mother."[39] Shame was a proper instinct but motherhood should trump it. As Lord Young explained: "I dare say you had good impulses upon you in trying to keep the thing secret—the respectability of your and your father's house. These impulses are intelligible enough. But you brought forth a living child and put it to death. That is not a mere transgression of immorality in a young woman yielding to temptations." Though this was by no means the first such case he had heard, Lord Young insisted, "Unnatural mothers who violently put an end to the life which they themselves have given to are, I am happy to say, rare in this country. . . . It does surprise me and distress me greatly and must surprise all right-minded people."[40] But however much the killing of newborns offended the sensibilities of Victorian judges, jurors, and journalists, their representatives in the government were not yet willing to shoulder the philosophical, political, and economic costs of preventing the circumstances that drove unwed mothers to such acts.

ILLEGITIMACY AND HOMICIDE

Cases in which a woman killed an illegitimate child after having made an effort to care for it created more serious problems. Once the victim was more than a few hours old, concealment charges were no longer an option. As Justice Day explained in a case in which a servant left her illegitimate infant on the road, "It was not a case of a woman, who maddened by pain, distress and want caused the death of a child but a case of manslaughter under circumstances of the most aggravated character." He sentenced the woman to twenty years.⁴¹ The mixed messages about shame and maternal instincts that were so prevalent in neonaticide cases were even stronger when the child was older. Throughout the United Kingdom, unwed mothers charged with killing infants they had at first tried to care for were more likely to be convicted than married women and sentences were much heavier. The *Times* insisted that maternal affection should win out despite the hardships. "Nature easily repairs the fault of circumstances, and many a parent learns to care for a child of shame as for any other. But Nature has no opportunity of repairing the fault and making maternal love triumph over shame" if the mother was allowed to abandon her infant.⁴²

But it was poverty as much as shame that most often led single mothers to kill. The same officials who were eager to brand women who killed their children unnatural were also loath to offer any aid to unwed mothers. Domestic servants could not keep their children with them, factory workers did not make enough money to pay for childcare, and extended families often either could not or would not provide support. Single mothers who tried desperately to care for children but were defeated by poverty and despair created painful situations for the courts throughout the United Kingdom. Sarah Crawford murdered her twenty-month-old illegitimate child after her landlady evicted her. At her trial the defense pointed out that she "had always been most kind to the child previously and latterly had been in great distress of mind from being out of work." She was found guilty of murder but recommended to mercy "for the peculiarly distressing circumstances."⁴³ But there was nothing peculiar about the circumstances.

Nearly three-quarters of unwed mothers charged with killing their children in England claimed poverty had motivated them. As one woman explained about the death of her fifteen-month-old daughter, "I took it out on Saturday night and strangled it; I am only a poor servant girl and could not afford to keep it."⁴⁴ Another told police: "I wish to tell the truth and plead for mercy; it was poverty and distress and not cruelty that made me drown my children. I have cried about my children every day since. I was destitute, I had no home or bed to lie on."⁴⁵ Both women were convicted of murder and sentenced to death though the sentences were commuted to life in prison.

An unwed mother in England who had attempted to care for her child and later drowned or poisoned the child to prevent a slow death from starvation was more likely to be convicted of *murder* than the average English killer. Forty-five percent of unwed mothers charged with killing their children were convicted of murder and another 22 percent were convicted of manslaughter.

The average sentence given to a single mother convicted of manslaughter for killing her own child was eighteen months longer than the overall average sentence for English manslaughter convictions. Though single mothers were the defendants in only a quarter of cases in which parents were accused of killing their children, they received 47 percent of the sentences of death or penal servitude given to homicidal parents.

Only two women in the United Kingdom were hanged for killing their own children between 1867 and 1892. Both cases were in England. Elizabeth Berry had poisoned her daughter for insurance money. Like most poisoners, she received no sympathy. The other mother who was hanged seems to have been the designated moral example. In 1878 Selina Wadge, a single mother of two, drowned her two-year-old after leaving the workhouse. She was convicted of murder and became the first person to be executed in Cornwall in sixteen years. The report of her execution noted that she had claimed she committed the crime because a man had promised to marry her if she got rid of the child.[46] While the callousness of choosing a man over her own child certainly did not improve her standing, Wadge was not the only mother to kill a child for this reason. Though Wadge was the only one to hang, twelve other Englishwomen convicted of killing a child to advance marital prospects were convicted of murder but had death sentences commuted.

Young unwed mothers who killed out of desperation rather than for ulterior motives were not usually perceived as monsters. They might even evoke sympathy. In 1876 Emily Church was tried at the Central Criminal Court for murdering her two-year-old illegitimate daughter. The *Times* noted that she had always been fond of her child and tried to earn a living. Her defense attorney argued that "she had been literally dependent on the charity and commiseration of neighbors from day to day and having exhausted that was driven to despair." The jury found Church guilty of murder though it strongly recommended mercy on grounds of poverty and youth. The *Times* reported that as the death sentence was pronounced on the "young, slender creature, who was so weak and overwhelmed with distress that she had to be supported by wardens in the dock, there was scarcely a dry eye in the Court. Strong men were entirely overcome by their feelings." The overwhelming display of sympathy in the courtroom was meant to demonstrate the right feeling of the men who had condemned Church to death. A week later the *Times* reported that the death sentence had been commuted, adding that "up to the time she met the child's father she'd been a respectable domestic servant."[47]

Occasionally judges and juries fell back on technicalities to avoid convictions. A servant accused of drowning her daughter explained that she had been driven to do it by the father of the child who had deserted her. She had tried to take her child to her sister but was refused. "She had tried to get work but everyone seemed to turn against her." Though the child's body was found in a pool of water, the defense argued that the cause of death had not been established. When a London jury seized on this fact to acquit her, the verdict was "received with cheers."[48] When a young servant's two-week-old infant was found in a ditch suffocated by a dress forced down its throat, Justice Cleasby instructed the jury that the child might have suckled the dress by accident and perhaps the woman had left the child in hopes someone would pick it up. The jury acquitted.[49] In another case a Leeds jury announced that they believed the defendant was guilty but they had not heard enough evidence and therefore acquitted her.[50] But far more often English jurors wept and pronounced the defendant guilty of murder.

Only five single mothers in Wales were indicted for killing children more than a day old. One was convicted of murder and three of manslaughter, but in 1890 a jury took pity on Elizabeth Vernon, who had left the workhouse with her toddler and a new baby. When the child's father turned her away, she told her family she was taking the child back to the workhouse. She returned without the infant, whose body was later found in a ditch. Despite medical evidence that the child had not died of natural causes, the jury acquitted her.[51]

As usual, Scottish courts insisted on atonement but mitigated punishment with mercy. Eighty-one percent of Scottish single women accused of killing their children were convicted, but none of them were convicted of the full offense of murder even though drowning was the cause of death in the majority of cases. Scottish courts recognized mental distress as mitigation. The average sentence in these cases was slightly more than six years; however, judges who gave very similar sentences offered very different explanations. A nineteen-year-old woman from Inverness drowned her toddler because her family would not help her and she had no job. The prosecution wanted a murder conviction, insisting this was "not like killing a new-born." The presiding judge, Lord Kingsborough, offered the jury the option that "if they thought she was sane than the crime was murder, but on the other hand, if they thought her mind was afflicted by the unhappy treatment to which she had been subjected, it might only be culpable homicide." The jury quickly concurred and Lord Kingsborough, noting that "the verdict was a great relief," sentenced her to seven years.[52]

In a very similar case from Dundee the defense attorney pointed out that the prisoner's mother was in a lunatic asylum and that she had been so depressed that a doctor had recommended she not have custody of her child. The prosecuting attorney argued the crime had been "an intelligible act and committed from intelligible motives by a person of some intelligence." The judge said the culpable homicide "verdict was a very merciful one. Such crimes as that of which the prisoner had been found guilty could not be tolerated in a civilized country."[53] He sentenced her to seven years penal servitude, just as the verbally more sympathetic Lord Kingsborough had done.

Lord Craighill offered no words of sympathy for Elspet Duncan, who pled guilty to culpable homicide in having drowned her three-month-old illegitimate son in a ditch. She had been paying fourteen shillings a month for childcare, but had run out of money. The poorhouse refused to accept a child without its mother. Desperate, she had actually begged the local constable's wife to take her child. Lord Craighill insisted the case was a moral lesson. "It is proof how dangerous it is to leave the path of virtue." He also said he believed the crime was murder, but because the advocate was willing to accept her guilty plea he sentenced her to eight years.[54]

Lord Young was even more merciful to a "young respectable looking woman" in Airdrie who had drowned her illegitimate twenty-month-old son. She had been seduced by a forty-five-year-old man "from a higher plane of life" who had promised marriage but abandoned her. She had recently lost her job and was too ashamed to go home to her parents, so she had drowned the child. Lord Young told her: "The Court shrinks from sending a comparative child like you into penal servitude but suffering of an exemplary kind must be inflicted on you." He sentenced her to only two years.[55] Though Lord Young generally gave lighter sentences than his colleagues, his comment does seem to reflect the general mood of Scottish courts toward young, unwed mothers: the courts shrank from convicting them of murder but insisted on some "suffering of an exemplary kind."

Unwed mothers made up only 40 percent of the Irish parents accused of killing their children, but they received 83 percent of the sentences of death or penal servitude given to Irish parents. But Irish women rarely came before the courts for killing their illegitimate children once past early infancy. This could be because the family structure in the Irish countryside meant unwed mothers had a greater support system or it could simply mean that Irish authorities chose not to investigate cases. One of the three cases in which an Irish unwed mother was convicted of murder indicates that family betrayal was at least part of the problem. When Ann Aylsward was convicted of murdering her toddler, the Kilkenny jury recommended her to mercy "on account of her youth, on account of her honest efforts to support the child for so long, and finally on account of the state of desperation to which she had been driven by the heartless desertion of the father of the child who had seduced her and his flight to America with her sister whom he also seduced."

Her death sentence was commuted to life in prison. The murder conviction may reflect the fact that Aylsward failed to live up to the image of loving Irish mothers. Her landlady testified that when she criticized Aylsward for beating the child, Aylsward said that "she could have no nature for the child for the father denied it."[56]

Clearly illegitimate children were particularly vulnerable. As one judge put it, he felt "bound to see that the lives of illegitimate children, especially illegitimate children were protected."[57] In England and Wales the illegitimacy rates per live births declined from 6 percent in 1870 to 4 percent by 1890, yet in over a third of all child homicide trials (*not* including neonaticides) in England and nearly a third in Wales between 1867 and 1892 the victims were illegitimate. The Scots had the highest recorded illegitimacy rate at 7 percent and the Irish the lowest at 3.2. Forty-eight percent of Scottish child homicide trials and 26.5 percent of Irish child homicide trials involved illegitimate children.[58] As the *Times* put it, "It cannot but be that they who come into the world without a right to do so, as society holds—without passport, credentials, introductions, friend—should find an indifferent reception and fare ill. It is not their fault, but they have no friends."[59] A defense attorney put it more bluntly, "Many bastards were born and many bodies were hidden."[60]

FATHERS AND ILLEGITIMACY

Not all of them were the victims of their desperate mothers. While the assumption was that maternal instincts should protect children, the natural instincts of fathers were more problematic. As the *Times* put it in an editorial, "Do the fathers suffer lifelong pangs and self-reproaches because they have ruined woman and left their off spring to perish? . . . *THEY* take it easily enough and are often most exemplary and most comfortable Christians in their way."[61] Judges often referred to the moral guilt of the father. After a Central Criminal Court jury returned a verdict of concealment in a case in which a young woman had stabbed her newborn seven times after the father refused to marry her, Justice Pollock said he "could only hope the man would feel it his duty to do that which was no doubt before God and man his bounden duty."[62] Justice Bovill told a young woman convicted of concealment, "This case will be a warning to him who caused your misery and to other young men."[63]

Though how much the fathers sympathized with the misery was subject to debate. In England the mother of an illegitimate child had twelve months to file a paternity suit against the father. Anne Noakes, a widow who worked as a laundress, had been seduced by a police constable who had promised to marry her but had failed to do so. On the child's first birthday, the father told Noakes that he had deliberately led her on to keep her from filing affiliation papers until it was too late. After leaving a note saying "she would no longer let herself be taunted and the talk of the neighborhood," Noakes cut the child's throat and her own. An unusually sympathetic London jury found her insane.[64]

An Irish judge told a servant whose infant had bled to death after being left in some bushes, "I think you are more sinned against than sinning—go and sin no more." Another judge expressed his regrets that "the female is generally the only sufferer in such cases." When a Cavan woman was accused of killing her infant, the defense attorney pointed out that "the real culprit, I say, is not in the dock. The real culprit is that beast, that brute who first destroyed this woman's virtue, then threw her upon the world an unfortunate wanderer." The judge directed the jury to recognize the benefit of the doubt and acquit.[65]

In Scotland Lord Young lamented that "the prisoner would suffer very greatly both in mind and body while the partner of her sin had altogether escaped the suffering."[66] But at least one Scottish judge suggested that the father's role was irrelevant to the charge. When the defense attorney asked the father of a dead infant what his wages were, Lord Craighill interrupted: "[N]o, we are not here trying the witness for not marrying the girl." But the defense may have worked on the jurors. Lord Craighill directed the jury to convict, but a majority of the jurors voted that the charges had not been proven.[67]

At least twelve men in the United Kingdom were charged with killing newborns. The common factor in these cases was that the father was either the employer or a relative of the infant's mother. In all but one of the cases in which the mother of the child was the father's employee, the father was acquitted. Predictably, the incest cases resulted in more serious consequences, even though incest was not a crime under English law.[68] The average sentence for fathers convicted of a crime in connection with the death of newborns in England was seventy months; for mothers the average was only twenty months. By far the harshest sentence for a man accused of killing a newborn was a case from York in which a man had fathered a child on his stepdaughter. The jury found the man guilty of manslaughter and the woman guilty of concealment. Justice Coleridge's indignation seemed to be aimed more at the sexual abuse of the stepdaughter than the death of the newborn: "I cannot and do not doubt for a minute that you ruined your young stepdaughter and that you shrank from no brutality however atrocious and revolting in the hope that it would conceal your crime from the censure of the world." Though the conviction was only for manslaughter, the judge concluded, "The jury have spared your life. It is not fit, however, in my judgment that you should contaminate society. I sentence you to slavery for the term of your natural life."[69]

Incest was also a factor in cases from Ireland and Wales. In Ireland a retired policeman in Galway and his niece were jointly charged with the murder of her newborn infant. A witness said that the couple had to kill the child as the priest refused to marry them since the child was the product of incest. The prisoners were convicted of concealment of birth and sentenced to nine months each.[70] A grand jury in South Wales threw out murder charges against half siblings whose infant was found in a coal heap. They were both convicted of concealment, the mother sentenced to one month and the father to four months.[71]

Scotland was the only part of the British Isles where incest was a crime in the nineteenth century. Forty-five incest trials were heard at the High Court of Justiciary between 1867 and 1892. However, the three cases in which Scotsmen were tried for killing newborns all involved relations between servants and employers. The only conviction was of a Lanark gamekeeper found guilty of "cruel and unnatural treatment of an infant" and sentenced to nine months.[72]

Despite the rhetoric, unless the father was guilty of incest or exceptional cruelty, the fathers of dead newborns usually escaped legal retribution. However, when couples united to rid themselves of an unwanted illegitimate child which had survived its first day, English judges punished fathers more severely. Elizabeth Porter, a twenty-four-year-old servant, and John Fenton, a twenty-five-year-old joiner, were jointly charged with the manslaughter of her infant child. Justice Charles said that "he fully believed she would never have done what she did but for the advice of the unworthy being who stood beside her." He sentenced her to eight months and Fenton to five years.[73]

Of nine single men in England tried for killing their illegitimate children more than a day old, six were convicted of murder and two were executed. But outside England the outcomes were less dire. There were three such cases in Ireland. One man was executed but he had also killed the child's mother. A jury in Dundee convicted a Scotsman of culpable homicide for poisoning his illegitimate three-week-old son with prussic acid, but recommended him to mercy on account of his good character. The judge said that "good character aggravated the case" and sentenced him to eight years.[74] A Welsh laborer charged with poisoning his illegitimate child as well as its mother had been heard to swear he would never pay child support despite an affiliation order. His defense attorney argued, however, that the mother had poisoned the child, and he was acquitted.[75]

MARRIED DEFENDANTS

Parents who killed illegitimate children were presumed rational, but married people who deliberately killed children were more likely to be found insane than any other accused killers. Forty-four percent of married Englishwomen tried for killing their children were found insane, even though the statements of these women were often very similar to those of unwed mothers who were convicted of murder. For example, Lydia Venables explained that she had killed her illegitimate daughter because "I knew I had no shelter for myself and my child and this caused me to do it." At her trial the defense attorney argued that "her previous good character, the affection which she had displayed towards the child, the straits to which they had been reduced had such an effect upon the mind of the prisoner as to render her incapable of understanding what she was doing." But Justice Quain insisted that there was nothing even to reduce the crime to manslaughter. "The statement of the prisoner although it must touch the heart of all who heard or read it, showed that she deliberately took the knife and cut her child's throat and also that she was perfectly conscious of what she was doing. That was what the law called murder." She was convicted of murder.[76]

Justice Quain's argument is a striking contrast to those judgments made regarding married women in England. In a case heard by Justice Pollock, a married woman who had been abandoned by her husband had killed her four-year-old daughter out of poverty and despair. Her words are very like those of the unwed mothers convicted of murder.

> The reason why I did it was because I dreaded to go back to the union [the poorhouse]. One thing, Gerty is in Heaven, she will not have to bear what I have gone through. I do not seem to feel anything; I wish I did. It would be better for me perhaps. My head feels dead. I wish my heart did.

The judge insisted there "could be no doubt the poor woman had been cruelly deserted by her husband and doubtless was distressed and distracted at the thought of her future." While Justice Pollock admitted that "[t]here was no medical evidence that the woman was so out of her mind as not to know the nature of the act she committed," so he suggested an alternative to the jury. "If the child had accidentally got into the water and the woman then became distracted and under the influence of distraction made the statement then she would not be guilty." She was found insane.[77]

Insanity in married women was often attributed to pregnancy, childbirth, or lactation. When Ann Nichols, the wife of a respectable chemist who "had a comfortable home and a kind husband," confessed to poisoning her child, her defense was that she had still been nursing the eight-month-old child. "Suckling children till they were big and strong was more than some women could bear . . . caused weakness, delusions and in fact temporary insanity. This kind of insanity was not of rare occurrence, it was well known; in such cases there was a predisposition to kill the child."[78]

The issues of shame, poverty, and hormones were all demonstrated in a Welsh case. In 1885 a pregnant woman from Carnarvon had cut the throat of her two-year-old daughter and then tried to cut her own because she had "got into a desponding state of mind." Her husband had joined the militia and her mother had gone to the workhouse. She was worried about money and as a newcomer to Carnarvon had no place to turn. After cutting the child's throat, she told a neighbor that "the child is in heaven and will not be in anybody's way again." Her crime seems to have been an attempt to escape desperate poverty and suffering for her child. But a physician testified that her action could be traced to her pregnancy. "In that condition her excitability would naturally be increased. Persons who were pregnant frequently did have homicidal tendencies." If that premise had been universally accepted, a great many unwed mothers might not have been convicted. But though the woman was found insane, Justice Stephen, who heard the case, was struck by the fact that when her husband asked why she did it she told him the child "will miss many a stone being thrown at her." After the verdict, Justice Stephen announced that he had discovered that the couple had not been legally married and told the father: "You have done her a great injury. You have been living with her and no doubt placed her in the painful position which she occupies today. . . . I think you will be a most degraded fellow if you do not do her the small justice you can by making her your wife."[79] In the defendant's mind the motive was poverty; the jury accepted that her pregnancy had made her insane; but for the judge the motive most in keeping with a woman's nature was shame.

In Ireland, as in England and Wales, when a married woman killed a child out of desperation, the outcome was likely to be an insanity verdict. Bridget Drennan, who cut her child's throat after her husband lost his job, was found insane as were 55 percent of married women tried for killing their children. But when Ellen Carroll, an unwed mother who cut her own throat as well as that of her child, offered insanity as a defense, she was convicted of murder and sentenced to death. No married woman in Ireland was found guilty of murdering her child and no Irish unwed mother who killed her child was found insane.[80] Every married Irish woman convicted of manslaughter in the death of her child served fewer than two years. Half of the convicted single mothers were sentenced to death or penal servitude.

Fifty percent of the married women accused of killing their children in Scotland were found insane. A Scottish physician testified that "[p]regnancy sometimes acts as an exciting cause to insanity."[81] Thirteen percent of all Scottish child homicides were attributed to puerperal insanity. But the Scots took a different perspective on poverty as a motive. No Scottish woman, married or single, who offered poverty as an explanation for killing her child was found insane. The Scots saw killing a child to escape poverty as a rational act—criminal but with extenuating circumstances.

Married men who killed their minor children were also more likely to be found insane than other killers were. However, the explanations for insanity were different for fathers than for mothers. Insanity in mothers was most often attributed to the precariousness of female mental stability particularly when reproductive biology was involved. One homicidal father blamed his action on childbirth. William Gouldstone felt his wife had been having children too quickly. When she gave birth to twins, he stopped speaking to her. A week later he killed their three young children and severely wounded the twins.[82] When arrested, he told the police: "I have done it like a man. . . . I thought it was getting too hot with five kids within three and a half years and I thought it was time to put a stop to it." His coworkers came to his defense and tried to raise money to hire an attorney, explaining, "We are quite sure he went out of his mind when his wife bore him twins."[83] It is striking that Gouldstone felt that his action was that of a man. While caring for one's family was certainly part of the Victorian masculine code, Gouldstone seemed to feel that fatherhood included the power of life and death. But if Gouldstone felt his decision was a masculine one, his attorney argued that his act was proof of insanity. He was "well-conducted and had gained the esteem of his employers, the confidence of his fellow workers and the love of his family." Further, there was no evidence of poverty: "There was no evidence of want, but on the contrary, every sign of those small comforts that people in their sphere of life might look for." Therefore, he must have been insane at the time. "He submitted that the prisoner's mind became unhinged before he committed the act and that unless it had become so it would have been impossible for him to have committed a deed of so awful a character."[84]

The jury convicted him of murder, a decision that the *Times* praised. But the *Times* also seemed to accept that Gouldstone was being driven by nature as much as women were driven by the hysteria of pregnancy: "We admit that he has acted after his kind; that he has done what his nature has led him to do but he has given to proof hereby that he is the type of man against whom our criminal code has been enacted and for whom the extreme penalty of the law is the appointed end."[85] When such a man acted according to his nature rather than his reason, he became a criminal, and a single mother who acted reasonably to spare her child starvation was a criminal. But when a married woman's nature drove her to kill, she was found insane

Unlike married women whose homicidal insanity was taken to be a product of their biology, homicidal insanity among fathers was more likely to be attributed to external factors, especially alcohol. In England fathers who had been drunk at the time they killed their children were more than three times more likely to be found insane than drunken mothers were. The difference stems partly from the fact that while 83 percent of drunken mothers were charged with homicide through neglect, 80 percent of drunken fathers had killed children during violent rages, the majority of them with lethal weapons. Under the circumstances the only options were murder or insanity. Though 20 percent of drunken fathers in England were found insane, 32 percent were convicted of murder and 10 percent of them were executed. The differences between the fathers who were found insane and those who were convicted of murder seemed to rest primarily with the persuasiveness of defense counsel and the sympathies of judges and juries. Medical experts testified that the men who were found insane were suffering from delirium tremens, but that was also true in nearly half the cases in which the father was found guilty of murder.

The *Times* generally did not approve of insanity verdicts in such cases, and apparently neither did the general public. In a case in which a London laborer had murdered his three-year-old son while in a drunken rage, the newspaper reported that the killer "shammed madness" after his arrest. His neighbors were unconvinced. When he was removed from the police station, he was "followed by a large crowd of people who hooted and hissed him. One woman followed up behind shouting 'Hang him! Hang him! He ought to be lynched! Hand him over to us women, and we'll limb him!' The prisoner who turned very pale, cast a terrified look behind him."[86] The insanity failed before a London jury, which convicted him of murder though he was later found insane and transferred to Broadmoor after the death sentence was commuted.

The other most common factor among fathers found insane in England and Wales was being either widowed or estranged from the child's mother. In 20 percent of the cases in which homicidal fathers were found insane, the man's insanity was attributed to the absence of a female caregiver for the child. A quarter of the widowers tried for child homicide in England were found insane. But as with drunkenness, the options were extreme: half of the widowers were found guilty of murder.

Of the twelve Scottish fathers accused of killing their own minor children, six were intoxicated at the time. Two who had violently killed infants while in a drunken rage were found insane; however, in a third very similar case the outcome was different. Andrew Wallace, a collier in Ayrshire who killed his two-year-old daughter while in a drunken rage, pled guilty to culpable homicide and was sentenced to twenty years— equaling the longest sentence given to a Scottish parent. The only judicial comment was that he probably deserved more.[87]

Wallace's sentence was a marked contrast to that given in a similar case in County Limerick, Ireland. After Patrick Conway crushed his daughter's skull and threw her body in the river, he told police, "I plead guilty to having killed my child while laboring under the influence of drink." At his trial the judge told the jury that "if they had any doubt, they should give the benefit of the doubt to the prisoner, and that manslaughter would be the safest verdict." After the jury convicted him of manslaughter, the judge said that "he had no doubt but he had been guilty of the crime and that he had been led into that crime by being a habitual drunkard." He was sentenced to only eighteen months because he had given himself up to the police.[88] Conway's sentence of eighteen months was the longest given to an Irish father who was drunk at the time of the homicide. A quarter of the accused were found insane and a third of them were acquitted completely.

NEGLECT

Throughout the United Kingdom, while violent homicides tended to get more attention and in most cases heavier sentences, children were more likely to die from neglect than from violence. Children died from starvation, a lack of medical attention, or other acts that might not have proved fatal to an adult. Between 1867 and 1892 on average, five parents per year in the United Kingdom were tried for homicide through neglect of their child, and the numbers remained surprisingly constant. But the suspicion was that such homicides were still underreported. The *Times* noted in 1891:

> We must add that the darker view of the facts is that entertained by several coroners who have excellent means of observation and who state that a verdict of "death from natural causes" or "accidental death" is often a decent way of describing the effect of slow starvation and that deaths by overlaying or by suffocation may mean the very worst crimes.[89]

The rate of such trials was twice as high in England and Wales as it was in Ireland and Scotland, suggesting that authorities were more inclined to prosecute such cases. Neglect was the cause of death in nearly a third of the cases in which English parents were tried for killing their children. About a third of English parents charged with manslaughter as a result of neglect were acquitted by English juries, though the reasoning was not always immediately apparent. The legal status of parents or guardians whose children died from neglect in England was subject to debate. In 1885 English Lord Chief Justice Coleridge told a jury that "if the prisoners had by culpable neglect caused the death of the child or shortened its life—that was, had tended to contribute to its death—then they were guilty of manslaughter." Coleridge explained that the provision was essential. "Otherwise, a long course of deliberate cruelty not perhaps intended to take life, but having the natural effect of shortening life continued (as he had known it continued) for years and ending in the slow but sure destruction of the life of a fellow-creature would not be punishable by the law." Coleridge was confident that such things could not happen in England. "By the law of England no particular act was necessary to constitute the crime of manslaughter; nor indeed, any act at all, and it would be a grave mischief to society if it were otherwise."[90]

In child neglect cases the prosecution had to prove that the parents had the means to provide for the child. Inquiries were usually made as to the parents' resources when a child died of starvation. When a coroner's jury in London heard a case in which an infant had starved to death, they heard testimony that the father made only ten shillings a week. The coroner's jury said the parents' "conduct to their children almost amounted to criminal neglect. The line drawn was a very fine one. But they returned a verdict of death from disease and want of food."[91] When the Board of Poor Law Guardians prosecuted a woman whose child died of malnourishment, the defense explained that her husband was away in the army and she earned eleven shillings a week with which she tried to support herself and four children. While she worked she left her children home alone, leaving sugar water to sustain them. Justice Grantham directed an acquittal since there was not sufficient evidence of negligence since she had to work.[92] In another case Justice Martin ordered a Lewes jury to acquit a man whose child had starved to death because "there was no evidence he had been in work or offered work."[93]

The outcomes of these cases indicate that there was some sympathy for poor parents, but at least until the late 1880s there were few indications that the courts thought that more direct measures should be taken by the state to prevent such deaths. In the spirit of laissez-faire, the *Times* insisted in 1883 that parents who could not care for their children could rely on "the competence of good Christian people. To lay down that a man can house, feed and clothe self, wife and four children on 12 shillings a week certainly is very hard lines. We admit very readily that a man in such a case is a proper object of charity—that is, of private charity."[94] The recorder at the Central Criminal Court insisted the poverty was no defense, as "the law provided, in cases where people were too poor to provide the necessaries, the workhouse where all that was requisite could be had at the public expense."[95] The recorder ignored the cruel reality that in the workhouse mother and child would be separated, but if the mother left the workhouse to try to find employment outside, she was required to take the child with her.

But even when a woman was willing to enter the workhouse, there was no guarantee of admission. In 1878 Ann Riley was charged at Manchester with the murder of her eleven-month-old daughter. She and her child had been evicted after her husband left her to look for work. When she tried twice to apply for Poor Relief, the relieving officer was too busy to meet with her. "She drowned the child because she had nowhere to go." The jury found her guilty of manslaughter but also voted to censure the relieving officer. Justice Manisty "remarked on the exceptional circumstance in which the crime was committed and said it was a fearful thing that a woman could in England be driven to desperation by the inadvertence or negligence of those who are appointed to administer relief. The prisoner was then sentenced to six calendar months' hard labour."[96] Exactly half of married parents in England who offered poverty as the defense for the death of a child through starvation were acquitted, but those convicted served very light sentences.

Occasionally the courts made an example of a public official although usually a fairly low-level one. In an extraordinary case in 1872, George Cannon, superintendent of the St. Giles' Workhouse, was charged with the manslaughter of a three-month-old child. He had refused to allow the child and its mother and two siblings into the casual ward on a cold, rainy night. Instead, he had insisted that the woman was drunk and tried to get her arrested. The police refused to charge her though the constable had taken her to the police station as "it was more humane than to leave them in the cold and wet yard." The police inspector had the woman and children sit by the fire and ordered food for them. The police surgeon wrote a certificate to get them admitted and still Cannon refused. When the infant died of pneumonia, Cannon was charged with manslaughter. The defense "[a]sked the jury not to be led away by prejudice . . . all that he could be guilty of was grievous error of judgment." After the jury convicted him of manslaughter, even his defense attorney spoke against him. Justice Quain said, "This was conduct which could not be lightly passed over. Looking at the importance of protecting that portion of the population which above all others required protection having nobody to look after them and nobody to appeal to and being entirely at the mercy of men in the position of the prisoner." He sentenced Cannon to twelve months at hard labor, "which would be a lesson to the prisoner and a warning to every relieving officer."[97]

But usually English courts assumed that women were responsible for childcare. In 90 percent of the trials in England in which married women were charged with killing their children, the cause of death was neglect. Fathers worked to provide means but might remain totally ignorant as to the physical well-being of their children. In one case in which an infant had starved though her father had good wages, prosecution witnesses testified with astonishment that the mother would "leave it to go out. The father in her absence had frequently been seen to feed the child." The mother was sentenced to ten months.[98]

In a case in which both parents were convicted, Justice Byles announced he needed time to consider the sentence for the husband. "With regard to the female prisoner he could have no hesitation because it was the mother's duty to attend to the child and she had dreadfully neglected that duty." He sentenced the mother to ten years penal servitude. The next day he said regarding the father, "[H]e had supplied his home with the proper resources, he had been from home all day and it was the duty of the wife to take care of the child and she had grossly neglected that duty. If the jury had acquitted him, he should not have been dissatisfied." He released the man on his own recognizance.[99] Often the implication was that the father's responsibility as patriarch was to make sure the mother performed her duties. After a husband and wife were both convicted for the death of their six-month-old daughter through neglect, Justice Lindley sentenced the mother to fifteen months and the father to three months as he "ought to have protected his child from his drunken wife."[100]

In England the average sentence for a mother convicted of manslaughter through neglect was 65 percent longer than that for fathers. Even when the woman was not the biological parent, the responsibility rested with her. In a case in which a man and his second wife were tried for the death of his daughter, Justice Coleridge "pointed out that there was a material difference between the cases of the father and the stepmother, he being a great deal from home; but if he knew of the ill-treatment, and did not object to it and allowed it then he would be guilty in point of law, and nearly as guilty (morally) as his wife." But the woman was the true culprit in the judge's eyes: "As to the stepmother, she was in the place of a mother to the child, and her duty was clear." After the jury returned a guilty verdict for both, Coleridge

told the couple that "they had been convicted on the clearest and most overwhelming evidence, and to his satisfaction of cruel, wicked, dastardly conduct towards this poor unoffending child. There was however a distinction
between their cases." He sentenced the father to eighteen months and the
mother to ten years.[101]

Among biological and stepparents of each gender in England, stepmothers
were the most likely to be convicted of manslaughter through neglect and
receive the heaviest sentences. The harshness may reflect the popular stereotype
of the wicked stepmother. Modern evolutionary theory also predicts that
stepchildren will be at greater risk.[102] The problem, however, was largely limited to England. Only nine trials in Ireland, Scotland, and Wales involved the
homicide of a minor stepchild. Further, even in England stepparents were the
accused killer in less than 5 percent of the child homicide trials. But a third of
the convictions for killing a stepchild in England led to executions. Gender
issues were also involved as the assumption that men were the breadwinners
and women the homemakers influenced outcomes. Though the numbers are
small when couples were jointly accused, stepmothers were the most likely to
be convicted (89 percent), followed by biological mothers (62 percent) and biological fathers (59 percent), with stepfathers the least likely to be convicted.

That women were held responsible is ironic since under English law until
midcentury the legal custody of legitimate children rested absolutely with the
father. In fact, in 1885, when a married woman was tried at the Central
Criminal Court for carrying her twenty-month-old child around in the cold
when the child was "wet, filthy, dirty and emaciated, weighing only ten
pounds," the Common Sergeant suggested that since the child was legitimate, the child's father bore the sole legal obligation to provide for it. He said
that the mother would be legally responsible only if the child was illegitimate.
His argument was certainly not generally accepted and in this case, despite
the Common Sergeant's explanation, the mother was convicted and sentenced to six months.[103]

Though single mothers received little sympathy, widowers were often
excused in cases of neglect. The defense attorney for a widower whose child
had starved to death suggested "[t]hat the prisoner was fond of the child there
could not be a doubt, remembering that he was attached to the child, it being
that of a good wife whom he had survived." The jury acquitted his client.[104]
Even more striking was the case of Arthur Teasel, a laborer from Norwich
who was accused of the murder of his infant son in 1889. Teasel's wife had
died in childbirth, leaving three young children. After relatives refused to take
the infant, Teasel took a train to London, carrying the child and a carpetbag.
When the train arrived, he no longer had the child. He told people the child

had been placed with a caretaker and two weeks later sent himself a telegram announcing the child's death. When suspicions were aroused based on testimony of people who had seen him with the child on the train, the police questioned him. Teasel told police, "[I]t is made away with. I threw the body over the bridge at Lynn, I never thought it would come to this." The police found the child's clothes and the bloodstained carpetbag in Teasel's room. Two months later a fisherman caught what he thought was the child's corpse but it fell back in the river and the body was never recovered. Teasel's defense attorney argued that there was no evidence the child had been murdered. His theory was that Teasel "had imprudently given to it an over-dose of cordial to keep it quiet, which had caused its death and that he foolishly threw the body into the river to prevent inquiry from being made." After a short deliberation, the jury acquitted Teasel.[105]

In another case in which a man was accused of drowning his fifteen-year-old daughter after he had been required to take her out of the workhouse, Justice Denman "in summoning up the case to the jury, took occasion to remark that there ought to be exceptions to the rule which compels a father to take his children with him on leaving the workhouse, as it seemed neither wise nor reasonable that a man who might be able to support himself should be prevented by being obliged to take his children." The man was acquitted. Had Denman's suggestion been applied to single mothers, it might have prevented a great many infanticides, but no judge suggested that it was unreasonable to oblige mothers to be responsible for their children.[106]

Women were supposed to care for children even if they had no money with which to do so, yet they faced prosecution if they left their children alone while they went out to work. Single mothers were expected to work but childcare was women's work, even if the child was motherless. When William Nottingham was charged with the manslaughter of his infant son, the defense argued that the death of his wife had so depressed Nottingham that he had become "an altered man that neglected his home and family." But more telling was the argument that his two older daughters (ages eight and twelve) "were capable of taking care of it but that they had since the death of their mother taken to 'gadding about; and neglected their duty.'" Nottingham was acquitted.[107]

Neglect was the cause of death in about a quarter of the Welsh trials in which parents were tried for killing their children, and mothers were twice as likely to be tried as fathers. All of the accused Welsh parents were convicted though the sentences were fewer than two years in all but one case. Though most of these cases fit a pattern similar to those of the English cases, one death from starvation was an extraordinary one that served to highlight the issues of state versus parental responsibility as well as the tensions between English and Welsh, and religious and scientific worldviews.

In 1869 an Anglican minister in rural Wales wrote a letter to the local press reporting that a young girl in his parish had not eaten in sixteen months.[108] Two months later he reported that four local men had watched the girl for two weeks and taken an oath that she had not eaten. He urged "such medical men as feel a real interest in the advancement of their science" to come and observe.[109] The London press viewed reports of the Welsh Fasting Girl with condescension. One Londoner wrote, "There is no doubt this is a mysterious case. Not how she exists without nourishment, but, how are the people gulled?"[110] The *Lancet* suggested that the parents were to blame and the issue of state intervention should be raised: "The girl doubtless brings much gain to her parents, besides making them the object of wondering interest to the Welsh mind; the question now arises whether the stupidity or selfishness of parents, as in this case, ought to be allowed to bar the way to their child's return to health and happiness."[111]

The letters to the local newspapers in Wales reflected a variety of views. One reader worried that "[s]ome English people say the Welsh are not truthful and with many of them this story of twenty months fasting will be considered sufficient to condemn the whole of Wales." But another correspondent (clearly a Welsh speaker) reported having seen the child and added, "No use for anybody to tell me that she is imposter or her father and mother a liar . . . I bet hundred pounds her don't eat or drink. . . . If doctors won't do this [take the challenge to investigate] let them hide in their confounded hedds and shut up their shops."[112] During the autumn, letters increasingly accused those who doubted the fasting girl of ignorant prejudice.

To resolve the question, a committee of respectable local farmers under the leadership of the vicar asked a physician at Guy's Hospital in London to send four nurses to the girl's home to watch around the clock. The editor of the *Carmarthen Weekly Reporter* was confident that the skeptics would be embarrassed. "What the *Lancet* and the members of the faculty will say to the final result—should all go satisfactorily—the public here are eager to know. It is an old saying that doctors differ but in this case, the doctors as a body it is not impossible will be outwitted."[113]

But the embarrassment went the other way. The girl died. As the Christmas issue of the *Carmarthen Weekly Reporter* reported, "She died on Friday afternoon, the 17th, after having really fasted for a period of eight days. The news of her death has doubtless served to undeceive the minds of many persons who were either avid believers or inclined to believe." The report did not mention that the editor himself had been among the believers, but an editorial stressed that gullibility was not unique to the Welsh. After citing recent examples of fortune-tellers and quack doctors in Somersetshire, the editorial concluded, "We could name many English counties in which from our acquaintance with them, we think it is more than probable that the case would have excited quite as much interest and credulity." The editorial also insisted that the parents had no ulterior motives. "The secluded situation in one of the most hilly and sparsely peopled part of Wales was such as to render it extremely improbable that a sufficiently large number of persons would visit the girl to make a pecuniary motive tenable."[114]

But the more pressing issue was that a child had starved to death while a number of adults looked on. "A grave responsibility for the death of the child rests somewhere. If her abstinence be traced only partially to her own will, who but her parents are responsible for her tragic end?" The *Carmarthen Weekly Reporter* absolved the medical personnel: "It was certainly not any part of the duty of either of the medical man or the nurse to feed the child. It is difficult to conceive how any degree of responsibility can attach to the nurses since they were subordinate to the medical gentleman and the committee."[115] The nurses had been told not to feed the child unless she asked for food and she did not. However, eight days after the nurses had been brought in it became clear that the girl's health was declining. One man resigned from the committee in protest but no one took any other steps. As the *Carmarthen Journal* put it, "[I]t is a great pity that the nurses were not at once withdrawn by the committee. What is more marvelous is they were not withdrawn on Friday when it was clear she was dying. We cannot help saying that some effort ought to have been made to save the child's life."[116] A local GP admitted that the father had told him he could offer the child food but "I thought it better not to for fear they might say something to me."[117]

A coroner's jury charged the father with manslaughter but absolved all the medical personnel and the committee members. The *British Medical Journal* noted defensively, "All candid minds will admit that it was the last thing to be expected that the child would allow herself to be starved to death, and that her parents would look calmly on."[118] But the *Times* expressed indignation: "If Welsh parents, doctors and clergymen are capable of such gross superstition as to believe that a human being can live without food, it is the duty of those who are better informed to set them a wholesome example." The *Times* clearly believed that allowances might be made for the Welsh: "It may have been worthwhile to seek some means of exposing the imposition among so credulous a people as the Welsh"; however, the fact that a London hospital had been involved was unforgivable. "It is monstrous that metropolitan aid should only have been granted in order to assist in culpable homicide." The

Times was particularly angry that no charges had been brought against the doctors involved. "A doctor who can consider a girl not in danger after an eight days fast must be an extraordinary specimen of his profession even in Wales." The editorial drew an angry retort from a Welsh doctor who pointed out that the nurses were from London.[119]

Another attempt to hold the doctors responsible was made before Welsh magistrates at Carmarthen. The prosecution alleged that the "medical men had entered into an illegal contract with an illegally constituted committee." However, the magistrates refused to commit the medical men for trial, though the girl's mother was indicted along with the father.[120] In something of an anticlimax, the girls' parents were tried at the July Assize before Justice Hannon. The defense argued that the child had been eating at night and the parents had been genuinely fooled. Nevertheless, both parents were convicted; the father was sentenced to twelve months and the mother to six.[121]

The case was remarkable in many ways, as it became a focus for competing images of the English and the Welsh. The English press never missed an opportunity to point out the backwardness of the Welsh. But the Welsh newspapers often stressed that those who failed to believe were in fact the ignorant ones. By the spring of 1870 the *Carmarthen Weekly Reporter* returned to its original position, arguing that the girl had not starved to death but had died from "excitement." The stress of dealing with the nonbelievers had been too much for her. An editorial urging readers to contribute to the legal defense fund being prepared for the father argued that the world needed "men who *can* believe more than they can understand, like the great Welshman Sir Isaac Newton."[122] Not only is it interesting that Newton (who was born in Lincolnshire) was claimed as a Welshman, but also that in defending what had been put forth as a religious miracle, the newspaper refers to the greatest hero of English science.[123] In addition to national antagonisms, the case is also significant in terms of the objectification of the child. It was only after her death that anyone asked whether it was appropriate for responsible adults to simply watch a child starve to death. Ultimately the courts fell back on the notion of parental responsibility, a position which certainly worked to the advantage of the medical personnel.

The rate of Scottish parents tried for killing a child through neglect was only half that of England and Wales. Though parents accused of killing their child through neglect were almost always convicted, sentences were a year or less in all but two cases. But community sanctions might have been more severe. The Scottish branch of the SPCC recognized the role of poverty in such cases. "On the whole it was only by thrift, industry, and sobriety that the majority of the people would be able to bring up their children in such a manner as was desirable in the interest of the whole community and until these qualities reached the lower circles of society they must be prepared to cope in the best possible way with the evil."[124] After hearing the case of a couple whose year-old daughter had weighed nine pounds at the time of her death, the judge sentenced them to twelve months each and told them they had the "condemnation of all human beings."[125]

Cases of children dying through neglect were rarely reported as homicides in Ireland. Only three deaths of children through the abuse or neglect of parents appear in the Outrage reports and nine other cases appear in the surviving court records. The longest sentence given in any of these cases was ten months. While it may be as the Irish press claimed, that fewer Irish children suffered from neglect, it is also possible that such cases were simply not perceived as homicides. Though the available information is limited, the report of one trial suggests that culpability required more than neglect. A father and stepmother in Kilkenny were accused of allowing his illegitimate daughter to die "by neglecting and withholding proper good food from his child." A doctor testified that "there was a complete absence of food. . . . I attribute the death of the child to an insufficiency of food continued for a month before death, the vermin was produced through want of care and filth." However, the newspaper report concludes that "the case having been fully gone into, the prisoner was acquitted and the court rose."[126]

Drink and Family Violence

Poverty and drink often made for a lethal combination throughout the United Kingdom. In more than 70 percent of English cases in which married women were charged with killing children through neglect, drink was mentioned as a factor. In these cases the courts were usually willing to accept drink as a mitigating factor. In early January 1867 the *Times* noted that seventeen infants in London had been accidentally suffocated during the last week of December. "The deaths of six children from burns and scalds were also recorded. After festive nights parents cannot take too much care of their children."[127] When Bridget Murphy, a married woman, was convicted of causing the death of her nine-week-old daughter through neglect, the jury recommended mercy on "account of her employment having drawn her from home." Justice Day rejected their suggestion. "The only evidence of any employment drawing the prisoner from home was that of frequenting public houses and leading a life of intemperance and worthlessness. It was necessary that an example should be made, to serve as a warning to other good-for-nothing women." He sentenced her to twelve months.[128] Elizabeth Large, a married woman "addicted to drink," had taken her nine-month-old son with her to a pub and forgotten where she left him. The child's body was found in a cesspool. Large told police, "I recollect him falling down. I thought we were abed and that he could cry himself to sleep." She was sentenced to three months.[129] Jane Jones had passed out from drink when her infant rolled off her lap. A London jury acquitted her of manslaughter, but the judge "commented strongly on her disgraceful habit of drunkenness."[130] Two-thirds of these women were convicted but over 80 percent of them served fewer than two years.

Drink was also a factor in the homicide trials of eight married mothers in Scotland. In a case from Inverness when a woman in a drunken stupor had allowed her child to roll off her lap into the fireplace, the judge said he was

> quite ready to believe that the sorrow the prisoner must have suffered by the painful death of her child caused by her own criminal negligence had been more severe than any sentence [but] it was necessary she should be sentenced because in the law the circumstances that the crime was the result of intoxication was not a defense which can be accepted in cases of this kind.

He sentenced her to six weeks.[131] When Elizabeth Penn, the wife of a soldier in the Highland Regiment, was accused of starving her infant son to death, the judge insisted that there "was no evidence of crime since dipsomania left her unable to care for her child. This was a case for moral improvement." As directed, the jury returned a not guilty verdict but included a reprimand with their verdict.[132] Two other women suffering from DTs were found insane but five married women who had overlain their infants while intoxicated were all acquitted, though the fact that the cases came to court at all may indicate that Scottish authorities were more inclined to prosecute than their neighbors.

The bishop of Limerick assured the SPCC that any cases of child abuse or neglect in Ireland were the result not "of deliberate cruelty or want of parental affection, but in almost every instance the outcome of drunkenness."[133] The implication was that if drunkenness was the cause, the parents were not culpable. In cases in which Irish parents were charged with killing their children while intoxicated, the incident usually occurred during a fight between the parents.[134] Irish courts were very lenient in such cases. More than half of them ended in acquittals, and of those convicted all but one was sentenced to time served. On Christmas Day 1892 Edward Fallon of Galway had poured a kettle full of boiling water on his child's cradle during a drunken fight with his wife. His wife explained to the police that "we did not live well together as he used to be drinking his wages." A neighbor claimed that the wife "had given to her husband some impudence." Fallon pled guilty to manslaughter and was sentenced to six months.[135] Other children had been dropped into fireplaces during violent struggles or stabbed when a parent threw a knife. But the judges and jurors seemed to share the sentiments of Justice O' Brien, who referred to the death of a child in a drunken tug-of-war between its parents on Christmas Eve as a "melancholy accident."[136]

Six English fathers were accused of accidentally killing their children while fighting with their wives. Justice Willes refused to consider manslaughter charges against a laborer who had knocked a candle over and set his child's bed on fire while chasing his wife: "The circumstances in the depositions proved no more than misconduct on the part of the prisoner in getting drunk and that an accident happened to his child in consequence of his drunkenness."[137] The other accused fathers, each of whom had thrown a poker or other heavy object at his wife and accidentally hit a child, were convicted, but the longest sentence was twelve months. In one case the judge "bid the prisoner to be warned by the grievous effect of his loss of temper and to endeavor to bear with his wife in future and to restrain his passions. The learned Judge sentenced him to three days from beginning of Assize, hence discharged."[138]

A Welsh case inspired similar leniency. A woman pled guilty to manslaughter after a poker she threw at her husband struck her child in the head. Justice Matthews sentenced her to just one day, adding that "she was free thereupon to walk home immediately to her husband and try to live happily with him."[139] A Scotsman who threw an iron rod at his wife and struck their fourteen-year-old son in the head was convicted of culpable homicide and sentenced to six weeks.[140] Though none of the accused in these cases had any intention of killing their children, it is striking that the tolerance for domestic violence was such that throwing a lethal weapon at a spouse could be overlooked.

CHASTISEMENT

The tolerance for violence in the home could also be seen in cases where children had died from the effects of parental chastisement. According to a contemporary guide to the English criminal law, "Where a parent is moderately correcting his child and happens to occasion his death, it is only a misadventure, for the act of correction was lawful; but if he exceeds the bounds of moderation either in the manner, the instrument, or the quantity of punishment, and death ensues, it is manslaughter at least."[141] The courts were particularly careful to preserve the parental right of chastisement. Though most of the accused were convicted, sentences were usually very light and judges seemed to be especially sympathetic to the defendants. In one case after a man was charged with the manslaughter of his nine-year-old daughter, Justice Huddleston cautioned the jury "against confounding proof of improper chastisement with evidence in support of the charge of manslaughter against the prisoner." Even though neighbors had testified that the child had been abused and ill-fed, the jury acquitted the father.[142]

The SPCC had encouraged the prosecution of Ellen Clarke for the death of her ten-year-old stepdaughter, who "had been very much ill-treated and neglected. She had beaten her with a strap, a broom, a hand-brush, or anything that came in her way. Witnesses had seen child tied to banister and every time Ellen passed she would strike child on her head and body." Clark "was loudly hooted when she left the Court in the custody of the police." But at her trial, Justice Wills directed for an acquittal of the manslaughter charge, though she was sentenced to five months for neglect.[143] A man who beat his eight-year-old son with a poker because he had failed to lay a fire was found guilty though the jury noted "the deceased boy had been very troublesome." Justice Hawkins, noting that "although correction was necessary parents should on no account use excessive violence, or more especially a weapon, towards their children," sentenced the father to one month hard labor.[144]

When a nine-year-old girl fell to her death while running from her father, the coroner's jury "having heard in evidence that the deceased was severely and unmercifully beaten by her father considered that he should be severely censured, his conduct in their opinion being more calculated to frighten and harden the child than improve its manners." The coroner "expressed his approval of the verdict and severely censured the father,"[145] but no further punitive action was taken. Juries might also make allowances for ignorance. When a woman "of good character and a teetotaler" was accused of beating her adopted daughter to death, the jury concluded that "because of her previous inexperience of children she went further in her correction of her child, than she intended to." Justice Pollack sentenced her to three months.[146]

The Celtic nations appear to have a lower tolerance for abuse. Catherine Roberts, a charwoman in North Wales, was accused of killing her eight-year-old daughter. She had told neighbors that "she would beat or starve the child to obedience." The neighbors testified of systematic cruelty. Physicians found eighty-six separate abrasions on the child's body. Roberts was convicted and Justice Lawson sentenced her to twenty years.[147]

When an Irishman in Lanark, Scotland, was charged with the culpable homicide of his twelve-year-old daughter through "starvation and beating with fists, belt and poker," the presiding judge "remarked that such a case of combined neglect and maltreatment had rarely come before any court in this country." He sentenced the man to five years.[148] His assessment was correct as there was no similar case in the records from 1867 to 1892.

The combined issues of chastisement and class were highlighted in an Irish case in 1892. Anne Margaret Montagu, the wife of a prominent Protestant landowner in Derry, was charged with killing her three-year-old daughter. As punishment for soiling herself, Montagu had tied a stocking around the child's arms at the elbow, looped the stocking over a nail five feet above the ground, and closed the door, leaving the child suspended in a dark, windowless closet for three hours. When Montagu returned, she discovered that the stocking had slipped over the child's throat, asphyxiating her. The case drew considerable coverage throughout the British Isles.[149]

The *Times* noted that in keeping with her status as the wife of a local justice of the peace, Mrs. Montagu was allowed to sit with her husband at the solicitor's table during the magistrate's hearing and "only officials and reporters were admitted to the Court." The chief witnesses for the prosecution were the servants who testified not only about the death of the little girl but also about systematic cruelty toward Montagu's seven sons. The defense attorney appealed to the sympathy of the court: "She had lost a beloved daughter. Was she to be punished further and her whole life blackened?" The magistrates bound her for trial but released her on £700 bail.[150]

At her trial in Dublin "the court was densely crowded. Mrs. Montagu was pale and seemed to feel her position but was firm and self-possessed." The prosecution stressed that such crimes were rare in Ireland and urged that regardless of her motive Montagu's actions were culpable, "unjust because extravagant, criminal because too severe." The defense "complained of a spirit of 'enthusiastic ferocity' which was abroad with respect to the prisoner who had been tried and found guilty in the Press . . . simple negligence was not a criminal offense." Though one defense witness did say the child was "of very independent will," the same witness admitted he had never seen a prison cell as poorly ventilated as the closet in which the child died. The jury returned a guilty verdict, adding that "the jury consider the treatment inflicted on the child was done under a mistaken sense of duty and therefore recommended her to mercy." The judge said "the course pursued by the prisoner was due to some mistaken and perverted sense of what was right and proper discipline. Even taking these circumstances into account he could not inflict fewer than twelve months imprisonment."[151]

Montagu's sentence was in line with those given to other parents, but as the *Times* admitted, the class and gender of the offender made it more significant. "It cannot be said that the sentence erred on the side of severity. For a woman of Mrs. Montagu's education and social position to stand in the dock is in itself a most painful thing and to be sentenced to any term of imprisonment is terrible; but if there is any crime that calls for sharp repression it is the crime of cruelty to those who have the strongest natural claim upon a woman's affection." The editorial went on to consider the forces behind cruelty to children in the form of discipline. "When the public reflects it cannot help coming to the conclusion that a 'mistaken sense of duty' may sometimes turn a woman into something monstrous and inhuman . . . [t]he law will deal severely with what the parent or the school master may fancy is only excessive care for the child's interest but what is really a specially cruel development of egoism."[152]

The *Times* compared the Montagu case to ones in which schoolmasters had killed students. Like parents, schoolteachers traditionally had the right to chastise their charges though the deaths of students at the hands of schoolteachers were rare by the late Victorian period. Five teachers in England and Wales and two each in Ireland and Scotland were accused of homicide through excessive chastisement. Generally violent chastisement was not fully condoned, but neither judges nor juries felt comfortable interfering with the rights of teachers. None of the English and Welsh teachers were convicted, though the accused were usually warned not to let it happen again. When a schoolmaster in London was accused of manslaughter after a ten-year-old boy died from a concussion, evidence showed he had struck the child on the top of the head. The recorder at the Central Criminal Court said, "[I]f the prisoner had in an unguarded moment, struck the unfortunate boy so violent a blow as to cause his death an example ought to be made of him; not merely in the light of punishment, but in order that little boys of tender age might be protected from any undue violence when at school." Perhaps because of the implicit threat of a heavy sentence, the jury acquitted the schoolmaster of both manslaughter and assault.[153] In another case in which a nine-year-old had died from brain inflammation after his boarding school headmaster beat him with a birch rod, the coroner's jury returned no indictment but the master was advised "not to chastise children privately in the future."[154]

The only conviction anywhere in the United Kingdom was of a schoolmaster in Scotland who had kicked a boy in the groin when the child refused to hold out his hand to be beaten. The schoolmaster told the boys' father: "He was a very forward boy and required to be kept under." The boy died of blood poisoning from the wound. The other children in the class supported the victim's version of events, but when the police interrogated the schoolmaster he said: "I do not remember the circumstances sufficiently well to answer questions." A jury in Perth acquitted the teacher of homicide charges but convicted him by a vote of eight to seven of assault. The judge admonished and released him on a £20 recognizance.[155]

In addition to parents and schoolteachers, other designated caregivers were sometimes accused of killing their charges through neglect or abuse. Within the family, grandparents were the relatives most often charged with child homicides. Perhaps because their legal responsibilities were less clear-cut, grandparents were very unlikely to be convicted even when the evidence was fairly strong. Unlike mothers, grandmothers might be excused from responsibility. For example, in a Welsh case a grandmother was accused of killing her three-month-old grandchild. "It appeared that the prisoner was so intoxicated as apparently to have no knowledge that she had the child and as she was probably in that state when she received it here was some doubt whether she was in a condition to undertake any duty with respect to the child. Under these circumstances the jury acquitted the prisoner."[156] When an Englishwoman was accused of starving her grandchild, Justice Brett stressed that she was not bound by law to take care of the child, but "as she chose to do so, she was bound to execute the charge without wicked negligence but if she had stopped at home she would have starved too." She was also acquitted.[157]

Two Scottish grandmothers acted deliberately, but the motives may have struck a sympathetic chord. One woman had strangled her three-day-old granddaughter and then bashed her head in because she wanted her daughter to go back to work. The woman's husband had said that the daughter could come live with them but not the child. Lord Deas charged for a murder verdict, but the majority of the Dumfries jurors voted that the charge was not proven.[158] Elizabeth Gillies allegedly poisoned her nineteen-month-old granddaughter, one of four illegitimate children she was keeping for her daughter. Gillies had been angry that the dead child's father had not been contributing to its support. When the child died, Gillies told police, "I am the criminal," and arsenic was found in an oatmeal stain on the child's dress. Nevertheless, the jury voted eight to seven that the charge had not been proven.[159] But "a quiet looking old woman" who had stabbed her grandchild to death for insurance money was convicted of murder by a Glasgow jury though her sentence was commuted.[160]

An English grandmother was actually executed for her grandchild's death. The case was exceptional in that the child's death had been intended to cause pain to its parents. The killer actually told her son-in-law, "It is the only thing that I can do to make your heart ache as you have made mine for so long."

The grandmother had drowned the little boy after a fight with her son-in-law and then written her daughter, "I have done murder and I want you to give me into the hands of justice. I have killed the dear boy." The jury found her guilty of murder but recommended her to mercy, and Justice Blackburn said during sentencing that "his own belief was that she did not intend any ill-will to the child at the time she removed it, but that some strange perversity of mind, subsequently induced her to commit the crime."[161] Despite the judge's suggestion that she had been insane, she became the only grandmother to be executed for killing her grandchild.

In England, in keeping with the belief that children were the responsibility of women, twice as many female relatives as male relatives were tried for killing a child. Women were more likely to be convicted and were given heavier sentences. One young woman was charged with the manslaughter of her infant stepbrother. When the infant's mother died, the father had taken his daughter out of the workhouse to care for the infant. When the child died from neglect and starvation, the stepsister was charged but not the father. Justice Coleridge said that legal responsibility rested with the father, but if the girl had undertaken the duty and neglected it she was guilty of manslaughter. She was convicted and sentenced to twelve months.[162]

Given that the courts preferred to leave responsibility for children in the hands of their parents, the deaths of children at the hands of people whom the parents had designated as caregivers again raised the question of exactly who could be held legally liable. For the youngest children, especially illegitimate children, parents often turned to baby farmers who would take the child into their home in return for a fee. In most cases, the parent paid on a weekly or monthly basis, and while the care was often minimal, the arrangement was often the only option for single mothers. The more dangerous format was one in which the parent (or sometimes grandparent) paid the baby farmer a lump sum to "adopt" the child. The survival rate for these children was very low, but since the parent usually had no plans to see the child again, there was rarely an interested party to investigate the outcome.[163]

English courts usually saw the neglect of infants by baby farmers as a lesser form of homicide. Thirty-two baby farmers were tried for homicide in England during the period. Nineteen of them were convicted, but 47 percent of the convictions led to sentences of fewer than two years. Two baby farmers were executed in England between 1867 and 1892. Annie Took was perhaps the more likely candidate. The mutilated remains of the nine-month-old child she was paid to care for were found in Essex in May 1879. Took confessed, saying that she had smothered the child though she would not have done it "if the mother's sister had not said that they never wanted to see or hear more of him." Took was convicted of murder and hanged.[164]

The other death penalty case was very different. Margaret Waters had the misfortune to be the chosen example of the evils of baby farming. Waters was indicted for murder based on evidence gathered by the grandfather of a child who died in her care and a journalist who wished to investigate baby farming. At her trial the public and the courts were presented with graphic descriptions of the reality of baby farming. Waters was charged with having murdered children through a systematic pattern of starvation and neglect. The prosecution described her crime as one of "the most heinous crimes that could possibly be tried in an English court of justice." The crime was certainly heinous but it was hardly unique. During the twenty-five years covered in this study, one hundred and seventy-eight people were charged in English courts with causing the death of a child through starvation and neglect. Margaret Waters was the only person to suffer the death penalty. After her conviction, Waters told the court that though "she had led a life of deceit and falsehood . . . guilty of murder she was not." Despite the accuracy of her protest that others guilty of the same offense had not been called murderers, the judge "said she had been convicted of the greatest crime that could be committed by a human being . . . it was necessary that the strong arm of the law should vindicate the justice of the country and take up the case of these poor innocent children." After sentencing Waters to death, the judge sentenced Waters's sister, who had been her accomplice, to only eighteen months, adding that it was "only in consideration of that sentence [given to Waters] which he trusted would have the effect of putting an end to these nefarious practices" that he gave her sister a light sentence.

The *Times* voiced its approval. "The outrage on every human, not to say womanly instinct involved in such conduct is frightful to contemplate. A conviction for Murder will, it may be hoped strike terror into all who share the responsibility of these shocking barbarities and will teach the licentious and cruel that 'he that hateth his child is a murderer.'" On the day after Waters was hanged the *Times* noted that "a most just sentence has thus been executed and the law has conspicuously fulfilled its appointed office of being a terror to evil-doers." However, the editorial also admitted that "we would not aggravate the wretched woman's criminality, nor do we for a moment dispute the justice of her assertion that many other persons were grievously implicated in her guilt." Nevertheless, Waters was properly punished as "the deepest instincts of a woman's heart must have been deadened before such slow murder could be perpetrated upon piteous little innocents."[165] While there is no evidence that Waters's heart was any more deadened than that of other baby farmers, her case had been highly publicized and she was the designated example.

Fewer than ten years later a couple in Birkenhead was convicted in very similar circumstances. The couple was convicted of manslaughter only and Justice Brett, noting that "their crime was but a hairsbreadth short of murder, and deserved the fullest penalty that could be inflicted," sentenced them both to life in prison. An editorial in the *Times* pointed out the similarities between the two cases and lamented that "something very like baby farming, though without its murderous intent, grows up almost of necessity in the lower classes of modern society." The editorial suggested that further regulation and licensing was required but did not offer a solution to the poverty and lack of support which led single mothers to use baby farmers in the first place.[166]

Jessie King, who was convicted of murdering at least three children whose parents had given her money to keep them, was the only Scottish woman hanged between 1867 and 1892.[167] King received no mercy for a number of reasons: she had killed for personal gain and she was, though the term was not used, a serial killer. King's case was most remarkable in that she had deliberately killed her victims. Six other Scots were tried for homicide when children they were paid to care for died, but because the children had died of neglect the deaths were not considered murders and none resulted in sentences of more than two years. Three Irish baby farmers were convicted when children in their care died from neglect. All were sentenced to only twelve months.

Household servants, staff at orphanages and workhouses, and people who had taken apprentices or servants from the poorhouse also came before the courts for killing children in their care. In eleven cases from England and Scotland teenage domestic servants were charged with the deaths of their employer's young children. What was most shocking about these cases is the deaths were not simply the result of neglect: four of the children had been poisoned, three of them drowned, and the other either beaten or suffocated. A thirteen-year-old girl in Cumberland had thrown her employer's six-month-old child down a well. She was convicted of murder though the death sentence was commuted. But the same day that the commutation was announced it was also reported that she had confessed to killing another child.[168] The motive in these cases was usually resentment. The servants, some as young as twelve, were single-handedly responsible for caring for several children as well as housekeeping. Judges and jurors often found it incredible that young girls could actually kill small children even though in most cases the girls were said to have confessed. Only four of the nine girls charged in England were convicted.

The two Scottish cases were both poisonings. Fifteen-year-old Elizabeth Gibson claimed she "merely wished to frighten the child's mother with whom she had had a disagreement." She pled guilty to culpable homicide and was sentenced to eighteen months.[169] In the other case a fourteen-year-old servant poisoned an infant and a toddler. She also pled guilty and explained that she "had not realized the consequences of her actions, which were meant to annoy her employer." She was sentenced to ten years.[170]

Young babysitters were not the only children accused of killing other children. Around 20 percent of the persons tried in UK courts for killing children (not including newborns) were under the age of nineteen. Children and teenagers, especially in England and Ireland, also killed each other in brawls. In fact, over a third of Irish homicide victims under the age of fourteen who were not killed by their own parents died in brawls.[171]

About 6 percent of the child homicides reported in the *Times* between 1867 and 1892 were apparently the work of strangers. The average number of such cases per year nearly doubled beginning in 1888, as the Ripper murders seem to have inspired imitation. Between 1888 and 1892 there were an average of 3.6 child murders per year reported in England. These cases provided enormous fodder for the press, but no arrests were made in about a third of the cases.

Nondomestic child homicides in England and Wales were most likely to be felonies committed by strangers. In Ireland children killed by nonrelatives were most likely to be killed in brawls, either as participants or bystanders. But in Scotland the plurality of child homicide trials involving nonrelatives were accidental deaths. Though the English and Irish press were far more likely to boast about the treatment of children in their nations, if road accidents are not included, Scotland's rate of nondomestic child homicide trials was 33 percent lower than England's and less than half that of Ireland.

Even so, in England, Ireland, and Wales the courts and press seemed confident that children were protected. When a Protestant clergyman in Ireland was tried for the manslaughter of children who had died of neglect in an orphanage he had founded, the *Times* reported with approval the conclusion of the presiding judge, "No one could help admiring a person who erected a charitable institution intended to receive the offspring of the lowest of mankind but they must remember that at the termination of the 19th century, they were not in a state in which children were allowed to die on the roadside."[172] His view seems to reflect that of authorities in England, Ireland, and Wales who were confident that the state had done what it could to protect children and all that remained was to punish the exceptional evil-doers.

But the *Scotsman* was not so positive that problems had been dealt with.

In fact, the editorials often criticized the courts themselves. One of the most moving of the editorials was in response to a case in which a group of boys, aged eleven to fifteen, had stowed away on a ship at Greenock. When the boys were discovered, the captain and the crew brutalized them and then forced them off the ship onto an ice floe off the shore of Greenland. The two youngest boys died on the ice. The captain and first mate were tried for manslaughter. The prosecution argued that the case was important as the powers of a ship's captain were so great that it was vital that society guard against their misuse. He urged the jury "not to shrink from the strict performance of their duty to protect the weak and helpless against the strong." The defense attorney claimed the prosecution's speech was pompous and scoffed at the sentiments of the general public. "Whatever might be the feeling out of doors it was for the jury to determine the case upon its own proper merits. It was obvious that lads like those who had concealed themselves on the Arran were of the very worst class . . . they forced the master to provide them with food which was not intended for their consumption." Since the bodies were never recovered, he insisted that there was no case. The defense's summation was met with applause in the courtroom but the judge responded to it. "Those unfortunate children could not act according to their own desires or interests . . . they were compelled to leave the ship by reason of threats and the exhibition of physical force." He also stressed that it was a very important case—the first of its kind. After a thirty-five-minute deliberation, the jury unanimously found the captain guilty of culpable homicide. The verdict was received with hisses in the courtroom.[173] The judge sentenced the captain to eighteen months—a sentence very much in line with those given elsewhere in the United Kingdom for cases in which young apprentices, servants, or workers had died of abuse.

But the *Scotsman* was not satisfied. In a scathing editorial it described the victims as "poor and young, foolish fanciful lads such as we find strolling and loafing about every seaport town." Interspersed with descriptions of the brutal treatment the boys received on ship was the refrain, "[T]he captain, being as everybody says, a very kind man." After noting that the first mate lashed a boy "with the lead line because he who had to live in filth and rags happened to be dirty," the editorial dropped sarcasm for pure emotion. "The heart sickens or the blood boils with indignation, and every feeling within one's breast calls aloud for punishment when we think of what that little band suffered. They left one of the children sitting on the ice to die." After quoting one of the sailors who testified that "we heard him greeting when we were a long way off," the editorial asked, "Can the most callow amongst us read or think of that child cast out by the 'good, kind' captain on that icy wilderness, and

there sitting down in unutterable loneliness and desolation to vent futile cries
to the cold bleak sky until frost and death at last kindly wrap him in obliv-
ion of his woes, without feeling a flood of sympathy well up and a mastering
flow of indignation and a demand for justice?" Though the captain had been
convicted, the editorial concluded, "We feel that we are apprehending an
anticlimax and narrating the end of some other and less sad story when we
mention that the captain received yesterday a sentence of only eighteen
months imprisonment. But then, as they say, he was a 'good, kind' captain
and he was a respected communicant of a respected church."[174] It was just one
case, but after the rhetoric of the *Times* finding "melancholy satisfaction" in
the suffering of sick children and the Irish press celebrating the fact that the
Irish were always kind to children, there is something bracing and positive
about the *Scotsman*'s refusal to be comforted.

Conclusion

Resolving the tensions between the Otherness of murder in the abstract and the quotidian reality of most actual homicides was a constant challenge for judges, jurors, and the press working to preserve the national image of the decent, respectable men like themselves. Throughout the United Kingdom, the first line was that murderers were foreigners—literally outsiders. Even native-born murderers were still Other—either insane or from a separate breed of monsters. But this differentiation did not square with the reality of most homicides since killers were often neither foreign nor psychotic. In addition to coming to terms with the fact that there might be killers in their midst, national identity was also impacted by how a nation dealt with killers.

In England two major trends were involved. One was the sense of Duty that the *Times* had described as essential to English character. "Our unwritten law is that everything is to be done in the best way possible, and that everybody is to act up to the most exalted canons of duty."[1] As the British Empire expanded and Britain's position of the world's greatest nation was both recognized and challenged, it became increasingly important that the British (read here definitely as English) be perceived not only as the richest and most powerful people in the world but also the noblest and best behaved. Those who failed to live up to the "exalted canons" were increasingly likely to suffer the consequences of that failure. The "unwritten law" and "exalted canons" were also being enforced by an expanding state power. The Englishman's duty included going through proper channels. Physically chastising an impudent servant, child, or spouse was becoming less acceptable. Violence inspired by provocation or a manly impulse, though still highly praised in some quarters, was increasingly likely to incur punishment. These changes were disproportionately geared toward improving the behavior of the working classes, women, and others outside the charmed circle of middle-class men, but even for them the law and its sanctions were growing less flexible. There was, however, also a realization that the residuum might be beyond civilizing; so long as both killer and victim were from this group, the deaths might be considered regrettable but inevitable. For them, the occasional example must be set by an execution, but otherwise the courts often dealt with them fairly leniently.

The Welsh took pride in the Cymry, even as their neighbors either ignored or made fun of them. Welsh homicide trials provide less useful information than those of the other nations. In part this is because the Welsh apparently had an extremely low level of interpersonal violence. Even the English recognized that the Welsh were a peaceful people. But the Welsh also seemed to prefer to settle things within their own culture. After hearing cases presided over by English judges according to English law, Welsh juries decided based on their own good judgment. The variance between the judge's charge and the jury verdict in part reflected communication issues, but it may have also reflected the sense that the Welsh had their own standards and values to uphold.

Scotland had its own judicial system and its own concept of accountability. The Scots were more likely to demand that every killer atone for his sin, even if the sin was totally unintentional. On the other hand, Scottish justice was much more likely to be tempered with mercy, especially if the accused were a native Scot. The Scottish courts were less concerned with class and more concerned with ethnicity in that the Other in Scottish courts was so clearly linked to Irish immigrants. When a native Scotsman killed, though he would usually be required to atone, every mitigating factor would be considered. As a Scottish judge explained, the goal for everyone was actually twofold: to "just act like a man of sense and do your duty."[2] While the Scottish courts upheld the law, good sense dictated that the punishments inflicted on respectable Scots should not be overly harsh. Equity and reason were both crucial in determining sentences. As the *Scotsman* frequently pointed out, the English were too rigid and thoughtless in their mindless conformity to Duty whether it made good sense or not. But good sense also dictated that mercy not be shown to the unworthy. The Irish were increasingly dealt with as hopeless savages who were not only ruining their own country but were polluting Scottish society as well.

The situation in Ireland was different. Not only were the Irish more tolerant of recreational violence, they were less willing to have their fellow citizens held accountable in courts that were still tainted with "British justice." For the Irish the dominant legal issues were about land and not about homicide or public behavior. Confident that brutal violence was an English characteristic, Irish juries were particularly willing to see homicides as the unintended consequence of the passionate nature of the Irish people.

Issues of gender and family further complicated reactions to homicides. Contradictory ideas about whether real manliness consisted in physical strength or self-restraint also created challenges for the courts. British courts were not willing to accept a purely physical definition of male strength, but judges and jurors often expressed a sneaking kindness for a good stand-up fight. Victorian ideals of femininity were often seriously at odds with the circumstances of real women. Both as defendants and as victims, women created problems for the all-male members of the court. In England women who fought each other were often seen as comical, but women who killed men could represent an insidious threat. Women who killed children were the antithesis of the nurturing female ideal, but social and economic realities meant children were the most frequent victims of female killers. English courts largely resolved these issues by differentiating between respectable women and lower-class females. The homicidal activities of respectable married women were viewed as evidence of insanity or as sensational deviations from the norm. Most female killers, however, were lower-class women or unwed mothers. Like their male counterparts, they were incapable of being civilized. They deserved punishment but they were not a threat to English society. Again, the occasional example sufficed. Despite the growing rhetoric about protecting infant life, the government still viewed the well-being of children, especially illegitimate ones, as solely the responsibility of their mothers.

Gender issues were less prominent in Welsh trials as there were so few cases involving female killers. They were no less likely to be convicted than male killers, but two-thirds of them served fewer than two years. But there is some evidence that the disapproval of the local community may have been considerably more severe.

The Scottish courts insisted that women, like men, were reasonable adults who should be accountable for their actions. But again the Scottish courts were more flexible, willing to see infanticide as a sin for which a woman must atone, but not necessarily as a sign of madness or a capital offense. Though not blind to gender issues, particularly in assessing the worthiness of female homicide victims, the Scottish courts were not willing to accept that women were naturally any less prone to violence or any less capable of reason and self-control.

The Irish courts made little distinction between male and female killers, but men who killed women were much more likely to be found insane than any other category of killer. The men found insane had usually killed a woman who was not only weaker but often older or ill. Irish homicides were usually the result of brawls between evenly matched opponents. Deviations from the pattern were more likely to be seen as signs of insanity than as capital crimes.

Ultimately the courts of each nation dealt not only with questions of guilt and innocence but with questions of national character, hierarchy, gender, and fundamental values. Each homicide had to be cast as an act of barbarism representative of an alien mentality, as a comprehensible response to provocation, as the unfortunate result of a careless moment, or as a fundamental threat to the existing social order. Which crimes fall in which category was determined by and in turn helped to define the national character. Whatever certain other countries might do, judges and juries were obligated to demonstrate what their own nation would and would not allow.

Notes

LIST OF ABBREVIATIONS

CCC Central Criminal Court
INA   Irish National Archives
NAS National Archives of Scotland

INTRODUCTION

1. The *Times,* 21 December 1872, 9ef.
2. *Carmarthen Weekly Reporter,* 4 December 1869.
3. *Scotsman* 1 October 1879.
4. *Cork Examiner,* 5 March 1877.
5. In addition to the works cited below that deal with Britain, a number of scholars in American and European history have also examined the cultural and social meaning of homicide. Vandal, *Rethinking Southern Violence: Homicides in Post-Civil War Louisiana, 1866–1884;* Monkkonen, *Murder in New York;* Adler, *First in Violence, Deepest in Dirt: Homicide in Chicago, 1875–1920;* Adler, "'My Mother-in-law Is to Blame, But I'll Walk on Her Neck Yet': Homicide in Late Nineteenth-Century Chicago"; Monkkonen, *Crime, Justice, History;* Brown, *No Duty to Retreat: Violence and Values in American History and Society;* McGrath, *Gunfighters, Highwaymen and Vigilantes: Violence on the Frontier;* Lane, *Violent Death in the City: Suicide, Accident and Murder in Nineteenth-Century Philadelphia;* and Ayers, *Vengeance and Justice: Crime and Punishment in the 19th-Century American South.* For a social science perspective, see Daly and Wilson, *Homicide,* and Archer and Gartner, *Violence and Crime in Cross-National Perspective.*
6. The dates for this study were initially determined by technical issues involving the sources. As is true with all historical work they are ultimately arbitrary.
7. See Elias, *The Civilizing Process: The History of Manners.* The seminal article on this period in English history is Gatrell, "The Decline of Theft and Violence in Victorian and Edwardian England." More recently the theme has been examined by Wiener in *Men of Blood: Violence, Manliness, and Criminal Justice in Victorian England;* Wood, *Violence and Crime in Nineteenth-Century England: The Shadow of*

211

Our Refinement; and Emsley, *Hard Men: Violence in England Since 1750.* For an examination of murder see D'Cruze, Walklate, and Pegg, *Murder: Social and Historical Approaches to Understanding Murder and Murderers.* For an examination of homicide trends in Britain over a longer period, see Lawrence Stone, "Interpersonal Violence in English Society, 1300–1980," and Sharpe and Stone, "Debate: The History of Violence in England: Some Observations: A Rejoinder." For trends in Europe, see Spierenburg, "Long-term Trends in Homicide: Theoretical Reflections and Dutch Evidence, Fifteenth to Twentieth Centuries."

8. The scholarship on larger issues of crime and society in Britain (and especially in England) has grown exponentially in the past few decades. The best place to start is Emsley, *Crime and Society in England, 1750–1900.* Regarding violent crime, see D'Cruze, ed., *Everyday Violence in Britain, 1850–1950,* and Jones, *Crime in Nineteenth Century Wales.* For earlier periods see Sharpe, *Crime in Early Modern England, 1550–1750.*

9. On the problems with English statistics, see Taylor, "Rationing Crime: The Political Economy of Criminal Statistics since the 1850s," and John Archer, "The Violence We Have Lost'? Body Counts, Historians and Interpersonal Violence in England." The statistics used here are based on all homicide trials reported in the *Times* between 1867 and 1892. Regarding the many variations and complications of the English justice system, see King, *Crime, Justice, and Discretion in England 1740–1820.* Though it deals with an earlier period, King brilliantly assesses the process in all its diversity. Also see May, *The Bar and the Old Bailey, 1750–1850.*

10. de Nie, *The Eternal Paddy, Irish Identity and the British Press, 1798–1882;* Curtis, *Anglo-Saxons and Celts: A Study of Anti-Irish Prejudice in Victorian England;* Curtis, *Apes and Angels: The Irishman in Victorian Caricature;* and Foster, *Paddy and Mr. Punch: Connections in Irish and English History.*

11. The question of Scottish national identity in the nineteenth century is a complex one, further complicated by the late twentieth-century reappearance of a Scottish parliament. On Scottish national identity, see Devine, *The Scottish Nation;* Lynch, *Scotland, A New History;* Donnachie and Whatley, *The Manufacture of Scottish History;* and Harvie, *Scotland and Nationalism: Scottish Society and Politics 1707 to the Present.*

12. See Williams, *When Was Wales?;* Morgan, *Rebirth of a Nation: Wales, 1880–1980.* Regarding British, English, and Welsh identities and their interworkings, see Ellis, "Reconciling the Celt: British National Identity, Empire, and the 1911 Investiture of the Prince of Wales."

13. The *Times,* 6 January 1876, 3f. Also see Jones, *Crime in Nineteenth-Century Wales,* 78.

14. Two of the best surveys of nineteenth-century Scotland are Smout, *A Century of the Scottish People 1830–1950,* and Lynch, *Scotland: A New History,* chap. 23.

15. Irish history is in a boom period. Some of the most impressive studies of the nineteenth century are Lee, *The Modernisation of Irish Society 1848–1918;* W. E. Vaughan, *Ireland under the Union;* and Hoppen, *Ireland since 1800: Conflict and Conformity.*

CHAPTER ONE

1. Quoted in the *Times,* 29 September 1871, 3f.

2. The *Times,* 6 January 1876, 3d. Regarding the problems of counting crimes from a contemporary standpoint, also see Morrison, "The Interpretation of Criminal Statistics"; and Grosvenor, "Statistics of the Abatement in Crime in England and Wales during the Twenty Years Ended 1887–1888."

3. Regarding the efficiency of coroner's juries, see Emmerichs, "Getting Away with Murder? Homicide and the Coroners in Nineteenth-Century London."

4. *Maidstone and Kentish Journal,* 16, 19, 23 April 1859. For other examples see Conley, *The Unwritten Law,* 55. Also see Archer, "The Violence We Have Lost'? Body Counts, Historians and Interpersonal Violence in England."

5. The *Times,* 15 June 1882, 4a.

6. For example, the *Times* noted that between 1860 and 1869 the coroner's inquest reported 2,495 murders in England and Wales, though only 376 people were actually convicted of murder. The *Times,* 31 March 1871, 4c.

7. *Carmarthen Weekly Reporter,* 29 May 1875.

8. The *Times,* 11 August 1874, 4f. Howard Taylor has argued that the decline in the number of homicides reported in England and Wales is primarily the result of the reluctance of authorities to pay for homicide investigations. Taylor, "Rationing Crime: The Political Economy of Criminal Statistics since the 1850s."

9. The *Times,* 29 October 1885, 4a.

10. *Scotsman,* 14 June 1881. The statistics for Scotland in this study are based on the records of the High Court of Justiciary in the National Archives of Scotland (AD 14) and the minute books of High Court circuits.

11. *Scotsman,* 25 September 1877. The National Archives of Scotland have extremely good records for the criminals the Fiscals brought before the criminal courts in Scotland; but there is no official record of those whose actions warranted investigation but no prosecution. The *Scotsman* reported that in 1875, eighty-eight cases were investigated by the procurator fiscal as potential homicides and only fifty-four led to criminal trials. In 1876 forty-eight trials resulted from ninety-two investigations. *Scotsman,* 30 May 1878.

12. Irish National Archives (INA), Return of Outrages Reported to the Constabulary Office, 1848–1878; 1879–1892, CSO ICR, vols. 1–2. A fire in the Irish Public Record Office destroyed most of the nineteenth-century Irish court records. The National Archives in Dublin (the successor to the Irish PRO has some assize and quarter sessions grand jury books, depositions, and/or records of indictments from seventeen Irish counties for the period 1867–1892. Though the records are sparse for most counties, the surviving records for Cavan, Kilkenny, Limerick, and Roscommon appear to be complete. Overall, about 3 percent of the homicides in the surviving trial records are not in the Outrage Papers, but there is no consistency from county to county. For a study of Irish homicides over a longer period, see O'Donnell, "Lethal Violence in Ireland, 1841–2003: Famine, Celibacy, and Parental Pacification."

13. Great Britain, Parliament, *Parliamentary Papers,* "Memorandum as to the Principle upon which Outrages Are Recorded," 1887, LXVIII, 25.

14. Though comparing rates is complicated by the fact that while the population on the Isle of Britain was growing during the period, Ireland's population was declining rapidly. This means that if the actual number of homicides occurring annually held constant throughout the United Kingdom, Ireland's homicide rate per 100,000 would rise while Britain's would decline. Further, the smaller the population the more drastically a slight variation in the number of actual homicides per year will alter the rate.

15. For an example of this, see Wiener, *Men of Blood*, 266.

16. *Glasgow Herald*, 22 December 1880.

17. The *Times*, 27 August 1867, 9c.

18. See Conley, *Melancholy Accidents*; also Crossman, *Politics, Law and Order in 19th Century Ireland*.

19. The *Times*, 17 July 1872, 7e.

20. *Roscommon Journal*, 16 December 1882.

21. Jones, *Crime in Nineteenth-Century Wales*, 4–13 and passim.

22. The *Times*, 2 November 1877, 10d. On the extent and distribution of Welsh speakers, see Ravenstein, "On the Celtic Languages in the British Isles: A Statistical Survey"; Parry and Williams, *The Welsh Language and the 1891 Census*. For a modern view of the problem, see Parry, "Random Selection, Linguistic Rights and the Jury Trial in Wales."

23. *Carmarthen Journal*, 9 October 1874.

24. The *Times*, 17 November 1871, 4f.

25. *Carmarthen Weekly Reporter*, 26 March 1870.

26. In 1885, in a homicide case from Bettwsycoed, the defense objected to the admission of the dying deposition because while the victim had given it in Welsh, it had been written down in English because the magistrate did not speak Welsh. *North Wales Chronicle*, 31 October 1885.

27. The *Times*, 14 November 1871.

28. The *Times*, 29 May 1885, 5d.

29. The *Times*, 8 May 1886, 5c. For more on this point, see Conley, *The Unwritten Law*.

30. The *Times*, 7 November 1884, 10b.

31. The *Times*, 13 March 13, 1868, 11c.

32. 24&25 Victoria, c.100, s.6.

33. Duncan, *Green's Glossary of Scottish Legal Terms*, 28. For a detailed discussion of the legal history of culpable homicide in Scots Law, see Farmer, *Criminal Law, Tradition and Legal Order: Crime and the Genius of Scots Law 1747 to the Present*, chap. 5. For a less scholarly take on Scottish crime, see Livingstone, *Confess and Be Hanged: Scottish Crime & Punishment through the Ages*.

34. The *Times*, 24 September 1874, 9a.

35. The *Times*, 16 July 1873, 12d.

36. The *Times*, 11 December 1868, 11c.

37. The *Times*, 28 October 1878, 11d.

38. The *Times*, 21 August 1868, 8e.

39. The *Times*, 9 December 1870, 9c.

40. The *Times*, 21 December 1874, 10d.

41. The *Times,* 15 July 1868, 11e.

42. The *Times,* 11 April 1876, 11d.

43. The *Times,* 4 July 1876, 10f.

44. The *Times,* 25 March 1872, 11b.

45. The *Times,* 18 November 1885, 7b.

46. The *Times,* 22 July 1867, 11b.

47. The *Times,* 18 July 1872, 12f.

48. *Limerick Reporter,* 7 March 1879.

49. *Clonmel Chronicle,* 7 December 1889.

50. *Glasgow Herald,* 4 May 1871.

51. For examples, see *Kilkenny Journal,* 7 March 1885; and *Cavan Weekly News,* 14 July 1870.

52. See Conley, *Melancholy Accidents,* 2. The sentiment is also like the one suggested by James Averill in his essay on anger and aggression: "If the rules of anger are met, the response may be interpreted as a passion rather than an action." Averill, *Anger and Aggression: An Essay on Emotion,* 125.

53. *Limerick Reporter,* 12 December 1879.

54. Breaky, *Handbook for Magistrates, Clerks of Petty Sessions, Solicitors, Coroners etc.,* 431.

55. Conley, *Melancholy Accidents,* 147.

56. *Glasgow Herald,* 14 September 1878.

57. *Glasgow Herald,* 21 April 1882.

58. NAS AD 14 73/323; *Glasgow Herald,* 12 April 1873; *Scotsman,* 12 and 16 April 1873.

59. *Carmarthen Weekly Reporter,* 4 December 1869.

60. Wiener, *Men of Blood,* is based in part on a study of the Home Office papers regarding capital sentences in the nineteenth century. Also see Emsley, *Hard Men: Violence in England since 1750.* For the earlier period, see Gatrell, *The Hanging Tree: Execution and the English People 1770–1868* and for a groundbreaking but still highly controversial take on the topic, see Hay, "Property, Authority and the Criminal Law."

61. *Sligo Chronicle,* 14 March 1891.

62. *Munster News,* 4 March 1874.

63. *Glasgow Herald,* 19 August 1881.

64. See Walker, *The Historical Perspective,* vol. 1 of *Crime and Insanity in England,* especially the preface where he discusses the myths perpetuated by earlier historians. Also see Guy, "On Insanity and Crime and On the Plea of Insanity in Criminal Cases."

65. The M'Naghten Rules were based on the answers given by the English judges when called before the House of Lords in 1843 after a man who had assassinated the prime minister's private secretary was found insane. The public outcry over the verdict prompted the Lords to submit a number of questions to the judges, who replied though with the proviso that English law did not lend itself to discussions in the abstract.

66. Quoted in Smith, *Trial by Medicine: Insanity and Responsibility in Victorian Trials,* 15.

67. Quoted in Smith and Sheldon, *Scots Criminal Law,* 136.

68. The *Times*, 19 August 1879, 9a.
69. The *Times*, 24 July 1875, 13ce
70. The *Times*, 13 September 1883, 8a
71. The *Times*, 20 October 1883, 9d
72. The *Times*, 6 November, 6e.
73. For example, see the *Times*, 27 February 1886, 12a; 6 October 1883, 5d; 6 November 1883, 6e; 11 April 1892, 6b.
74. For a discussion of the debate between medical experts and legal authorities over the insanity defense in the period 1840–1870, see Smith, *Trial by Medicine*.
75. The *Times*, 19 July 1890, 13e.
76. The *Times*, 15 January 1873, 10e.
77. The *Times*, 29 November 1876, 3f.
78. The *Times*, 7 November 1878, 10d.
79. See Smith, *Trial by Medicine*, 143–60; Zedner, *Women, Crime and Custody in Victorian England*, 264–96.
80. The definitive work on the treatment of the insane in Ireland during this period is Finane, *Insanity and the Insane in Post-Famine Ireland*. Regarding the ratio of male to female admissions, see pages 130–31.
81. *Kilkenny Journal*, 11 October 1884; everywhere, "committed as a criminal lunatic" meant detention at "Her Majesty's Pleasure," which in essence meant until the Home Secretary authorized discharge. Smith, *Trial by Medicine*, 23.
82. NAS AD 67/192; the *Scotsman*, 21 September 1867; *Glasgow Herald*, 20 September 1867; Walker, *Crime and Insanity in England*, vol. 1, 142; Smith, *Trial by Medicine*, 85–89.
83. The *Times*, 28 September 1875, 8c.
84. The *Times*, 14 March 1878, 10c.
85. Parliamentary Papers Judicial Statistics 1874, vol. 71, 348.
86. On drink and violence, see Rowbotham, "'Only When Drunk': The Stereotyping of Violence in England, c. 1850–1900," 155–69. For drink in the nineteenth century, see Thompson, *The Rise of Respectable Society*, chap. 8; Harrison, *Drink and the Victorians: The Temperance Question in England 1815–1872;* Malcolm, *Ireland Sober, Ireland Free: Drink and Temperance in Nineteenth-Century Ireland;* Smout, *A Century of the Scottish People, 1830–1950*, chap. 6. The issue of drink and culpability was also challenging American courts: see Martin, "Violence, Gender and Intemperance in Early National Connecticut."
87. The *Times*, 9 April 1873, 10f.
88. NAS AD 14 74/553, *Glasgow Herald*, 12 September 1874; AD14 87/169; *Glasgow Herald*, 26 August 1887.
89. *Kilkenny Journal*, 2 January 1880.
90. The *Times*, 18 July 1878, 10c.
91. The *Times*, 26 October 1877, 11e.
92. The *Times*, 26 May 1886, 5d.
93. The *Times*, 16 July 1869, 11c.
94. The *Times*, 2 November 1878, 11b.
95. The *Times*, 25 January 1886, 10d; for another example of one judge expressly refusing to accept a precedent set by another, see The *Times*, 26 October 1877, 11d.

96. The *Times,* 6 May 1886, 7e.

97. *Carmarthen Journal,* 30 July 1875.

98. *Mayo Examiner,* 21 March 1891.

99. *Carmarthen Weekly Reporter,* 3 January 1873.

100. *Scotsman,* 8 October 1874; for examples, see NAS, AD14 73/321, 73/45, 84/287 77/89.

101. *Scotsman,* 17 September 1877.

102. Walford, "On the Number of Deaths from Accidents, Negligence, Violence and Misadventure in the United Kingdom and Some Other Countries."

103. The *Times,* 25 August 1873, 9d.

104. The *Times,* 31 October 1874, 11c.

105. The *Times,* 31 July 1879, 11e.

106. The *Times,* 12 January 1882, 4e.

107. The *Times,* 1 August 1892, 10a.

108. The *Times,* 26 October 1892, 4e.

109. *Scotsman,* 12 April 1869.

110. NAS AD14 73/84; *Glasgow Herald,* 3 October 1873.

111. A study for the Statistical Society performed in 1881 found that between 1867 and 1879 an average of 1,076 people per year were killed in railway accidents in England and Wales. Walford, "On the Number of Deaths from Accidents," 488. According to the *Times* in 1875, 1,290 people were killed in rail accidents in the United Kingdom and another 5,755 were injured. The *Times,* 17 April 1876, 7f.

112. The *Times,* 1 October 1869, 7c.

113. The *Times,* 28 March 1878, 11f.

114. The *Times,* 18 March 1876, 13d.

115. The *Times,* 20 March 1877, 11d.

116. The *Times,* 29 March 1869, 6f.

117. The *Times,* 20 October 1869, 7e.

118. The *Times,* 8 April 1875, 11d.

119. The *Times,* 9 April 1875, 9e.

120. *Scotsman,* 5 September 1868.

121. *Scotsman,* 2 June 1868.

122. NAS AD14 73/321; *Glasgow Herald,* 11 April 1873.

123. *Scotsman,* 26 February 1878.

124. NAS AD14 73/125; *Inverness Advertiser,* 22 April 1873.

125. *Scotsman,* 26 April 1873.

126. The *Times,* 9 November 1889, 9c; 26 October 1889, 9e; 28 October 1889, 7b.

127. The *Times,* 26 May 1870, 9d. Late nineteenth-century criminologists were fascinated by the physical attributes of criminals, though British experts were more skeptical than their European counterparts. See Wiener, *Reconstructing the Criminal: Culture, Law and Policy in England, 1830–1914.* On the European developments, see Gibson, *Born to Crime: Cesare Lombroso and the Origins of Biological Criminology.*

128. The *Times,* 20 March 1868, 9d.

129. A number of scholars have examined the Victorian press and its fascination

with murderers: see Knelman, *Twisting in the Wind: The Murderess and the English Press;* Robb, "The English Dreyfus Case: Florence Maybrick and the Sexual Double-Standard"; Taylor, "Beyond the Bounds of Respectable Society: The 'Dangerous Classes' in Victorian and Edwardian England." For another take on the role of the press, see Early, "Keeping Ourselves to Ourselves: Violence in the Edwardian Suburb," 170–84.

130. The Ripper murders have also inspired many historians. One of the best works on the larger context of the crime is Walkowitz, "Jack the Ripper and the Myth of Male Violence."

131. *Scotsman,* 14 February 1891.

132. The *Times,* 8 September 10c; 9 September, 12a; 10 September, 12b; 12 September, 6b; 23 October, 8f, 1873.

133. The *Times,* 22 February 1889, 10e.

134. The *Times,* 3 May 1892, 9d.

135. The *Times,* 15 July 1878, 11d.

136. The *Times,* 31 March 1870, 10f.

137. The *Times,* 16 May 1870, 12e.

138. The *Times,* 12 January 1878.

139. The *Times,* 21 May 1891, 6c.

140. The *Times,* 9 May 1871, 12b.

141. The *Times,* 30 May 1869, 12e.

142. The *Times,* 7 August 1870, 7c.

143. The *Times,* 21 May 1891, 6c; 21 August 1891, 12c.

144. The *Times,* 11 June 1891, 9e; 23 June 1891, 11c; 3 August, 9f, 1891.

145. The *Times,* 12 December 1891, 9f; 21 December 10e, 1891.

146. The *Times,* 8 April 1892, 12b.

147. *The Times,* 27 November, 5d; 29 November, 8b; 20 December, 10d; 21 December, 5f, 1888. On children who killed other children, see Abbott, "The Press and the Public Visibility of Nineteenth-Century Criminal Children," 23–39.

148. Quoted in The *Times,* 11 August 1874, 4f.

149. On reactions to violent robberies, see Davis, "The London Garroting Panic of 1862: A Moral Panic and the Creation of a Criminal Class in Mid-Victorian England."

150. The *Times,* 11 December 1874, 11f.

151. *Scotsman,* 12 April 1878.

152. *Scotsman,* 27 May 1870.

153. *Scotsman,* 10 April 1879.

154. On reactions to nonfatal rapes, see Stevenson, "'Crimes of Moral Outrage': Victorian Encryptions of Sexual Violence"; Conley, "Rape and Justice in Victorian England."

155. The *Times,* 24 November, 11c; 26 November 12b, 1882.

156. The *Times,* 3 August 1882, 9b.

157. *Scotsman,* 11 January 1876.

158. NAS 69/36; *Glasgow Herald,* 2 August; 6 October 1869.

159. NAS 90/71; *Glasgow Herald,* 4 July 1890; *Scotsman,* 4 July 1890.

160. NAS 73/34; *Scotsman,* 6 November 1872; NAS 92/14.

CHAPTER TWO

1. Most of the work on the making of the British national identity focuses on earlier periods than the one covered here. The leading work is Colley, *Britons: Forging the Nation 1707–1837.*

2. Regarding English identity in the late nineteenth century, see *Englishness: Politics and Culture 1880–1920,* ed. Colls and Dodd.

3. The *Times,* 6 May 1868, 14f.

4. The *Times,* 11 December 1877, 9e.

5. The *Times,* 21 March 1887, 6e. For the major study of this idea in an earlier period, see Colley, *Britons: Forging the Nation 1707–1837.*

6. The *Times,* 25 March 1887, 9f.

7. The *Times,* 13 October 1887, 11d.

8. The *Times,* 21 March 1887, 6e.

9. The *Times,* 12 May 1886, 7c. While an argument could be made that the late nineteenth-century English were a relatively orderly lot, this was a very recent development. See Shoemaker, *The London Mob: Violence and Disorder in Eighteenth-Century England.*

10. The *Times,* 4 October 1881, 10d.

11. The *Times,* 24 November 1888, 11e.

12. On this point in another context, see Wiener, "The Sad Story of George Hall: Adultery, Murder and the Politics of Mercy in Mid-Victorian England," and Hall, "The Nation Within and Without."

13. The *Times,* 20 December 1876, 10d.

14. The *Times,* 9 September 1874, 8c.

15. The *Times,* 3 August 1888, 10a. On youth gangs, see Davies, "Youth Gangs, Masculinity and Violence in Late Victorian Manchester and Salford."

16. The *Times,* 28 August 1883, 9e.

17. The *Times,* 21 December 1872, 9ef.

18. Quoted in the *Times,* 11 August 1874, 4f.

19. The *Times,* 11 August 1890, 6f.

20. Quoted in the *Times,* 18 December 1874, 9f. On the idea of the working classes as an alien world, see Dodd, "Englishness and the National Culture."

21. The *Times,* 8 October 1877, 9bd.

22. The *Times,* 22 August 1882, 7bc.

23. For a full account, see Waldron, *Maamtrasna: The Murders and the Mystery.*

24. The *Times,* 21 August 1882, 5d.

25. The *Times,* 16 November 1882, 6c.

26. The *Times,* 13 January 1889, 13a.

27. The *Times* 24 May 1871, 12c.

28. Though backwardness and superstition were not limited to Wales. In 1875 the *Times* reported a case from Warwick "that shows that there is a general belief in witchcraft at Long Compton and other villages of South Warwickshire among a certain class of the agrarian population." A man of "good character" had stabbed an eighty-year-old woman with a pitchfork because he "was and still is under the impression

that there are fifteen or sixteen witches who live in the village and that she was one of them, and that they had bewitched him and prevented him from doing his work." Justice Bramwell said he "never remembered a sadder case than seeing a half-witted man stand charged with the murder of a poor inoffensive old woman, whom he had killed under an impulse arising from a belief in witchcraft which would be discreditable to a set of savages." The defendant was found insane. *Times,* 17 December 1875.

29. The *Times,* 28 August 1868, 9f.

30. The *Times,* 23 February 1867, 9f.

31. The *Times,* 2 July 1868, 5f.

32. The *Times,* 25 December 1889, 7d.

33. The *Times,* 11 December 1877, 9de.

34. The *Times,* 26 December 1887, 8a–e.

35. The *Times,* 23 August 1889, 7a–b.

36. *Carmarthen Weekly Reporter,* 29 June 1870

37. *North Wales Chronicle,* 30 May 1885. Some English editors even acknowledged the tendency to create stories from a safe distance. The *Maidstone and Kentish Journal* reported "in the old days of journalism it was said to be the custom to 'kill a child in Liverpool' or invent some other mild and vague catastrophe of the kind, whenever a corner paragraph was required to fill the newspapers." *Maidstone and Kentish Journal.* 29 November 1875.

38. *Carmarthen Weekly Reporter,* 18 November 1871. The Welsh Language Census of 1891 found that 54 percent of the population over the age of two spoke Welsh. Parry and Williams, *The Welsh Language and the 1891 Census,* 11.

39. *Carmarthen Weekly Reporter,* 4 December 1869.

40. *Carmarthen Journal,* 21 March 1875.

41. *Carmarthen Journal,* 24 July 1875.

42. The *Times,* 26 July 1876, 11d.

43. *Herald of Wales,* 10 September 1892.

44. *North Wales Chronicle,* 4 June 1881.

45. *North Wales Chronicle,* 10 December 1881.

46. *Carmarthen Weekly Reporter,* 26 February 1870.

47. *Scotsman,* 9 December 1868.

48. The *Times,* 25 December 1872, 6b.

49. *Scotsman,* 19 February 1891.

50. *Glasgow Herald,* 15 July 1872.

51. *Scotsman,* 2 January 1868.

52. At the battle of Bannockburn in 1314 a Scottish army under the leadership of Robert Bruce won a decisive victory against the English, thus ending the threat of the English conquest of Scotland.

53. *Scotsman,* 28 June 1870.

54. *Scotsman,* 4 January 1868.

55. *Scotsman,* 29 September 1890.

56. *Scotsman,* 21 February 1877.

57. *Scotsman,* 9 January 1869.

58. *Scotsman,* 11 May 1878.

59. *Scotsman* 12 June 1879.

60. *Scotsman,* 9 June 1881.

61. *Scotsman,* 27 November 1882.

62. *Scotsman,* 8 January 1884.

63. *Scotsman,* 18 May 1886.

64. *Scotsman,* 21 May 1886.

65. *Scotsman,* 11 June 1886.

66. *Dundee Advertiser,* 5 January 1889.

67. *Scotsman* 21 August 1891.

68. *Scotsman,* 30 May 1888.

69. *Cavan Weekly News,* 8 November 1872.

70. *Kilkenny Journal,* 3 March 1875.

71. *Kilkenny Journal,* 24 June 1876.

72. *Roscommon Journal,* 18 October 1879.

73. *Limerick Reporter,* 1 November 1881.

74. *Clonmel Chronicle,* 9 July 1892.

75. *Kilkenny Journal,* 2 January 1889.

76. *Munster News,* 26 March 1870.

77. *Kilkenny Journal,* 26 June 1872.

78. The *Times,* 6 January 1876

79. The *Times,* 28 October 1875, 6a.

80. See Swift, "Behaving Badly? Irish Migrants and Crime in the Victorian City"; Swift and Gilley, eds., *The Irish in the Victorian City;* Swift and Gilley, eds., *The Irish in Britain 1815–1939;* Swift and Gilley, eds., *The Irish in Victorian Britain: The Local Dimension;* MacRaild, *Irish Migrants in Modern Britain, 1750–1922;* Lees, *Exiles of Erin: Irish Migrants in Victorian London;* Finnegan, *Poverty and Prejudice: A Study of Irish Immigrants in York 1840–1875;* Swift, "'Another Stafford-Street Row': Law, Order and the Irish in Mid-Victorian Wolverhampton"; Neal, "A Criminal Profile of the Liverpool Irish."

81. The *Times,* 6 February 1873, 11c.

82. The *Times* 16 January 1869, 11f.

83. The *Times,* 3 March 1870, 11e.

84. The *Times,* 8 September 1868, 10a.

85. The *Times,* 5 December 1868, 11a.

86. See Aspinwall and McCaffrey, "A Comparative View of the Irish in Edinburgh"; Smout, *A Century of the Scottish People, 1830–1950,* 91.

87. *Scotsman,* 18 May 1886.

88. Ibid.

89. Ibid.

90. The *Times,* 6 January 1876, 3e.

91. *Glasgow Herald,* 17 September 1875.

92. Lynch, *Scotland, A New History,* 360, 395–96.

93. NAS AD 14 70/275; *Glasgow Herald,* 11 January 1870.

94. NAS AD 14 72/112; *Glasgow Herald,* 25 September 1872; 15 July 1872; the *Times,* 15 July 1872, 7d.

95. NAS AD 14 69/3, *Glasgow Herald,* 22 April 1869; the *Times,* 5 January 1869, 9d.

96. NAS AD 14 78/143; *Glasgow Herald,* 14 September 1878.

97. *Scotsman,* 18 May 18, 1886.

98. *Carmarthen Weekly Reporter,* 31 August 1877.

99. *Carmarthen Weekly Reporter,* 4 December 1869.

100. *Llannelly Guardian,* 19 July 1877.

101. *Carmarthen Weekly Reporter,* 25 August 1876.

102. *Carmarthen Weekly Reporter,* 4 September 1869.

103. *Carmarthen Weekly Reporter,* 31 August 1877.

104. *Carmarthen Journal,* 12 March 1875.

105. *North Wales Guardian,* 13 November 1880. Note the use of the spelling "Briton," which usually referred to the earliest Celtic occupants of Britain, that is, the ancestors of the Welsh who had been displaced by the Anglo-Saxon ancestors of the English.

106. The *Times,* 20 July 1871, 10f; 18 October 1870, 5d.

107. The *Times,* 18 December 1871, 11d.

108. The *Times,* 21 March 1874, 12f. The incident bears a considerable likeness to Irish faction fights. On faction fights, see O' Donnell, *The Irish Faction Fighters of the Nineteenth Century,* and Conley, *Melancholy Accidents: The Meaning of Violence in Post-Famine Ireland,* 20–24.

109. The *Times,* 29 July 1878, 4c.

110. The *Times,* 4 August 1882, 5f.

111. For more on ethnic battles, see Conley, "War among Savages: Homicide and Ethnicity in the Victorian United Kingdom." Also see Swift, "'Another Stafford-Street Row': Law, Order and the Irish in Mid-Victorian Wolverhampton,",and "Crime and the Irish in Nineteenth-Century Britain."

112. For example, see the *Times,* 19 April 1867, 11e (Belgium); 16 August 1869, 4d (Italy); 25 September 1869, 9b (France); 28 December 1872, 8a–c (United States); 3 January 1873 3e (United States and France).

113. The *Times* 15 June 1872, 12c.

114. The *Times,* 17 August 1867, 11a.

115. The *Times,* 26 December 1874, 4b; 14 January 1875, 7c.

116. *Scotsman,* 8 January 1890, 17 January 1890; NAS AD 14 90/105.

117. The *Times,* 24 June 1867, 9b.

118. *Kilkenny Journal,* 12 March 1879.

119. The *Times,* 13 April 1867, 11d.

120. The *Times,* 17 November 1879, 11f.

121. *Dundee Advertiser,* 16 September 1867.

122. On this point, see Emsley, *Hard Men,* chap. 7; Wiener, *State of Mind,* 55–59; Wood, *Violence and Crime in Nineteenth-Century England,* chap. 4; Conley, *Unwritten Law,* chap. 2.

123. *Tonbridge Telegraph,* 15 March 1873.

124. *Maidstone and Kentish Journal,* 10 December 1861.

125. See Wiener, *Men of Blood,* 55–56, 61–62; 75, 162–63, 170, 195–96, 251–55, 264–70.

126. *North Wales Guardian,* 24 January 1880.

127. The *Times,* 30 July 1885, 12b.

128. *Limerick Reporter,* 4 July 1871.
129. *Limerick Chronicle,* 12 January 1869.
130. INA Return of outrages for Cavan 1870.
131. *Cork Examiner,* 18 December 1886.
132. The *Times,* 17 April 1889, 6f.
133. The *Times,* 8 August 1877, 11f.
134. The *Times,* 21 December 1887, 7e.
135. The *Times,* 31 July 31, 1890, 3e.
136. The *Times,* 13 September 1890, 12b.
137. The *Times,* 6 February 1891, 9b, 6b.
138. The *Times,* 24 November 1869, 8b.
139. For a very different interpretation of gun regulation in England, see Malcolm, *Guns and Violence: The English Experience.*
140. The *Times,* 8 August 1867, 11b.
141. The *Times,* 26 November 1881, 12b.
142. The *Time,* 24 September 1881, 9e.
143. The *Times,* 8 February 1890, 12d.
144. The *Times,* 14 August 1868, 9a.
145. The *Times,* 10 April 1876, 11b; 11 April 1876, 11d.
146. The *Times,* 21 December 1887, 7e.
147. The *Times,* 19 October 1881, 4b.
148. NAS AD 14 77/222; *Scotsman,* 11 September 1867, 13 September 1877.
149. *Scotsman,* 28 April 1870; NAS AD 14 70/209.
150. NAS AD 14 78/314; *Glasgow Herald,* 9 September 1878.
151. *North Wales Guardian,* 5 September 1891.
152. *Herald of Wales,* 2 January 1892.
153. *Herald of Wales,* 6 February 1892.

CHAPTER THREE

1. To get some sense of the complexity and the ongoing debates, see Cannadine, *The Rise and Fall of Class in Britain.*
2. Quoted in the *Times,* 29 January 1872, 5e.
3. The *Times,* 14 April 1879, 3f.
4. The *Times,* 26 February 1879, 10c.
5. The *Times,* 11 August 1874, 4f; 18 December 1874, 11f.
6. The *Times,* 6 July 1880, 12b.
7. The *Times,* July 14, 1879, 8b.
8. The *Times,* 1 August 1879, 11d.
9. The *Times,* 1 August 1879, 11e.
10. The *Times,* 12 August 1879, 9c–d.
11. Basing the punishment on the status of the victim rather than that of the accused harkens back to Celtic and Anglo-Saxon traditions in which the compensation a killer was required to pay was specifically based on the wergild or man-worth of the victim.

12. The *Times,* 10 February 1887, 6f.

13. The *Times,* 2 December 1875, 5a.

14. The argument that English courts were growing less tolerant has been made in Wiener, *Men of Blood;* Wood, *Shadow of Our Refinement;* and in a more nuanced argument in Emsley, *Hard Men.*

15. The *Times,* 29 March 1870, 11e.

16. The *Times,* 31 January 1868, 9b.

17. The average sentence for manslaughter convictions between 1867 and 1879 was 76.7 months, for 1880 to 1892 it was 78 months.

18. The *Times,* 26 March 1878, 4c.

19. The *Times,* 28 February, 12a; 2 March 1882, 7e.

20. Davies, "Youth Gangs, Masculinity and Violence in Late Victorian Manchester and Salford," 349–69.

21. The *Times,* 3 August 1888, 10a.

22. Regarding the transition, see Archer, "'Men Behaving Badly'? Masculinity and the Uses of Violence, 1850–1900"; Wood; Wiener, *Men of Blood;* and Emsley, *Hard Men.* Also see the essay by Wiener, "The Victorian Criminalization of Men." For an American perspective, see Courtwright, *Violent Land: Single Men and Social Disorder from the Frontier to the Inner City.*

23. See the collection of essays edited by Spierenburg, *Men and Violence.* Regarding England, see Shoemaker, *The London Mob: Violence and Disorder in Eighteenth-Century England,* chap. 7. Also Wood, chap. 1; Wiener, *Men of Blood,* chap. 2; and Emsley, *Hard Men,* chap. 3.

24. The *Times,* 9 April 1875, 11e.

25. The *Times,* 7 March 1876, 5f.

26. The *Times,* 18 October 1883, 3d.

27. The *Times,* 22 January 1880, 11d.

28. The *Times,* 29 July 1880, 11d.

29. The *Times,* 7 May 1874, 10e.

30. The *Times,* 5 March 1877, 11b.

31. The *Times,* 17 December 1888, 10f.

32. The *Times,* 18 July 1878, 11c.

33. The *Times,* 5 March 1877, 10f.

34. The *Times,* 4 February 1879, 6f.

35. The *Times,* 13 June 1867, 11c.

36. The *Times,* 8 May 1879, 4d.

37. The *Times,* 9 April 1875, 11e; on this point, see Emsley, *Hard Men,* chap. 3.

38. The *Times,* 22 January 1880, 11d.

39. The *Times,* 20 August 1868, 11a.

40. *North Wales Guardian,* 24 January 1880.

41. *Carmarthen Journal,* 30 July 1875.

42. The *Times,* 13 March 1867, 12d.

43. For a carefully reasoned discussion of the treatment of drunkenness by Welsh authorities, see Jones, *Crime in Nineteenth Century Wales,* 68–69, 89–94.

44. *Carmarthen Weekly Reporter,* 13 December 1873.

45. *Scotsman,* 10 April 1868.

46. *Scotsman,* 5 November 1868.
47. *Scotsman,* 14 December 1886.
48. NAS AD 14 73/156; *Glasgow Herald,* 25 December 1873.
49. NAS AD14 75/57; *Glasgow Herald,* 14 September 1875; the *Times,* 15 September 1875.
50. Quoted in Mitchison, *A History of Scotland,* 142. Also see Brown, *Bloodfeud in Scotland 1573–1625: Violence, Justice and Politics in an Early Modern Society;* Whatley, "How Tame Were the Scottish Lowlanders during the Eighteenth Century?"
51. NAS AD14 67/226
52. NAS AD14 74/356; *Glasgow Herald,* 27 April 1874.
53. NAS AD14 91/170; *Dundee Advertiser,* 4 September 1891.
54. On drink, violence, and recreation among the working classes, see T. C. Smout, *A Century of the Scottish People, 1830–1950,* chap. 6, esp. 133–39.
55. *Glasgow Herald,* 23 December 1868.
56. NAS AD14 91/19; *Glasgow Herald,* 5 March 1891.
57. NAS AD14 74/30; *Glasgow Herald,* 9 October 1874.
58. For further discussion of class and violence in Ireland, see Clark, *Social Origins of the Irish Land War,* and "The Importance of Agrarian Classes: Agrarian Class Structure and Collective Action in Nineteenth-Century Ireland."
59. *Limerick Reporter,* 12 December 1881; *Mayo Examiner,* 13 July 1889.
60. *Roscommon Journal,* 12 March 1892.
61. *Cavan Weekly News,* 2 March 1877
62. *Munster News,* 23 March 1874.
63. For more on Irish attitudes toward brawls, see Conley, "The Agreeable Recreation of Fighting."
64. *Roscommon Journal,* 16 July 1887.
65. *Limerick Report,* 12 July 1892.
66. NAS AD14 86/223; *Scotsman,* 23 June 1886; *Scotsman,* 24 April 1886.
67. INA, 1888.
68. The *Times,* 3 July 1884, 9e.
69. The *Times,* 9 April 1875, 9c.
70. *Scotsman,* 16 April 1873.
71. *Scotsman,* 17 June 1879.
72. D'Cruze, Walklate, and Pegg, *Murder,* 47. The literature on gender and violence in British history is extensive. On the role of gender in the "construction" of homicide, see pages 39–43 and 46–68. For a slightly earlier period, see Hurl-Eamon, *Gender and Petty Violence in London, 1680–1720.* Regarding women as criminals, see Zedner, *Women, Crime, and Custody in Victorian England,* especially pages 38–39, and Emmerichs, "Trials of Women for Homicide in Nineteenth-Century England."
73. Hartman, *Victorian Murderesses: A True History of Thirteen Respectable French and English Women Accused of Unspeakable Crimes;* Knelman, *Twisting in the Wind: The Murderess and the English Press;* Robb, "The English Dreyfus Case: Florence Maybrick and the Sexual Double Standard"; and Ruddick, *Death at the Priory: Sex, Love, and Murder in Victorian England.*
74. For a list and brief account of all the women executed in Britain between 1843 and 1955, see Wilson, *Murderess: A Study of the Women Executed in Britain since 1843.*

75. The *Times*, 8 July 1870, 4d; 3 July 1879, 11c; 1 April 1879, 5e. For a different, feminist reading of the Webster case, see D'Cruze, *Murder*, 52–58.

76. NAS AD14 74/285; *Glasgow Herald*, 10 May 1876.

77. Conley, "No Pedestals: Women and Violence in Late Nineteenth-Century Ireland." For general studies of women in nineteenth-century Ireland, see Luddy and Murphy, eds., *Women Surviving: Studies in Irish Women's History in the 19th and 20th Centuries;* MacCurtain, O'Dowd, and Luddy, "An Agenda for Women's History in Ireland, 1500–1900"; Fitzpatrick, "The Modernisation of the Irish Female," 166; and Rhodes, *Women and the Family in Post-Famine Ireland: Status and Opportunity in a Patriarchal Society,* 153.

78. The *Times*, 13 February 1891, 8c; 27 February 1891, 7e.

79. Quoted in the *Times*, 4 June 1867, 13a.

80. The *Times*, 26 June 1880, 12d.

81. Excerpt in the *Times*, 12 April 1872.

82. *Scotsman*, 19 March 1878.

83. INA Carlow Assize Files 1891; *Carlow Sentinel*, 14, 18 July 1891; *Limerick Chronicle*, 25 January 1873.

84. The *Times*, 18 July 1879, 4f.

85. The *Times*, 7 January 1867, 9f.

86. *Glasgow Herald*, 28 December 1872; NAS 72/130.

87. *Kilkenny Journal*, 4 January 1882. For other examples, see Conley, *Melancholy Accidents*, 95–97.

88. The *Times*, 14 August 1873, 8e.

89. The *Times*, 4 March 1869, 11b.

90. The *Times*, 11 March 1874, 14b.

91. The *Times*, 28 February 1879, 11c.

92. The *Times*, 4 February 1875, 12a.

93. *Limerick Reporter*, 20 October 1871; 8 March 1872.

94. *Glasgow Herald*, 11 April 1867.

95. *Scotsman*, 5 December 1882.

96. *Glasgow Herald*, 16 August 1889.

97. The *Times*, 5 August 1870, 9c.

98. The *Times*, 4 January 1869, 10a.

99. The *Times*, 4 December 1890, 9c.

100. The *Times*, 17 January 1872, 12d.

CHAPTER FOUR

1. Arensberg and Kimball, *Family and Community in Ireland,* 52, 55, 56; Daly, *Social and Economic History of Ireland Since 1800,* 91–95; Goldstrom and Clarkson, eds., *Irish Population, Economy and Society: Essays in Honour of the Late K. H. Connell,* 167; Connell, *Irish Peasant Society;* Connell, "Peasant Marriage in Ireland: Structure and Development Since the Famine"; Brendan M. Walsh, "Marriage Rates and Population Pressure: Ireland, 1871 and 1911"; Walsh, "A Perspective on Irish Population Patterns"; Fitzpatrick, "Irish Emigration in the Later Nineteenth

Century." For more on the contribution this trend made to violence, see Conley, *Melancholy Accidents,* chapters 2 and 3.

 2. INA, Outrage returns, Roscommon, 1885, 7.

 3. The *Times,* 1 May 1883, 12c.

 4. NAS AD14 71/324; *Glasgow Herald,* 20 November 1871.

 5. The *Times,* 26 June 1885, 7e.

 6. The *Times,* 20 December 1870, 3f; 30 March 1871, 11d.

 7. The *Times,* 3 May 1887, 10f; Outrage papers 1883, 7.

 8. The *Times,* 27 January, 9f; 29 June, 11f; 31 January, 7e; 1 February, 7e–f; 4 February, 6c; 18 February, 12c, 1890.

 9. The *Times,* 18 March 3e; 21 March 10e–f, 1890.

 10. The *Times* 22 March, 4f; 7 April 9e; 10 April 8c; 2 April 7b; 5 April 10b; 7 April 9c; 8 April, 3f; 9 April, 7f, 12b; 10 April, 6a, 1890.

 11. The *Times,* 28 October 1884, 8d.

 12. The *Times,* 28 February 1870, 5f; 8 April 1870, 11f. For other examples, see the *Times,* 3 March 1870, 11a; 13 April 1876, 9f; 14 April 1876, 8f; 5 August 1876, 11d.

 13. The *Times,* 2 March 1871, 11d.

 14. The *Times,* 16 November 1877, 10e.

 15. INA, Outrage returns Limerick, 1872, 10; *Limerick Reporter,* 25 February 1873.

 16. The *Times,* 9 December 1886.

 17. The *Times,* 23 March 1890, 5e.

 18. INA Outrage Papers, Mayo 1880.

 19. *Scotsman,* 20 May 1879.

 20. NAS AD 14 82/279; *Glasgow Herald,* 14 April 1882.

 21. *Glasgow Herald,* 24 December 1879.

 22. NAS AD 14 72/323; *Scotsman,* 23 January 1872.

 23. NAS AD 14 72/113; *Glasgow Herald,* 27 September 1872.

 24. NAD AD 14 77/116; *Glasgow Herald,* 25 April 1877.

 25. The *Times,* 4 November 1873, 7d; 18 December 1873, 12a.

 26. The *Times,* 12 October 1888, 5e; 15 December 1888, 12b.

 27. The *Times,* 28 June 1883, 7e.

 28. The *Times,* 15 January 1879, 11d; 4 August 1886, 6f.

 29. The *Times,* 9 March 1867, 11e.

 30. The *Times,* 15 April 15, 1878, 10f.

 31. *Glasgow Herald,* 19 January 1886.

 32. *Scotsman,* 28 April 1881.

 33. NAS AD 14 90/52; *Glasgow Herald,* 26 February 1890.

 34. NAS AD14 89/119; *Glasgow Herald,* 17 October 1889; the *Times,* 28 July 1889, 6f.

 35. NAS AD14 85/88; *Glasgow Herald,* 20 October 1888.

 36. The *Times,* 18 January 1879, 11f.

 37. The *Times,* 6 February 12b.

 38. *Clonmel Chronicle,* 6 December 1890; INA Return of Outrages, Tipperary 1890, 13.

39. Return of Outrages, Cavan 1867, 3; *Cavan Weekly News,* 11 October 1867.
40. *Limerick Reporter,* 9 July 1880.
41. NAS AD 14 89/208; *Glasgow Herald,* 22 February 1889.
42. For anonther example, see NAS AD14 83/2; *Scotsman,* 13 March 1883.
43. NAS AD14 83/162; *Glasgow Herald,* 28 August 1883; 20 October 1883.
44. NAS AD14 70/147; *Glasgow Herald,* 29 December 1870.
45. *Pall Mall Gazette,* quoted in the *Times,* 19 March 1875, 8a.
46. The *Times,* 22 November 1881, 12b.
47. The *Times,* 3 December 1873, 12a.
48. NAS AD 14 91/122; *Glasgow Herald,* 8 May 1891.
49. The *Times,* 16 March 16, 1877, 11b.
50. The *Times,* 13 August 1874, 11c.
51. The *Times,* 2 April 1874, 11e.
52. The *Times,* 4 August 1889, 10de.
53. The *Times,* 18 February 1888, 11b.
54. The *Times,* 8 July 1876, 13e.
55. The *Times,* 31 July 1885, 10e.
56. The *Times,* 3 August 1874; 14 January 1886; 18 February 1888.
57. *Glasgow Herald,* 8 September 1878.
58. *Glasgow Herald,* 10 May 1892.
59. NAS AD14 82/319; *Dundee Advertiser,* 2 February 1882.
60. The *Times,* 26 July 1886, 6d; INA Return of Outrages, Cork 1886.
61. The *Times,* 1 May 1879, 11d.
62. *Scotsman,* 15–17 September 1890.
63. The *Times,* 24 October, 10c; 25 October, 12a, 1890.
64. The *Times,* 12 July 1871, 12f.
65. The *Times,* 17 July 1871, 12d–f.
66. *Dundee Advertiser,* 16 September 1867.
67. The *Times,* 14 March 1878, 10c.
68. The *Times,* 12 November 1887, 9e. For an analysis of romantic homicides in nineteenth-century America, see Hatton, "He murdered her because he loved her."
69. The *Times,* 30 July 1884, 11c.
70. *Dundee Advertiser,* 6 February 1888.
71. *Scotsman,* 30 March 1878.
72. The *Times,* 6 April 1869, 4e.
73. The *Times,* 31 July 1877, 3e; 9 November, 1877, 8e.
74. The *Times,* 28 March 1872, 10c; INA Cavan Assize Books, 1870; INA Return of Outrages Cavan, 1870; *Cavan Weekly News,* 21 July 1870, 3 March, 21 July 1871; 23 February 1872, 24 March 1872, 21 July 1872, 29 November 1872.
75. *Carmarthen Weekly Report,* 2 November 1877; *Llannelly Guardian,* 26 July 1877; the *Times,* 2 November 1877, 10d.
76. The *Times,* 17 June 1871, 10f.
77. Ibid., 12d–f.
78. INA Return of Outrages, Tipperary, 1869.
79. The *Times,* 29 July, 1884, 5d.
80. NAS AD14 68/52; *Scotsman,* 15 January 1868.

81. NAS AD14 68/266; *Glasgow Herald,* 9 April 1868.

82. The *Times,* 4 December 1890, 9c.

83. The *Times,* 16 July 1872, 11b.

84. The *Times,* 26 October 1872, 10d–f.

85. The *Times,* 16 January 1872, 11ef, 12a.

86. The *Times,* 17 January 1872, 12a–d

87. The *Times,* 17 January 1872, 9c–d.

88. *Spectator* quoted in the *Times,* 29 January 1872, 5e.

89. *Scotsman* 18 January 1872.

90. *Scotsman,* 16 March 1868.

91. The *Times,* 9 March 1868, 10d–f.

92. The *Times,* 6 April 1868, 10d.

93. INA Return of Outrages, Clare, 1882.

94. NAS AD14 67/287; *Scotsman,* 17 September 1867; the *Times,* 21 November 1867, 8d

95. NAS AD14 85/23; *Glasgow Herald,* 17 November 1885.

CHAPTER FIVE

1. The pioneering works on domestic violence in England were Tomes, "'A Torrent of Abuse': Crimes of Violence between Working Class Men and Women in London, 1840–1873"; Ross, "'Fierce Questions and Taunts': Married Life in Working Class London, 1870–1914"; more recently see Wiener, *Men of Blood: Violence, Manliness, and Criminal Justice in Victorian England;* Hammerton, *Cruelty and Companionship: Conflict in Nineteenth-Century Married Life;* D'Cruze, *Crimes of Outrage: Sex, Violence and Victorian Working Women;* and Clark, "Domesticity and the Problem of Wifebeating in Nineteenth-Century Britain: Working-Class Culture, Law and Politics." For a very interesting study of domestic violence among various ethnic groups in Chicago, see Adler, "'We've Got a Right to Fight; We're Married': Domestic Homicide in Chicago, 1875–1920." Other works on domestic violence in the United States include: *Over the Threshold; Intimate Violence in Early America,* ed. Daniels and Kennedy, especially the essay by Roth, "Spousal Murder in Northern New England, 1776–1865," 65–93; del Mar, *What Trouble I Have Seen: A History of Violence against Wives;* Adler, "'I Loved Joe, but I Had to Shoot Him': Homicide by Women in Turn-of-the-Century Chicago"; Moore, "'Justifiable Provocation': Violence against Women in Essex County, New York, 1799–1860."

2. The *Times,* 21 October 1873, 5d.

3. The *Times,* 18 March 1869, 4d.

4. *Glasgow Herald,* 27 April 1877.

5. *Carmarthen Weekly Reporter,* 4 April 1884.

6. *Kildare Observer,* 22 March 1884.

7. *Kilkenny Journal,* 13 June 1885.

8. *Limerick Reporter,* 1 November 1881.

9. Wiener, *Men of Blood,* esp. chap. 4.

10. *Scotsman,* 12 April 1878. For an earlier period, see Leneman, "'A Tyrant and

Tormentor': Violence against Wives in Eighteenth- and Early Nineteenth-Century Scotland."

11. *Glasgow Herald,* 7 May 1880.

12. The *Times,* 28 March 1867, 11b.

13. The *Times,* 1 December 1886, 8c.

14. The *Times,* 6 May 1886, 7e.

15. The *Times,* 29 June 1876, 13e.

16. Fitzpatrick, "Divorce and Separation in Modern Irish History." A. R. Gillis has pointed out that domestic homicide rates declined in France as divorce and marital separation became easier. (Gillis, "So Long as They Both Shall Live: Marital Dissolution and the Decline of Domestic Homicide in France, 1852–1909").

17. *Scotsman,* 12 April 1878.

18. The *Times,* 16 March 1869, 5e.

19. *Carmarthen Weekly Reporter,* 11 September 1874.

20. The *Times,* 8 March 1875, 11b.

21. *Carmarthen Weekly Reporter,* 20 August 1870.

22. The *Scotsman,* 24 April 1875.

23. The *Times,* 18 December 1874, 9e.

24. NAS AD14 87/149; *Glasgow Herald,* 26 October 1886.

25. *North Wales Chronicle,* 17 December 1887.

26. The *Times,* 2 August 1890, 10d; 31 July 1891, 4f; 9 August 1879, 10f; 26 October 1877, 11d; 16 September 1874, 5e.

27. The *Times,* 6 January 1869, 11e.

28. The *Times,* 31 October 1876, 9a.

29. The *Times,* July 11 1867, 11e.

30. The *Times,* 24 February 1877, 11b.

31. The *Times,* 11 December 1869, 11d.

32. *Scotsman,* 11 September 1877.

33. *Munster News,* 3 July 1869.

34. *Leinster Express,* 5, July 1890.

35. *Glasgow Herald,* 18 December 1867.

36. *Cavan Weekly News,* 1 March 1872.

37. The *Times,* 18 July 1872, 12f.

38. Ross, "'Fierce Questions and Taunts'"; Tomes, "A Torrent of Abuse"; and D'Cruze, *Crimes of Outrage.*

39. The *Times,* 10 June 1875, 10e.

40. The *Times,* 15 December 1871, 11f.

41. The *Times,* 7 August 1868, 9c.

42. The *Times,* 26 October 1869, 11c.

43. The *Times,* 12 April 1877, 11e.

44. The *Times,* 4 August 1886, 6f.

45. The *Times,* 9 August 1878, 4e.

46. The *Times,* 29 January 1879, 11d.

47. The *Times,* 18 December 1889, 7b.

48. The *Times,* 29 June 1876, 13e.

49. The *Times,* 6 March 1877, 11e.

50. The *Times,* 27 March 1868, 12c.

51. The *Times,* 24 February 1877, 11b–c.

52. *Limerick Reporter,* 25 February 1873.

53. INA Crown Files at Assize Galway, 1888.

54. INA Return of Outrages, Cork, 1878.

55. *Scotsman,* 11 May 1878.

56. *Scotsman,* 12 April 1878.

57. *Scotsman,* 18 April 1878.

58. *The Times,* 3 April 1875, 11b.

59. *Limerick Reporter,* 6 March 1866.

60. NAS AD14 87/74; *Glasgow Herald,* 24 February 1887.

61. The *Times,* 11 November 1884, 10e.

62. The *Times,* 2 March 1870, 12e.

63. *Glasgow Herald,* 28 January 1883.

64. INA Crown Files at Assize Tipperary, 1891 (Nenagh); Reports of Outrage Tipperary.

65. The *Times,* 31 January 1884, 3f.

66. The *Times,* 20 July 1874, 13d.

67. The *Times,* 6 June 1868, 11e.

68. The *Times,* 3 May 1888, 12a.

69. *Scotsman,* 12 April 1878.

70. The *Times,* 22 July 1867, 11b.

71. The *Times,* 27 October 1883, 6a.

72. *Glasgow Herald,* 29 October 1890.

73. The *Times,* 28 September 1874, 5e; 17 December 1874, 11d.

74. The *Times,* 5 November 1884, 10c.

75. INA Crown Files at Assize Carlow, 1887.

76. *Glasgow Herald,* 22 April 1875; NAS AD14 75/148.

77. *Scotsman,* 3 September 1890.

78. *Glasgow Herald,* 5 October 1870

79. *Scotsman,* 12 April 1878.

80. *Times* 16 July 1869, 11c.

81. *Times,* 21 December 1872, 9e–f.

82. *Times,* 12 January 1870, 11c.

83. Quoted in the *Times,* 1 August 1872, 4f.

84. The *Times,* 8 August 1881, 9d.

85. The *Times,* 11 August 1887, 11f.

86. See Dobash and McLaughlin, "The Punishment of Women in Nineteenth-Century Scotland: Prisons and Inebriate Institutions."

87. *Scotsman,* 12 April 1878.

88. *Glasgow Herald,* 12 September 1879.

89. NAS AD14 86/216; *Dundee Advertiser,* 20 January 1886.

90. Walker, *Crime and Insanity in England,* vol. 1, 142; NAS AD14 67/192.

91. The *Times,* 8 April 1872, 13b.

92. The *Times,* 15 January 1885, 12a.

93. NAS AD14 91/123; *Glasgow Herald,* 8 May 1891.

94. The *Times*, 11 May 1877, 10e–f; CCC, vol. 86, 1877; The *Times*, 21 September 1877, 12b; 25 September 1877, 10f; *Scotsman*, 27 September 1877.

95. The *Times*, 15 October 1877, 9c.

96. The *Times*, 14 April 1880, 13e.

97. The *Times* 8 May 1873, 13d.

98. The *Times* 24 February 1880, 11b.

99. The *Times*, 25 February 1880, 11b.

100. Ibid., 9c–d.

101. The *Times*, 5 August 1880, 4e.

102. The *Times*, 12 January 1882, 4e.

103. The *Times*, 19 November 1891, 14c.

104. The *Times*, 12 October 1871, 5d.

105. The *Times*, 13 October 1871, 9a.

106. The *Times*, 1 January 1872, 9a–b.

107. The *Times*, 2 January 1872, 11a–c

108. The *Times*, 13 January 1872, 11abc.

109. The *Times*, 17 December 1874, 11d; 5 January 1875, 5f.

110. *Spectator*, quoted in the *Times*, 29 January 1872, 5e. Not all the *Times* correspondents were so sympathetic. One wit actually amused himself by writing Latin puns about the crime.

111. *Limerick Reporter*, 15 August 1883.

112. The *Times*, 15 December 1887, 6a–b.

113. The *Times*, 17 December 1887, 9a.

114. The *Times*, 19 December 1887, 7a–b.

115. *Scotsman* 2 January 1873.

116. Lang's is one of eight cases from England and Scotland in which husbands had killed their wives by vaginally penetrating them with foreign objects. While in most cases the crime appears to have been at least in part one of drunkenness, the motive often usually involved a suspicion of infidelity. Only one of these cases led to a conviction in Scotland: a miner was sentenced to fifteen years. As a miner he would have been entitled to no benefit of the doubt based on class, as was clearly the case with Lang. All of the English cases resulted in sentences of penal servitude for manslaughter. The judge's comment in a case which was not fatal suggests that the symbolic intent was clear. Lord Deas suggested that a man who had stabbed his sweetheart "intended to either destroy her life or destroy her as a woman. It was difficult to say which of the two was the most atrocious." NAS AD73/119; the *Times*, 2 February 1873, 12a; *Glasgow Herald*, 4 February 1873; NAS AD 67/219; *Glasgow Herald*, 16 September 1867.

117. *Glasgow Herald*, 24 January 1873; *Scotsman*, 24 April 1873; NAS AD14 73/23.

118. NAS AD 14 78/341.

119. *Scotsman*, 10 May 1878.

120. *Scotsman*, 11 May 1878.

121. The *Times*, 11 May 1878, 12e.

122. *Scotsman*, 1 June 1878.

123. NAS AD14 91/154.

124. Ibid.
125. The *Times,* 21 October 1873, 5d.
126. The *Times,* November 25, 1869, 11a.
127. *Glasgow Herald,* 14 May 1880.
128. *Mayo Examiner,* 23 July 1892.
129. The *Times,* 11 March 1873, 11d; *Carmarthen Weekly Reporter,* 29 March 1873.
130. *Scotsman,* 1 September 1890.
131. The *Times,* 1 February 1887, 10e.
132. The *Times,* 11 June 1878, 10d.
133. The *Times,* 28 July 1877, 11e.
134. The *Times,* 8 October, 1888, 11d.
135. The *Times,* 21 September 1871, 11c.
136. The *Times,* 27 May 1881, 12a.
137. *Scotsman,* 17 April 1878.
138. *Scotsman,* 9 March 1868.
139. The *Times,* 8 August 1889, 7b. On female poisoners, see Robb, "Circe in Crinoline: Domestic Poisonings in Victorian England." Also see Emsley, *Elements of Murder,* 171–96 for an account of Florence Maybrick, one of the period's most celebrated suspected poisoners.
140. The *Times,* 7 May 1879, 7f.
141. The *Times,* 19 July 1875, 11e.
142. The *Times,* 18 November 1887, 12b.
143. The *Times,* 12 July 1871, 11b.
144. The *Times,* 22 February 1877, 11c; *PRO* ASSI36, Box 22.
145. *Limerick Reporter,* 11 December 1879; Outrage paper, Limerick 1879; the *Times,* 18 December 1879, 4f.
146. *Scotsman,* 28 March 1878; the *Times,* 28 March 1878, 11a.
147. NAS AD14 78/244; *Glasgow Herald,* 5 and 6 September 1878; *Scotsman,* 21 June 1878.
148. The *Times,* 19 March 1888, 7f.
149. *Carmarthen Weekly Reporter,* 4 April 1884.
150. *Carmarthen Weekly Reporter,* 9 May 1884.

CHAPTER SIX

1. Regarding the reforms, see Behlmer, *Child Abuse and Moral Reform in England, 1870–1908;* for a contemporary view, see Jones, "The Perils and Protection of Infant Life." For the changing perspectives of American courts toward family violence, see Pleck, "Criminal Approaches to Family Violence, 1640–1980."
2. The *Times,* 26 May 1870, 9f.
3. The *Times,* 8 August 1878, 10a.
4. Aries, *Centuries of Childhood: A Social History of Family Life.*
5. Some scholars suggest that infanticides should not be included in general studies of homicides. On the problems of counting infanticides, see Emmerich, "Trials of Women for Homicide in Nineteenth-Century England"; Emsley, *Crime*

and Society in England 1750–1900, 100–101; Monkkonen, *Crime, Justice History,* 80; Sharpe, *Crime in Early Modern England,* 60–62; and Lane, *Violent Death in the City: Suicide, Accident, and Murder in Nineteenth-Century Philadelphia,* 96–100.

6. The *Times,* 22 January 1890, 10a.

7. The *Times,* 12 March 1874, 12a.

8. *Carmarthen Weekly Reporter,* 24 February 1888; 2 March 1888.

9. *Carmarthen Weekly Reporter,* 9 August 1878.

10. Behlmer, *Child Abuse;* Jackson, *Child Sexual Abuse in Victorian England;* Conley, *The Unwritten Law: Criminal Justice in Victorian Kent;* Barret-Ducroq, *Love in the Time of Victoria: Sexuality, Class, and Gender in Nineteenth-Century England.*

11. The *Times,* 14 July 1870, 9d–e.

12. *Carmarthen Weekly Reporter,* 9 February 1877.

13. *Limerick Reporter,* 11 March 1892.

14. Hoff and Yeates suggest that many child homicides reported as accidents were actually similar to the case described below:

> At the Petty Session of Clonmel yesterday two women named Rourke and Cummins were prosecuted for having on April 22 burnt a child three years old, named John Dillon by placing him naked on a hot shovel. The act was the result of gross superstition on their part, the two women alleging that he was an old man left by the fairies as a substitute for a real child whom they had taken from its mother. The charge was proved against Rourke and she was sentenced to a week's imprisonment, the magistrate being of the opinion that as she had been in custody since the occurrence the addition of a week's imprisonment would satisfy the demands of justice. He strongly characterized the ignorance and superstition which she had shown. (*The Times,* 26 May 1884, 8b)

15. United Kingdom, Parliament, *Report of the Capital Punishment Commission,* 1866, 291.

16. The *Times,* 29 February 1888, 12a.

17. Hoffer and Hull, *Murdering Mothers: Infanticide in England and New England, 1558–1803;* Mark Jackson, ed., *Infanticide: Historical Perspectives on Child Murder and Concealment, 1550–2000;* Jackson, *New-Born Child Murder: Women, Illegitimacy and the Courts in Eighteenth-Century England;* Arnot, "Understanding Women Committing Newborn Child Murder in Victorian England"; Kilday, "Maternal Monsters: Murdering Mothers in South-West Scotland, 1750–1815"; Abrams, "From Demon to Victim: The Infanticide Mother in Shetland, 1699–1899"; Knelman, *Twisting in the Wind: The Murderess and the English Press,* chaps. 5–6; and Rose, *The Massacre of the Innocents: Infanticide in Britain, 1800–1939.* For an anthropological perspective, see Hrdy, *Mother Nature: Maternal Instincts and How They Shape the Human Species.* A very valuable survey of the treatment of infanticide in Europe is Tinkova, "Protéger ou punir? La mère infanticide entreseuil 'mère affreuse,' 'fille malheurese' et 'femme alienée' au seuil de la société civile" ["To Protect or Punish? The Infanticidal Mother's Transition from 'a Dreadful Mother,' 'Unfortunate Girl,' and 'Alienated Woman' in Civil Society"].

18. "The statute 43 George 3, c 58 which repeals the 21 Jac1.c 27 and the Irish

Act 6 Anne provides that the trials in England and Ireland of women charged with the murder of any issue of their bodies which being born alive would be by law be bastard shall be proved by the like rules of evidence and presumption as are allowed to take place in respect to other trials for murder." And the statute further enacts

> that it shall and may be lawful for the jury, by whose verdict any prisoner charged with such murder as aforesaid shall be acquitted, to find, in case it shall so appear in evidence that the prisoner was delivered of issue of her body, male or female, which if born alive, would have been bastard; and that she did, by secret burying, or otherwise, endeavor to conceal the birth thereof; and thereupon it shall be lawful for the court before which such prisoners shall have been tried to adjudge that such prisoner shall be committed to the common gaol. Or house of correction. For any time not exceeding two years. Included in Criminal Law Consolidation Act of the 24 and 25 Victoria. C.100, s.60—misdemeanor maximum penalty of 2 years.

Scotland Statute 49 Geo.3, c. 14 enacts that

> if any woman in Scotland shall conceal her being with child during the whole period of her pregnancy and shall not call for and make use of help or assistance in the birth and if the child be found dead or be missing, the mother being lawfully convicted thereof shall be imprisoned for a period not exceeding two years, in such common gaol or prison as the court before which she is tried shall direct and appoint.

19. The *Times,* 8 April 1886, 12c.
20. *Cork Examiner,* 11 December1878.
21. *Weekly Mail,* 17 May 1890; the *Times,* July 28, 1890, 4d.
22. The *Times,* 11 December 1891, 6f.
23. The *Times,* 29 October 1886, 10d.
24. The *Times,* 1 April 1867, 11b.
25. The *Times,* 18 December 1874, 9d.
26. *Carmarthen Weekly Reporter,* 13 February 1869.
27. *Carmarthen Weekly Reporter,* 9 February 1877.
28. *Carmarthen Weekly Reporter,* 8 September 1876; 16 December 1876.
29. The *Times,* 8 August 1881, 9f.
30. NAS 89/185; *Glasgow Herald,* 23 January 1889.
31. NAS 68/311; *Scotsman,* 7 July 1868.
32. *Roscommon Journal,* 1 October 1881. INA Limerick Quarter Sessions Grand Jury Books, 1886. The popular attitude toward illegitimacy is hard to discern. In her study of folklore, Anne O'Connor found evidence of sympathy for the unwed mother, including a story in which a curate who defies a priest's orders and gives last rites to an unwed mother is blessed by the Virgin and inherits the benefice after the Virgin helps bring about the priest's death. O'Connor, "Women in Irish Folklore: The Testimony Regarding Illegitimacy, Abortion and Infanticide," 316.
33. *Carmarthen Journal,* 12 March 1869.

34. *Carmarthen Weekly Reporter,* 18 July 1874.

35. The *Times,* 7 March 1867, 11b.

36. *Kilkenny Journal,* 14 July 1875.

37. INA Crown Files of Assize, 1892.

38. NAS, 86/22; *Scotsman,* 18 May 1886.

39. The *Times,* 22 November 1883, 7c.

40. *Scotsman,* 18 May 1886.

41. The *Times,* 31 May 1886, 6e.

42. The *Times,* 14 July 1870, 9e.

43. The *Times,* 16 March 1869, 4d.

44. The *Times,* 9 May 1879, 11d.

45. The *Times,* 2 August 1878, 4a.

46. The *Times,* 29 July 1878, 4c; 16 August 1878, 5c.

47. The *Times,* 24 November 1876, 10f; 1 December 1876, 11c.

48. The *Times,* 11 January 1884, 12a.

49. The *Times,* 19 December 1868, 11d.

50. The *Times,* 19 May 1890, 7d.

51. The *Times,* 6 December 1890, 8f.

52. NAS AD 14 90/18; *Inverness Courier,* 9 May 1890.

53. NAS AD 14, 82/345; *Dundee Advertiser,* 12 April 1882.

54. NAS 76.306; *Daily Free Press,* 6 April 1876.

55. *Glasgow Herald,* 24 August 1882.

56. *Kilkenny Journal,* 2 April 1871.

57. *Leinster Express,* 14 December 1889.

58. Connolly, *Priests and the People in Pre-Famine Ireland 1780–1845,* 189; Howarth, "Gender, Domesticity and Sexual Politics," 167; Thompson, *The Rise of Respectable Society: A Social History of Victorian Britain, 1830–1900,* 112.

59. The *Times,* 14 July 1870, 9e.

60. The *Times,* 16 March 1868, 11c.

61. The *Times,* 14 July 1870, 9d.

62. The *Times,* 1 April 1876, 12a.

63. The *Times,* 7 March 1867, 11b.

64. The *Times,* 30 April 1880, 11c.

65. O'Corrain, "Women in Early Irish Society," in MacCurtain and O'Corrain, 8; *Sligo Champion,* 10 December 1892; *Kildare Observer,* 12 March 1886; Kildare Assize Files 1886; *Cavan Weekly News,* 6 March 1868; Kildare Assize Files 1886.

66. NAS AD 90/70; *Glasgow Herald,* 3 July 1890.

67. NAS AD 90/70; *Scotsman,* 3 July 1890.

68. The first incest legislation was not passed until 1908. Anthony Wohl suggests that the idea of incest was just too horrible to be considered. See Wohl, "Sex and the Single Room: Incest among the Victorian Working Class," and Anderson, "'The Marriage of a Deceased Wife's Sister Bill' Controversy: Incest Anxiety and the Defense of Family Purity in Victorian England."

69. The *Times,* 23 March 1875, 11e.

70. INA Crown Files at Assize Galway; *Galway Express,* 22 March 1890.

71. The *Times,* 3 May 1887, 10f.

72. AD 14 75/190; *Glasgow Herald,* 24 December 1875.

73. The *Times,* 23 March 1889, 4e.

74. NAS AD 14 69/130; *Glasgow Herald,* 10 September 1869.

75. The *Times,* 8 February 1879, 11e.

76. The *Times,* 15 and 23 August 1872.

77. The *Times,* 31 July 1882, 5e.

78. The *Times,* 15 December 1871, 11e; also see Showalter, *The Female Malady: Women, Madness and English Culture, 1830–1980.*

79. *North Wales Chronicle,* 16 May 1885; 25 July 1885.

80. INA Record of Outrages Kildare, 1885; *Kilkenny Journal,* 1 March 1872.

81. *Dundee Advertiser,* 12 April 1882.

82. The *Times,* 9 August 1883, 9f.

83. The *Times,* 6 September 1883, 5f.

84. The *Times,* 15 September 1883, 12a–c.

85. The *Times,* 15 September 1883, 9e–f.

86. The *Times,* 21 August, 10c; 27 August 10d; 19 October 8a; 6 November, 6e, 1883.

87. NAS AD 14 74/92; the *Times,* 19 November 1874, 4f.

88. *Kilkenny Moderator,* 10 July 1880.

89. The *Times,* 4 August 1891, 7c.

90. The *Times,* 16 February 1885, 10f.

91. The *Times,* 29 October 1875, 3f.

92. The *Times,* 16 September 1887, 10a.

93. The *Times,* 23 December 1871, 11c.

94. The *Times,* 22 November 1883, 9d–e.

95. The *Times,* 23 November 1880, 11b.

96. The *Times,* 30 October 1878, 11f; 31 October 1878, 11d.

97. The *Times,* 19 December 1872, 9a.

98. The *Times,* 5 December 1867, 12f.

99. The *Times,* 11 March 1867, 11d; the *Times,* 12 March 1867, 12c.

100. The *Times,* 8 August 1878, 10a.

101. The *Times,* 16 February 1885, 10f.

102. Daly and Wilson, *Homicide,* 83–93.

103. The *Times,* 29 May 1878, 6c.

104. The *Times,* 14 December 1877, 11f.

105. The *Times,* 22 July 1889, 11d.

106. The *Times,* 31 July 1876, 11d–e.

107. The *Times,* 20 August 1874, 9e.

108. *Carmarthen Journal,* 19 February 1869.

109. *Carmarthen Journal,* 2 April 1869.

110. Quoted in *Carmarthen Journal,* 10 September 1869.

111. Quoted in the *Times,* 17 September 1869, 10e.

112. *Carmarthen Weekly Reporter,* 10 July 1869.

113. The *Times,* 3 December 1869, 9f; *Carmarthen Weekly Reporter,* 18 December 1869.

114. *Carmarthen Weekly Reporter,* 25 December 1869.

115. Ibid.

116. *Carmarthen Journal,* 24 December 1869.

117. Ibid.

118. Ibid.

119. The *Times,* 24 December 1869, 7d; 27 December 1869, 5e.

120. The *Times,* 1 March 1870, 12b; 9 March 1870, 5b; 16 March 1870, 12f.

121. *Carmarthen Weekly Reporter,* 16 July 1870.

122. *Carmarthen Weekly Reporter,* 19 March 1870; 23 April 1870.

123. Of course, Newton was a man of faith as well as science and also very interested in alchemy. See Kearney, *Science and Change 1500–1700.*

124. *Scotsman,* 16 October 1884.

125. NAS AD 14 88/28; *Glasgow Herald,* 12 September 1888; *Scotsman,* 25 June 1888.

126. *Kilkenny Journal,* 17 July 1878.

127. The *Times,* 9 January 1867, 9a.

128. The *Times,* 22 October 1881, 10b.

129. The *Times,* 11 December 1876, 11f.

130. The *Times,* 18 August 1871, 9a.

131. NAS AD 14 85/248; *Inverness Courier,* 23 April 1885.

132. NAS AD 14 89/98; *Glasgow Herald,* 16 August 1869.

133. *Limerick Reporter,* 11 March 1892.

134. Conley, "No Pedestals."

135. INA Crown Files at Assize Galway, 1892; Record of Outrages, 1892, 8.

136. *Limerick Reporter,* 4 March 1892.

137. The *Times,* 13 June 1867, 11c.

138. The *Times,* 13 February 1879, 11c.

139. *Herald of Wales,* 6 August 1892.

140. *Scotsman,* 17 October 1884.

141. Jervis, *Archbold's Pleading and Evidence in Criminal Cases,* 690.

142. The *Times,* 5 April 1876, 13c.

143. The *Times,* 6 May 1892, 11c; 30 June 1892, 3c.

144. The *Times,* 24 November 1882, 8e.

145. The *Times,* 17 January 1887, 6b.

146. The *Times,* 3 February 1887, 3e.

147. *North Wales Guardian,* 25 July 1891.

148. NAS AD 14 78/295; *Glasgow Herald,* 24 April 1878; *Scotsman,* 24 April 1878.

149. *The Herald of Wales* carried the story on the front page. See *Herald of Wales,* 9 April 1892.

150. The *Times,* 26 February 1892, 8c.

151. The *Times,* 5 April 1892, 10bc. In a nearly identical case in which a London laborer had suspended his son with a rope around his arms and the child had died, the father was sentenced to nine months. See the *Times,* 12 February 1881, 7e.

152. The *Times,* 5 April 1892, 9e.

153. The *Times,* 25 November 1868, 9d.

154. The *Times,* 24 June 1874, 6b.

155. NAS AD 14, 68/240; *Scotsman,* 16 April 1868.

156. The *Times,* 7 August 1872, 9d.

157. The *Times,* 12 December 1874, 12a.

158. AD 14 71/237; *Galloway Advertiser and Wigtownshire Free Press,* 11 May 1871.

159. *Scotsman,* 13 September 1877.

160. NAS AD 14 88/119; *Glasgow Herald,* 25 October 1888.

161. The *Times,* 11 June 1874, 10e.

162. The *Times,* 10 December 1890, 10c.

163. Regarding baby farming, see Arnot, "Infant Death, Child Care and the State: The Baby-Farming Scandal and the First Infant Life Protection Legislation of 1872"; Bentley, "She Butchers: Baby-Droppers, Baby-Sweaters and Baby-Farmers"; Knelman, *Twisting in the Wind,* chap. 6.

164. The *Times,* 19 May 1879, 8c; 23 July 1879, 4f; 12 August 1879, 5e.

165. The *Times,* 22 September 1870, 9b; 24 September 1870, 11b, c, 4e, g; 12 October 1870, 9e–f.

166. The *Times,* 13 October 1879, 9f; 29 October 1879, 12c–d; 30 October, 9cde.

167. For more on this case see NAS AD 89/146 and *Scotsman,* 2 February 1889.

168. The *Times,* 6 July 1881, 12c; 3 November 1881, 9e; 11 November 1881, 8e.

169. NAS AD14 67/134; *Glasgow Herald,* 14 September 1867.

170. NAS AD 14, 71/57; *Glasgow Herald,* 3 May 1871.

171. On children as offenders, see Abbott, "The Press and the Public Visibility of Nineteenth-Century Criminal Children."

172. The *Times,* 30 March 1872, 7f.

173. *Scotsman,* 24 November 1868.

174. *Scotsman,* 26 November 1868.

CONCLUSION

1. The *Times,* 8 October 1877, 9b–d.

2. *Scotsman,* 26 April 1873.

Bibliography

Primary Sources

Irish National Archives

Return of Outrages Reported to the Constabulary Office, 1848–1878; 1879–1892. CSO ICR Volumes 1 and 2.
Crown Files at Assize. Carlow. 1887–1891.
Crown Books at Assize. Cavan. 1866–1892.
Crown Files at Assize. Cavan. 1866–1892.
Crown Books at Quarter Sessions. Cavan. 1870–1892.
Crown Files at Assize. Clare. 1865, 1890, 1891.
Crown Files at Assize. Galway. 1888–1892.
Crown Books at Assize. Kildare. 1884–1892.
Crown Files at Assize. Kildare. 1885–1892.
Crown Books at Assize. Kilkenny. 1866–1892.
Crown Files at Assize. Kilkenny. 1875, 1891.
Crown Books at Quarter Session. Kilkenny. 1870–1892.
Crown Files at Assize. Leitrim. 1888–1892.
Grand Jury Indictment Books. Limerick. 1866–1892.
Crown Files at Assize. Limerick. 1889–1892.
Crown Books at Quarter Sessions. Limerick. 1866–1892.
Crown Books at Assize. Mayo. 1884, 1889–1892.
Crown Files at Assize. Mayo. 1889–1892.
Crown Books at Assize. Queens. 1889.
Crown Files at Assize. Queens. 1889–1892.
Crown Books at Assize. Roscommon. 1866–1892.
Crown Files at Assize. Roscommon. 1890.
Crown Books at Quarter Sessions. Roscommon. 1884–1892.
Crown Files at Assize. Sligo. 1885, 1890–1892.
Crown Books at Assize. Tipperary. 1888–1892.
Crown Files at Assize. Tipperary. 1888–1892.
Crown Files at Assize. Westmeath. 1882, 1892.

Parliamentary Debates, Papers, and Acts

U.K. Hansard Parliamentary Debates (Commons), 3rd ser., vol. 310 (1887).

U.K. Parliament. Judicial and Criminal Statistics for Ireland. 1867–1892.

U.K. Parliament. Judicial and Criminal Statistics for England and Wales. 1867–1892.

_____. Memorandum as to the Principle upon which outrages are recorded as agrarian. 1887, vol. LXVIII, 25.

_____. Peace Preservation (Ireland) Act, 1870, 33 and 34 Vict., c.9.

_____. Protection of Life and Property in Certain Parts of Ireland Act, 1871, 22 and 35 Vict., c. 25.

_____. Protection of Person and Property (Ireland) Act. 1881, 44 and 45 Vict., c.4.

_____. Act for the Prevention of Crime in Ireland, 1882, 45 and 46 Vict., c. 25.

_____. Criminal Law and Procedure (Ireland) Act, 1887, 50 and 51 Vict.

_____. Criminal Law Consolidation Act, 1861–62. 24 and 25 Vict. c. 100.

_____. *Report of the Capital Punishment Commission,* 1866.

Newspapers

England
The *Times*
Maidstone and Kentish Journal
Pall Mall Gazette
The Daily Free Press
The Spectator

Ireland
The Cork Examiner
Carlow Sentinel
Limerick Chronicle
Kilkenny Journal
Kilkenny Moderator
Clonmel Chronicle
Cavan Weekly News
Kildare Observer
Munster News
Leinster Express
Mayo Examiner
Roscommon Journal
Sligo Chronicle
Sligo Champion

Wales
Carmarthen Weekly Reporter
Carmarthen Journal

Cheshire Observer and Chester, Birkenhead, Crewe and North Wales Times
Cardiff Times
The Carnarvon and Denbigh Herald
North Wales Chronicle
North Wales Guardian
The Herald of Wales
The Llannelly Guardian
The Weekly Mail

Scotland
The Glasgow Herald
The Scotsman
The Dundee Advertiser
Inverness Courier
North Telegraphic News (Aberdeen)
The Daily Free Press (Aberdeen)
Stirling Journal and Advertiser
Inverness Advertiser
The Teviotdale Record and Jedburgh Advertiser
Galloway Advertiser and Wigtownshire Free Press
Ayr Observer

National Archives of Scotland
AD 14 Records of High Court of Justiciary, 1867–1892
JC 8: 78–86 Minute Books Court of Justiciary, Edinburgh
JC 11:104–115 Minute Books Court of Justiciary, Northern Circuit
JC 12: 52–55 Minute Books Court of Justiciary, Southern Circuit
JC 13: 103–118 Minute Books Court of Justiciary, Glasgow Second Circuit
JC 14: 8–21 Minute Book Court of Justiciary, Western Circuit

Books, Articles, etc.

Breaky, Alex. *Handbook for Magistrates, Clerks of Petty Sessions, Solicitors, Coroners, etc.* Dublin: A. Thom and Co. Ltd., 1904.
Grosvenor, George. "Statistics of the Abatement in Crime in England and Wales during the Twenty Years Ended 1887–1888." *Journal of Royal Society of Statistics* 53, no. 3 (September 1890): 377–419.
Guy, William A. "On Insanity and Crime and On the Plea of Insanity in Criminal Cases." *Journal of Statistical Society of London* 32, no. 2 (June 1869): 159–91.
Jervis, John. *Archibald's Pleadings and Evidence in Criminal Cases.* 19th ed. London: H Sweer, 1878.
Jones, Hugh R. "The Perils and Protection of Infant Life." *Journal of the Royal Statistical Society* 57 (1894): 1–103.
Morrison, William Douglas. "The Interpretation of Criminal Statistics." *Journal of the Royal Society* 60 (1897): 1–32.

Ravenstein, E. G. "On the Celtic Languages in the British Isles: A Statistical Survey." *Journal of the Statistical Society of London* 42, no. 3 (September 1879): 608–624.

Walford, Cornelius. "On the Number of Deaths from Accidents, Negligence, Violence, and Misadventure in the United Kingdom and Some Other Countries." *Journal of the Statistical Society.* London,: 1881.

SECONDARY SOURCES

Abott, Jane. "The Press and the Public Visibility of Nineteenth-Century Criminal Children." In *Criminal Conversations: Victorian Crimes, Social Panic, and Moral Outrage.* Judith Rowbotham and Kim Stevenson, editors, 23–39. Columbus: Ohio University Press, 2005.

Abrams, Lynn. "From Demon to Victim: The Infanticidal Mother in Shetland, 1699–1899." In *Twisted Sisters: Women, Crime, and Deviance in Scotland since 1400,* Yvonne Galloway Brown and Rona Ferguson, editors, 180–203. East Linton, Scotland: Tuckewell Press, 2002.

Adler, Jeffery. *First in Violence, Deepest in Dirt: Homicide in Chicago, 1875–1920.* Cambridge, MA: Harvard University Press, 2006.

_____. "I Loved Joe, but I Had to Shoot Him: Homicide by Women in Turn-of-the-Century Chicago." *Journal of Criminal Law and Criminology* 92 (2002): 867–97.

_____. "'My Mother-N-Law is to Blame, But I'll Walk on Her Neck Yet': Homicide in Late Nineteenth-Century Chicago." *Journal of Social History* 31 (1997): 253–77.

_____. "'We've Got a Right to Fight: We're Married': Domestic Homicide in Chicago, 1875–1920." *The Journal of Interdisciplinary History* 34 (2003): 27–48.

Anderson, Nancy Fix. "'The Marriage of a Deceased Wife's Sister Bill' Controversy: Incest Anxiety and the Defense of Family Purity in Victorian England." *Journal of British Studies* 21 (1982): 67–86.

Archer, Dane, and Rosemary Gartner. *Violence and Crime in Cross National Perspective.* New Haven, CT: Yale University Press, 1984.

Archer, John. "'Men Behaving Badly?': Masculinity and the Uses of Violence, 1850–1900." In *Everyday Violence in Britain, 1850–1950,* Shani D'Cruze, editor, 41–54. London: Pearson, 2000.

_____. "The Violence We Have Lost? Body Counts, Historians, and Interpersonal Violence in England." *Memoria y Civilizacion* 2 (1999): 171–90.

Arensberg, Conrad, and Solon Kimball. *Family and Community in Ireland.* 2nd ed. Cambridge, MA: Harvard University Press, 1986.

Aries, Phillipe. *Centuries of Childhood: A Social History of Family Life.* New York: Vintage, 1962.

Arnot, Margaret. "Understanding Women Committing Newborn Child Murder in Victorian England." In *Everyday Violence in Britain, 1850–1950,* D'Cruze, editor, 55–69. London: Pearson, 2000.

Aspinwall, Bernard, and John McCaffery. "A Comparative View of the Irish in Edinburgh." In *The Irish in the Victorian City,* Roger Swift and Sheridan Gilley, editors, 130–57. London: Croom-Helm, 1985.

Averill, James R. *Anger and Aggression: An Essay on Emotion.* New York: Sprier-Verligg, 1982.

Ayers, Edward L. *Vengeance and Justice: Crime and Punishment in the Nineteenth-Century American South.* New York: Oxford University Press, 1984.

Barret-Ducroq, Françoise. *Love in the Time of Victoria: Sexuality, Class, and Gender in Nineteenth-Century England.* New York: Verso, 1991.

Behlmer, George K. *Child Abuse and Moral Reform in England, 1870–1908.* Stanford: Stanford University Press, 1982.

Bentley, David. "She Butchers: Baby-Droppers, Baby-Sweaters and Baby-Farmers." In *Criminal Conversations: Victorian Crimes, Social Panics, and Moral Outrage,* Judith Rowbotham and Kim Stevenson, editors, 198–214. Columbus: Ohio State University Press, 2005.

Broeker, Galen. *Rural Disorder and Police Reform in Ireland, 1812–36.* London: Routledge and Kegan Paul, 1970.

Brown, Keith M. *Bloodfeud in Scotland, 1573–1625: Violence, Justice, and Politics in an Early Modern Society.* Edinburgh: John Donald Publishers, Ltd., 1986.

Brown, Richard Maxwell. *No Duty to Retreat: Violence and Values in American History and Society.* Norman, OK: University of Oklahoma Press, 1991.

Cannadinne, David. *The Rise and Fall of Class in Britain.* New York: Columbia University Press, 1999.

Clark, Anna. "Domesticity and the Problem of Wifebeating in Nineteenth-Century Britain: Working Class Culture, Law, and Politics." In *Everyday Violence in Britain, 1850–1950: Gender and Class,* Shani D'Cruze, editor, 27–40. London: Pearson, 2000.

Clark, Samuel. "The Importance of Agrarian Classes: Agrarian Class Structure and Collective Action in Nineteenth-Century Ireland." In *Irish Studies 2. Ireland: Land Politics and People,* P. J. Drudy, editor. 14–30 Cambridge: Cambridge University Press, 1982.

_____. *Social Origins of Irish Land War.* Princeton, NJ: Princeton University Press, 1979.

Colley, Linda. *Britons: Forging the Nation, 1707–1837.* New Haven, CT: Yale University Press, 1992.

Colls, Robert, and Philip Dodd, eds. *Englishness: Politics and and Culture, 1880–1920.* London: Croom Helm, 1986.

Conley, Carolyn. "The Agreeable Recreation of Fighting." *Journal of Social History* 33 (1999): 57–73.

_____. *Melancholy Accidents: The Meaning of Violence in Post-Famine Ireland.* Lanham, MD: Lexington Books, 1999.

_____. "No Pedestals: Women and Violence in Late Nineteenth-Century Ireland." *Journal of Social History* 28 (1995): 801–19.

_____. "Rape and Justice in Victorian England." *Victorian Studies* 29 (1986): 519–34.

_____. *The Unwritten Law: Criminal Justice in Victorian Kent.* London: Oxford University Press, 1992.

_____. "Wars among the Savages: Homicide and Ethnicity in the Victorian United Kingdom." *Journal of British Studies* 44 (2005): 775–95.

Connell, K. H. *Irish Peasant Society.* Oxford: Clarendon Press, 1968.

_____. "Peasant Marriage in Ireland: Structure and Development since the Famine." *Economic History Review* 14 (1961–62): 502–523.

Connolly, S. J. *Priests and the People in Pre-Famine Ireland, 1780–1845.* New York: St. Martin's Press, 1982.

_____. "Violence and Order in the Eighteenth Century." In *Rural Ireland 1600–1900: Modernization and Change,* Patrick O'Flanagan, Paul Ferguson, and Kevin Whelan, editors, 42–61. Cork: Cork University Press, 1987.

Courtwright, David T. *Violent Land: Single Men and Social Disorder from the Frontier to the Inner City.* Boston: Harvard University Press, 1996.

Crossman, Virginia. *Politics, Law, and Order in 19th Century Ireland.* New York: St. Martin's, 1996.

Curtis, L. P. *Anglo-Saxons and Celts: A Study of Anti-Irish Prejudice in Victorian England.* Bridgeport, CT: University of Bridgeport Press, 1968.

_____. *Apes and Angels: The Irishman in Victorian Caricature.* Washington, D.C.: Smithsonian, 1971.

Daly, Martin, and Margo Wilson. *Homicide.* New York: Aldine de Gruyter, 1988.

Daly, Mary. *Social and Economic History of Ireland since 1800.* Dublin: Educational Company, 1981.

Daly, Martin, and Margo Wilson. *Homicide.* New York: Aldine de Gruyter, 1988.

Daniels, Christine, and Michael Kennedy, eds. *Over the Threshold: Intimate Violence in Early America.* New York: Routledge, 1999.

Davies, Andrew. "Youth Gangs, Masculinity, and Violence in late-Victorian Manchester and Salford." *Journal of Social History* 32 (1998): 349–69.

Davis, Jennifer. "The London Garroting Panic of 1862: A Moral Panic and the Creation of a Criminal Class in Mid-Victorian England." In *Crime and the Law: The Social History of Crime in Western Europe Ssince 1500,* V. A. C. Gatrell, Bruce Lenman, and Geoffrey Parker, editors, 190–213. London: Europa Publications, 1980.

Devine, T. M. *The Scottish Nation.* New York: Viking, 1999.

D'Cruze, Shani. *Crimes of Outrage: Sex, Violence, and Victorian Working-Women.* DeKalb, IL: Northern Illinois University Press, 1998.

_____, ed. *Everyday Violence in Britain, 1850–1950.* New York: Pearson, 2000.

del Mar, David Peterson. *What Trouble I Have Seen: A History of Violence against Wives.* Cambridge, MA: Harvard University Press, 1996.

de Nie, Michael. *The Eternal Paddy: Irish Identity and the British Press, 1798–1882.* Madison, WI: University of Wisconsin Press, 2004.

Dobash, Russell, and Pat McLaughlin. "The Punishment of Women in Nineteenth-Century Scotland: Prisons and Inebriate Institutions." In *Out of Bounds: Women in Scottish Society, 1800–1945,* Esther Breitenbach and Eleanor Gordon, editors, 65–94. Edinburgh: Edinburgh University Press, 1992.

Donnachie, Ian, and Christopher Whatley. *The Manufacture of Scottish History.* Edinburgh: Polygon, 1992.

Donnelly, James. "The Social Composition of Agrarian Rebellions in Early Nineteenth Century Ireland: The Case of Carders and Cravats, 1813–16." In *Radicals, Rebels, and Establishments: Historical Studies XV,* P. J. Corish, editor,151–69. Belfast: Appletree Press, 1982.

Duncan, A. G. M. *Green's Glossary of Scottish Legal Terms*. Edinburgh: Sweet and Maxwell, 1992.

Early, Julie English. "Keeping Ourselves to Ourselves: Violence in the Edwardian Suburb." In *Everyday Violence in Britain, 1850–1950: Gender and Class*, Shani D'Cruze, editor, 170–184. New York: Pearson, 2000.

Elias, Norbert. *The Civilizing Process: The History of Manners*. Translated by. Edmund Jephcott. New York: Urizen Books, 1978.

Ellis, Joseph S. "Reconciling the Celt: British National Identity, Empire, and the 1911 Investiture of the Prince of Wales." *The Journal of British Studies* 37 (1998): 391–418.

Emmerichs, Mary Beth Wasserlein. "Getting Away with Murder? Homicide and the Coroner in Nineteenth-Century London." *Social Science History* 25 (2001): 92–99.

_____. "Trials of Women for Homicide in Nineteenth-Century England." *Women and Criminal Justice* 5 (1993): 99–109.

Emsley, Clive. *Crime and Society in England, 1750–1900*. 3rd ed. New York: Pearson Longman, 2005.

_____. *Hard Men: Violence in England since 1750*. London: Hambledon and London, 2005.

Emsley, John. *Elements of Murder*. New York: Oxford University Press, 2005.

Farmer, Lindsay. *Criminal Law, Tradition, and Legal Order: Crime and the Genius of Scots Law, 1747 to the Present*. Cambridge: Cambridge University Press, 1997.

Finane, Mark. *Insanity and the Insane in Post-Famine Ireland*. London: Croom-Helm, 1981.

Finnegan, Frances. *Poverty and Prejudice: A Study of Irish Immigrants in York, 1840–1875*. Cork: Cork University Press, 1982.

Fitzpatrick, David. "Divorce and Separation in Modern Irish History." *Past and Present* 144 (1987): 172–96.

_____. "Irish Emigration in the Later Nineteenth Century." *Irish Historical Studies* 22 (1980–81): 126–41.

_____. "The Modernization of the Irish Female." In *Rural Ireland 1600–1900: Modernization and Change*, Patrick O'Flanagan, Paul Ferguson, and Kevin Whelan, editors, 162–80. Cork: Cork University Press, 1987.

Foster, R. F. *Paddy and Mr. Punch: Connections in Irish and English History*. New York: The Penguin Press, 1993.

Gatrell, V. A. C. "The Decline of Theft and Violence in Victorian and Edwardian England." In *Crime and the Law: The Social History of Crime in Western Europe since 1500*, V. A. C. Gatrell, Bruce Lenman, and Geoffrey Parker, editors, 238–37. London: Europa Publications, 1980.

_____. *The Hanging Tree: Execution and the English People, 1770–1868*. Oxford: Oxford University Press, 1986.

Gatrell, V. A. C., Bruce Lenman, and Geoffrey Parker, eds. *Crime and the Law: The Social History of Crime in Western Europe since 1500*. London: Europa Publications, 1980.

Gibson, Mary. *Born to Crime: Cesare Lombroso and the Origins of Biological Criminology*. Westport, CT: Praeger, 2002.

Gillis, A. R. "So Long as They Both Shall Live: Martial Dissolution and Decline of Domestic Homicide in France, 1852–1909." *American Journal of Sociology* 101 (1996): 1273–1305.

Goldstrom, J. M., and L. A. Clarkson, eds. *Irish Population, Economy and Society: Essays in Honour of the late K. H. Connell.* New York: Oxford University Press, 1981.

Hall, Catherine, Keith McClelland, and Jane Rendall, eds. *Defining the Victorian Nation: Class, Race, Gender, and the Reform Act of 1867.* Cambridge: Cambridge University Press, 2000.

Hammerton, A. J. *Cruelty and Companionship: Conflict in Nineteenth-Century Married Life.* New York: Routledge, 1992.

Harrison, Brian. *Drink and the Victorians: The Temperance Question in England, 1815–1872.* Pittsburgh, PA: University of Pittsbugh Press, 1971.

Hartman, Mary S. *Victorian Murderesses: A True History of Thirteen Respectable French and English Women Accused of Unspeakable Crimes.* New York: Schocken Books, 1977.

Harvie, Christopher. *Scotland and Nationalism: Scottish Society and Politics, 1707 to the Present.* 3rd ed. New York: Routledge, 1998.

Hatton, Ed. "He Murdered Her because He Loved Her." In *Over the Threshold: Intimate Violence in Early America,* edited by Christine Daniels and Michael Kennedy, editors, 111–34. New York: Routledge, 1999.

Hay, Douglas. "Property, Authority, and the Criminal Law." In *Albion's Fatal Tree: Crime and Society in Eighteenth-Century England,* Douglas Hay, editor, 17–63. London: Pantheon, 1975.

Hoff, Joan, and Marian Yeates. *The Cooper's Wife Is Missing: The Trials of Bridget Cleary.* New York: Basic Books, 2000.

Hoffer, Peter, and N. E. H. Hull. *Murdering Mothers: Infanticide in England and New England, 1558–1803.* New York: New York University Press, 1981.

Hoppen, K. T. *Ireland since 1800: Conflict and Conformity.* New York: Longman, 1989.

Howarth, Janet. "Gender, Domesticity, and Sexual Politics." In *The Nineteenth Century: The British Isles, 1815–1901,* Colin Matthew, editor, 163–93. Oxford: Oxford University Press, 2000.

Hrdy, Sarah Blaffer. *Mother Nature: Maternal Instincts and How They Shape the Human Species.* New York: Ballantine, 1999.

Hurl-Eamon, Jennine. *Gender and Petty Violence in London, 1680–1720.* Columbus: Ohio State University Press, 2005.

Jackson, Louise. *Child Sexual Abuse in Victorian England.* London: Routledge, 2000.

Jackson, Mark, ed. *Infanticide: Historical Perspectives on Child Murder and Concealment, 1550–2000.* London: Ashgate, 2000.

———. *New Born Child Murder: Women, Illegitimacy and the Court in Eighteenth Century England.* Manchester, 1996.

Johnson, Eric A., and Eric Monkkonen. *The Civilization of Crime: Violence in Town and Country since the Middle Ages.* Urbana, IL: University of Illinois Press, 1996.

Jones, David. *Crime in Nineteenth Century Wales.* Cardiff: University of Wales, 1992.

Kearney, Hugh. *Science and Change, 1500–1700.* New York: McGraw-Hill, 1971.

Kilday, Anne Marie. "Maternal Monsters: Murdering Mothers in South-West Scotland, 1750–1815." In *Twisted Sisters: Women, Crime, and Deviance in Scotland since 1400,* Yvonne Galloway Brown and Rona Ferguson, editors, 156–79. East Linton, Scotland: Tuckewell Press, 2002.

King, Peter. *Crime, Justice, and Discretion in England, 1740–1820.* Oxford: Oxford University Press, 2000.

Knelman, Judith. *Twisting in the Wind: The Murderess and the English Press.* Toronto: University of Toronto Press, 1998.

Lane, Roger. *Violent Death in the City: Suicide, Accident, and Murder in Nineteenth-Century Philadelphia.* Columbus: Ohio State University Press, 1999.

Lee, Joseph. *The Modernization of Irish Society, 1848–1918.* Dublin: Gill and MacMillian, 1973.

Lees, Lynn Hollen. *Exiles of Erin: Irish Migrants in Victorian London.* Ithaca, NY: Cornell University Press, 1979.

Leneman, Leah. "'A Tyrant and Tormentor':Violence against Wives in Eighteenth- and Early Nineteenth-Century Scotland." *Continuity and Change* 12 (1997): 31–54.

Livingston, Shelia. *Confess and Be Hanged: Scottish Crime and Punishment through the Ages.* Edinburgh: Birlinn Ltd., 2000.

Luddy, Maria, and Cliona Murphy, eds. *Women Surviving: Studies in Irish Women's History in the 19th and 20th Centuries.* Dublin: Poolbeg Press, 1990.

Lynch, Michael. *Scotland: A New History.* London: Pimlico, 1991.

MacCurtain, Margaret, Mary O'Dowd, and Maria Luddy. "An Agenda for Women's History in Ireland, 1500–1900." *Irish Historical Studies* 109 (1992): 1–37.

MacRaild, Donald M. *Irish Migrants in Modern Britain, 1750–1922.* New York: St. Martin's Press, 1999.

Malcolm, Elizabeth. *Ireland Sober, Ireland Free: Drink and Temperance in Nineteenth-Century Ireland.* Syracuse, NY: Syracuse University Press, 1986.

———. "Popular Recreation in 19th Century Ireland." In *Irish Culture and Nationalism, 1750–1950,* Oliver MacDonagh, W. F. Mandle, and Pauric Travers, editors, 40–51. London: MacMillan, 1985.

Malcolm, Joyce Lee. *Guns and Violence: The English Experience.* Cambridge, MA: Harvard University Press, 2002.

Martin, Scott. "Violence, Gender, and Intemperance in Early National Connecticut." *Journal of Social History* 34 (2000): 309–25.

May, Allyson N. *The Bar and The Old Bailey, 1750–1850.* Chapel Hill: University of North Carolina Press, 2003.

McGrath, Roger. *Gunfighters, Highwaymen, and Vigilantes: Violence on the Frontier.* Berkeley: University of California Press, 1984.

Mitchison, Rosalind. *A History of Scotland.* London: Methuen, 1970.

Monkkonen, Eric. *Crime, Justice, History.* Columbus: Ohio State University Press, 2002.

———. *Murder in New York City.* Berkeley: University of California Press, 2001.

Moore, Sean T. "'Justifiable Provocation': Violence against Women in Essex County, New York, 1799–1860." *Journal of Social History* 35 (2002): 889–918.

Morgan, Kenneth. *Rebirth of a Nation: Wales, 1880–1980.* New York: Oxford University Press, 1981.

Neal, Frank. "A Criminal Profile of the Liverpool Irish." *Transactions of the Historic Society of Lancashire and Cheshire* 131 (1991): 161–99.

O'Corrain, Donncha. "Women in Early Irish Society." In *Women in Early Modern Ireland,* Margaret Maccurtain and Mary O'Dowd, editors, 1–16. Dublin: Dublin Wolfhound Press, 1991.

O'Connor, Anne. "Women in Irish Folklore: The Testimony Regarding Illegitimacy, Abortion, and Infanticide." In *Women in Early Modern Ireland,* Margaret Maccurtain and Mary O'Dowd, editors, 304–317. Dublin: Dublin Wolfhound Press, 1991.

O'Donnell, Ian. "Lethal Violence in Ireland, 1841–2003: Famine, Celibacy, and Parental Pacification." *British Journal of Criminology* 45 (2005): 671–95.

O'Donnell, Patrick. *The Irish Faction Fighters of the Nineteenth Century.* Dublin: Anvil Book, 1975.

Parry, Gwenfair, and Mari Williams. *The Welsh Language and the 1891 Census.* Cardiff: University of Wales Press, 1999.

Parry, Gwynedd R. "Random Selection, Linguistic Rights and the Jury Trials in Wales." *Criminal Law Review* (October 2002): 805–816.

Pleck, Elizabeth. "Criminal Approaches to Family Violence, 1640–1980." *Crime and Justice* 11 (1989): 19–57.

Rhodes, Rita. *Women and the Family in Post-Famine Ireland: Status and Opportunity in a Patriarchal Society.* New York: Garland Publishing, 1992.

Robb, George. "Circe in Crinoline: Domestic Poisonings in Victorian England." *Journal of Family History* 22 (1997): 176–90.

_____. "The English Dreyfus Case: Florence Maybric and the Sexual Double-Standard." In *Disorder in the Court: Trials and Sexual Conflict at the Turn of the Century,* George Robb and Nancy Erber, editors, 57–77. New York: New York University Press, 1998.

Roberts, Paul. "Caravats and Shanavests." In *Irish Peasants: Violence and Political Unrest, 1780–1914,* Sam Clark and James Donnelly, editors, 66–91. Madison, WI: University of Wisconsin Press, 1983.

Rose, Lionel. *The Massacre of the Innocents: Infanticide in Britain, 1800–1939.* London: Routledge and Keegan Paul, 1986.

Ross, Ellen. "'Fierce Questions and Taunts': Married Life in Working Class London, 1870–1914." *Feminist Studies* 8 (1982): 575–602.

Roth, Randolph. "Spousal Murder in New England, 1776–1865." In *Over the Threshold: Intimate Violence in Early America,* Christine Daniels and Michael Kennedy, editors, 65–93. New York: Routledge, 1999.

Rowbotham, Judith. "'Only When Drunk': The Stereotyping of Violence in England, c.1850–1900." In *Everyday Violence in Britain, 1850–1950: Gender and Class,* Shani D'Cruze, editor, 155–69. London: Pearson, 2000.

Sharpe, J. A. *Crime in Early Modern England, 1550–1750.* Longman, 1984.

_____. "The History of Violence in England: Some Observations." *Past and Present* 108 (1985): 206–215.

Shoemaker, Robert. *The London Mob: Violence and Disorder in Eighteenth-Century England.* London: Hambledon and London, 2004.

Showalter, Elaine. *The Female Malady: Women, Madness, and English Culture, 1830–1980.* London: Virago Press, 1987.

Smith, R. A. A. McCall, and David Sheldon. *Scots Criminal Law*. 2nd ed. Edinburgh: Butterworths, 1977.

Smith, Roger. *Trial by Medicine: Insanity and Responsibility in Victorian Trials*. Edinburgh: Edinburgh University Press, 1981.

Smout, T. C. *A Century of the Scottish People, 1830–1950*. New Haven, CT: Yale University Press, 1986.

Spierenburg, Peter. "Long-term Trends in Homicide: Theoretical Reflections and Dutch Evidence, Fifteenth to Twentieth Centuries." In *The Civilization of Crime: Violence in Town and Country since the Middle Ages,* Eric A. Johnson and Eric H. Monkkonen, editors, 63–105. Urbana, IL: University of Illinois Press, 1996

_____. *Men and Violence: Gender, Honor, and Rituals in Modern Europe and America*. Columbus: Ohio State University Press, 1998.

Stevenson, Kim. "'Crimes of Moral Outrage': Victorian Encryptions of Sexual Violence." In *Criminal Conversations: Victorian Crimes, Social Panic, and Moral Outrage,* Judith Rowbotham and Kim Stevenson, editors, 232–46. Columbus: Ohio State University Press, 2005.

Stone, Lawrence. "The History of Violence in England: Some Observations: A Rejoinder." *Past and Present* 108 (1985): 216–24.

_____. "Interpersonal Violence in English Society, 1300–1980." *Past and Present* (101): 22–33.

Swift, Roger. "'Another Stafford-Street Row': Law, Order, and the Irish in Mid-Victorian Wolverhampton," In *The Irish in the Victorian City,* Roger Swift and Sheridan Gilley, editors, 181–206. London: Croom-Helm, 1985.

_____. "Behaving Badly? Irish Migrants and Crime in the Victorian City.," In *Criminal Conversations: Victorian Crimes, Social Panic, and Moral Outrage,* Judith Rowbotham and Kim Stevenson, editors, 106–125. Columbus: Ohio State University Press, 2005.

_____. "Crime and the Irish in Nineteenth-Century Britain." In *The Irish in Britain, 1815–1939,* Roger Swift and Sherdian Gilley, editors, 163–82. Savage, MD: Barnes and Noble, 1989.

Swift, Roger, and Sheridan Gilley, eds. *The Irish in Britain, 1815–1939*. Savage, MD: Barnes and Noble, 1989.

_____, eds. *The Irish in Victorian Britain: The Local Dimension*. Dublin: Four Courts Press, 1999.

_____, eds. *The Irish in the Victorian City*. London: Croom-Helm, 1985.

Taylor, David. "Beyond the Bounds of Respectable Society: The 'Dangerous Classes' in Victorian and Edwardian England." In *Criminal Conversations: Victorian Crimes, Social Panic, and Moral Outrage,* Rowbotham and Kim Stevenson, editors 3–22. Columbus: Ohio State University Press, 2005.

Taylor, Howard. "Rationing Crime: The Political Economy of Criminal Statistics since the 1850s." *Economic History Review* 51 (1998): 569–90.

Thompson, F. M. L. *The Rise of Respectable Society*. Cambridge, MA.: Harvard University Press, 1988.

Tinkova, Daniela. "Proteger ou punir? La mère infanticide entreseuil 'mère affreuse,' 'fille malheurese' et 'femme alienée' au seuil de la société civile." An unpublished paper presented at the International Association for the History of Crime and Criminal Justice conference in Paris, June 2003.

Tomes, Nancy. "'A Torrent of Abuse': Crimes of Violence between Working Class Men and Women in London, 1840–1873." *Journal of Social History* 11 (1978): 328–46.

Townshend, Charles. *Political Violence in Ireland: Government and Resistance since 1848.* New York: Oxford University Press, 1983.

Vandal, Gilles. *Rethinking Southern Violence: Homicides in Post-Civil War Louisiana.* Columbus: Ohio State University Press, 2000.

Vaughan, W. E. *Ireland under the Union.* New York: Oxford University Press, 1989.

Vicinus, Martha. *Suffer and Be Still: Women in the Victorian Age.* Bloomington, IN: Indiana University Press, 1977.

Waldron, Jarleth. *Maamtrasna: The Murders and the Mystery.* Dublin: Edmund Burke Publisher, 1992.

Walker, Nigel. *Crime and Insanity in England.* Vol. 1. Edinburgh: Edinburgh University Press, 1968.

Walklate, Sandra, Shani D'Cruze, and Samantha Pegg. *Murder: Social and Historical Approaches to Understanding Murder and Murderers.* Portland, OR: Willan Publishing, 2006.

Walkowitz, Judith. "Jack the Ripper and the Myth of Male Violence." *Feminist Studies* 8 (1982): 542–74.

Walsh, Brendan M. "Marriage Rates and Population Pressure: Ireland, 1871 and 1911." *English Historical Review* 23 (1970): 148–62.

_____. "A Perspective on Irish Population Patterns." *Eire* 3 (1969): 3–21.

Whatley, Christopher A. "How Tame Were the Scottish Lowlanders during the Eighteenth Century?" In *Conflict and Stability in Scottish Society, 1700–1850,* T. M. Devine, editor, 1–30. Edinburgh: John Donald Publishers, Ltd., 1990.

Wiener, Martin. *Men of Blood: Violence, Manliness, and Criminal Justice in Victorian England.* Cambridge: Cambridge University Press, 2004.

_____. *Reconstructing the Criminal: Culture, Law, and Policy in England, 1830–1914.* Cambridge: Cambridge University Press, 1990.

_____. "The Sad Story of George Hall: Adultery, Murder, and the Politics of Mercy in Mid-Victorian England." *Social History* 24 (1999): 173–95.

_____. "The Victorian Criminalization of Men." In *Men of Violence: Gender, Honor, and Rituals in Modern Europe and America,* Pieter Spiernburg, editor, 197–212. Columbus: Ohio University Press, 1998.

Williams, Gwyn. *When Was Wales?* London: Black Raven Press, 1985.

Wilson, Patrick. *Murderess: A Study of Women Executed in Britain since 1843.* London: Michael Joseph Ltd., 1971.

Wohl, Anthony S. "Sex and the Single Room: Incest among the Victorian Working Class." In *Suffer and Be Still: Women in the Victorian Age,* Martha Vicinus, editor, 197–216. Bloomington, IN: Indiana University Press, 1977.

Wood, J. Carter. *Violence and Crime in Nineteenth-Century England: The Shadow of Our Refinement.* London: Routledge, 2004.

Zedner, Lucia. *Women, Crime, and Custody in Victorian England.* Oxford: Oxford University Press, 1991.

Index

accidental deaths, 26–31; railway accidents, 29–31; traffic accidents, 27–29

Act of Union for Ireland (1801), 2

Act of Union for Scotland (1707), 10

alcohol, 23–26, 70, 75–76, 79–80, 81–82, 97, 101, 103–5, 112, 135, 138–43, 144–46, 183–84, 193–95; insanity and,140–42, 157, 183–84

Aylsward, Ann, 176

beating deaths, 60–61

Berry, Elizabeth, 174

brawls, 71–82

capital punishment, 1, 18–19, 38, 99–100

Chantrelle, Eugene, 150–52

chastisement, 100–101, 103, 109–10, 134–38. *See also* children; spousal violence

children: chastisement of, 195–205; fathers,177–79; homicides of, 34, 162–205; illegitimacy, 172–80; neglect, 184–93, 200; neonaticide, 166–72, 178; parental responsibility, 164, 185; public interest in, 162–65; stepparents, 100, 102; unwed mothers, 174–178, 180; widowers and, 183

Church, Emily, 174

civilizing process, 3

class, 68–72, 76–78, 80, 86, 91, 103, 114–15, 116, 118–20, 127–28, 131–32, 141–42, 143–52, 157; brawling and, 71–82; justice and,

68–82, 127–28, 142, 143–53; working-class as alien, 42, 208

cohabitation, 156–57

concealment of birth or pregnancy, 167

Conway, Patrick, 184

Coroner's juries, 8

courtship and homicide, 113–15, 120–22

Crawford, Sarah, 123

crimes of passion, 2, 115–20

Cross, Philip, 148–49

culpable homicide, 15, 82

death sentence, 18–19, 34, 35, 37, 78, 149, 199, 201–2

Dingwall case, 23, 141–42

Dorty, Letitia, 168

Edmunds, Christiana, 118–20

Elias, Norbert, 3

England: attitudes toward other cultures, 3–4, 40, 41, 42–45, 51–52; judicial process, 14; self-identification, 39–45, 67, 206–7

estranged couples, 155

ethnic conflict, 56–58, 67

fair-fights, 60–61, 67, 72–76, 78–81, 87–90, 91

family homicides, 95–110; female killers, 107–9; female victims, 107–10; fratricide, 96–98; gender and, 107–10, 111–12; in-laws, 105–8; matricide, 103–5, 108; patricide, 98–103, 107–8; privacy, 129–32, 164–66; seduction, revenge

HISTORY OF CRIME AND CRIMINAL JUSTICE
DAVID R. JOHNSON AND JEFFREY S. ADLER, SERIES EDITORS

The series explores the history of crime and criminality, violence, criminal justice, and legal systems without restrictions as to chronological scope, geographical focus, or methodological approach.